CRITICAL THINKING

A SHEPHERD'S GUIDE TO TENDING SHEEP

A Text and Reader

Second Edition

Revised Printing

Jason McFaul

KENDALL/HUNT PUBLISHING COMPANY
4050 Westmark Drive   Dubuque, Iowa 52002

Dedication

To my mom, who didn't think I could read—
and to my dad, who kept reassuring her that I could.

Cover art *Rubes* by Leigh Rubin, Creators Syndicate.

Copyright © 2000, 2002 by Jason McFaul

Revised Printing: 2006

ISBN 978-0-7575-2939-9

Printed in the United States of America
10   9   8

Contents

Preface

Welcome to America, home of the gobemouche, the credulous, the sheep.

Yes, America is a shepherd's dream! But here is the funny thing: the sheep are so disoriented they can't even spy their flock's silhouette. And even funnier, they wax individualistic. Ask an American if he is an individual, and he will answer with a resounding, "obviously." Yes, the omnipresence of sheep in America is daunting. I'm reminded of words uttered by George Carlin: "Never underestimate the power of stupid people in large groups." I must clarify, however, that I am not ready to brand America's sheep as "stupid." Stupid people are slow-thinking and dull. America's sheep are simply misdirected. Because they have been following a few shepherds for most of their lives, their conformity is more pathological than conscious. For this reason, I believe we can arouse the sheep from their mentally indolent stupor; we can wake them up!

My father used to say, "If four of your friends jumped off the Brooklyn Bridge, would you?" It is, in my opinion, a loaded question. To answer in the affirmative is to sound like a mindless conformist. To answer with a simple "no" seems the logical choice. But now, twenty years later, I find myself interested in the "Brooklyn Bridge question." As a born-again critical thinker, I would like to question my father's question before I satisfy him with a response. I would like to ask my father "why?" Why are my friends jumping off the Brooklyn Bridge? Is it on fire? If so, jumping sounds like a reasonable alternative. I also, because of the advent of bungee jumping, might ask him if my four friends have bungee chords tied to their ankles. If so, I would jump, for I am quite fond of extreme sports. In other words, I would force my father to define his reality so that I really know what he is asking.

In part, this is what we will be doing in *Critical Thinking: A Shepherd's Guide to Tending Sheep*. The goal is to not only motivate students to begin asking questions but to teach students how to create the right questions. Students should begin thinking about their thinking while they're thinking in order to make their thinking better. Students should learn how to look at situations objectively and from a variety of perspectives. This, coupled with terrific readings and applications, should begin a metamorphosis, one which eventually turns sheep into shepherds.

Acknowledgments

While writing this book, I received support and suggestions from the following professors at Mt. San Antonio College: Julian Medina, Gary Enke, and Paul O'Brien. Thank you for taking the time to help make this vision a reality. Additionally, I'd like to thank professors Todd Davis and Dan Onorato at Modesto Junior College, and I'd like to thank Jay Rubin, professor of English at Las Positas College. Retired professors of English Paul Neumann and Gary Phillips also deserve much thanks, for they taught me more about teaching critical thinking than any course or textbook ever did. And thank you Jon St. Amant for your dedication to making the illustrations adhere so specifically to the book's theme. Finally, I'd like to thank Matthew Begersdorf and Eric MacDonald for their suggestions specific to the Second Edition.

To Instructors

Unlike many textbooks claiming to teach critical thinking, this book is different for one reason: it offers instructors a program which, if adhered to, can be completed in eighteen weeks. Instead of mincing, dicing, and excerpting sections from various chapters (something many must do because of textbook incohesion), *Critical Thinking: A Shepherd's Guide to Tending Sheep* can provide instructors and students with a comprehensive curriculum, something which definitely promotes the delivery of responsible, cogent, explicit arguments, germane to both spoken and written discourse.

Critical Thinking: A Shepherd's Guide to Tending Sheep begins by asking students to create their constitutions. Once students know what they stand for and why, it is much easier to note why they embrace certain issues and avoid others. This exercise promotes awareness, and it keeps students from engaging in what Jung considered the greatest sin: being unconscious.

Next, students are offered different methodologies to which critical thinkers might adhere. Because most people have never been formally taught how to think, the chapter on methodologies is essential to students' growth as thinkers. Again, they must become conscious of different "ways" to think. In order to remedy any ailment (in this case, thinking irresponsibly or not thinking at all), one must first become aware of the ailment itself.

Students are now ready to begin critically analyzing written arguments. In Chapter 3, students are presented with an opportunity to learn about the three claims which most often appear in arguments: claims of value, claims of fact, and claims of policy. Once students have completed this chapter, they will become aware of an integral component to responsible argumentation: addressing one claim at a time. Though it may be rather cosmopolitan to digress (more often in spoken arguments), students will learn that most digressions are the result of inadequate support on behalf of the person shifting from one claim to the next.

In Chapter 4, students are asked to write Issue/Problem (I/P) Papers. Now that students can articulate their morals/beliefs (via their constitutions), and now that students are familiar with different methodologies for thinking, they are much more aware of why and *how* they think what they think. And now that students can responsibly identify claims, it is time for them to begin committing claims to paper. Issue/Problem Papers afford students this opportunity. Issue/Problem Papers also introduce students to the concept of refuting the opposition. (Additionally, I/P Papers help instructors pinpoint students' locations on the critical-thinking evolutionary scale, i.e., where they are now, and where they need to go.) Because I/P Papers are short (they shouldn't exceed one page), students are tempted to engage in fallacious reasoning, for they often do not have enough room to adequately support their claims. This is excellent, for it justifies the length of future papers assigned by instructors. Students realize how much easier it is to state a claim and proceed to support it if they are asked to fit it into four pages instead of one.

Once students have written two I/P Papers (students should find the first one quite difficult), they should progress to Chapter 5, Writing Argument Papers. Though a comprehensive checklist is provided for writing argument papers, prompts are not, for many instructors have their own agenda regarding paper topics. In writing many argument papers, much focus should be placed on proper refutation of the opposition. Students should learn that to not address the opposition is to, in essence, only address the proponents—people who already agree and, hence, need not be persuaded.

In Chapter 6, students are introduced to whistle blowers. Though this term may be foreign to many, the actions of a whistle blower are not. In fact, this chapter was included for one very important reason: since students now know what they stand for (via their constitutions), they need to begin thinking about whether or not they'd take action if they witnessed an injustice, some anathematic event which demands a whistle be blown. Ralph Waldo Emerson writes: "Good and bad are but names very readily transferable to that or this; the only right is what is after my constitution; the only wrong what is against it." When students witness a wrong, something against their constitutions, what will they do? This chapter helps provide some insight for students; it provokes them, forcing them to consider whether or not they'd "walk their talk."

In Chapter 7, students learn about fallacies. Now students will have more ammunition with which to combat the opposition. Students should also note impurities, or fallacious reasoning, in their own arguments.

At this point in the course, students should be prepared for the satire. Ostensibly one of the most fascinating forms of argument, the satire delights, amuses, confuses, and offends. However, it is effective. Though writing satires will be much easier for some students than others, formal study and creation are important to truly understanding why such a rhetorical form can be so poignant. Besides, in an age of encouraged classroom "edutainment," it isn't surprising that many will flock to read the satire yet flounder helplessly when presented with an argument written in a more traditional manner.

The final chapter focuses on debate and the eventual construction and delivery of an oral presentation. The oral presentation, which might more aptly be termed "a persuasive speech" or an "oral argument," should require students to amalgamate many of the concepts covered in the course into a presentation of ten to fifteen minutes. For instructors and students, this is usually the most exciting part of the semester.

Something not yet mentioned is the quality of readings included in *Critical Thinking: A Shepherd's Guide to Tending Sheep*. Aside from terrific essays by Mark Twain, Michael Moore, Jonathan Swift, Plato, and many others, the section entitled Additional Readings includes works from Ralph Waldo Emerson, Henry David Thoreau, Niccolo Machiavelli, and others.

In the appendix, instructors will find a section on Precision Language Exercises (PLE) and a section including other exercises conducive to teaching critical thinking; both should provide excellent stimuli for students. Also, the appendix houses a section on inferences and a section on grammar.

New to this second edition is a section titled "Critical Exercises" and more student examples. The rationale for such an addition was this: many people learn through a combination of comprehension and realization. Student examples, or essay "models," promote comprehension while the "Critical Exercises" definitely promote realization. When combined, they should compel students' critical thinking abilities to further evolve.

Overall, this textbook should provide students with a firm foundation, one which someday may be unshakable. Instructors can expect to benefit from the straightforward, pragmatic approach of *Critical Thinking: A Shepherd's Guide to Tending Sheep*.

What Is Critical Thinking?

If critical thinking were a publicly-traded company, its stock would probably plummet. Unfortunately, thinking is, in a sense, phobic. It often leads to headaches and neck pains, causing one to rely too heavily on aspirin, hoping the pain will "just go away." But still, colleges across the country are touting the benefits of critical thinking: "It will benefit you in *so* many ways." This book is designed to show you how critical thinking may benefit you and, more importantly, why you may wish to make critical thinking a *critical* part of your life.

First of all, what is critical thinking? Well, though it looks like a noun, you should see it as a verb, for critical thinking demands action. *You must take action.* Thinking will not simply come to you like a lost puppy. It is the reward one receives for learning the skill, the art of thinking. Critical thinking forces one to evaluate and weigh, interpret and ponder. To think critically involves patience, for critical thought cannot be applied on a whim.

Picture, for instance, a dead body. You are being asked to perform the autopsy. At first, you have no idea what may be the cause of death; however, you begin taking samples. You cut, scrape, pull, prod, dissect—and whammo, you dig to the root, the source. This same method can be applied when confronted with an issue or problem. Dissect it.

Say you want to go to the circus. You're excited. You can see Bozo. You can taste the cotton candy. You can see the ring leader and his handle-bar mustache. Then you overhear one of your friends say, "I heard the animals are constantly mistreated at circuses. I heard they are abused, and I heard they're miserable as a result." Now you're thinking, "Wow, I am a professed animal lover. I can't support the mistreatment of animals. I will not go to the circus." But it's not that easy.

As a critical thinker, you must take a look at this situation as a whole to see if it jibes when scrutinized. You *must* ask questions: Is my friend credible? Where did she get this information? Is the provider of that information credible? What do I know about circuses? What information is available? What are my positions on animal cruelty? Why do I feel this way? Is this the way *I* feel, or am I merely a sheep, a product of my conditioning?

What if you're asked to take a stand on abortion? The most cosmopolitan thing to do is say, "Well, there are so many variables, so many reasons for and against abortion. It all really depends. . . ." You may continue, communicating with obscure nonverbal gestures, grappling for an exit, the freedom from actually committing. However, as a critical thinker, you must commit. You cannot vacillate. You must figure out what weighs and what does not. Then you must take a stand! People euphemize uncertainty by saying, "Oh, he's still on the fence post." Critical thinkers do not have the motivation to learn how to balance on white picket fence posts' pointed tips. No! Aside from encouraging awkward posture, it is a waste of time, a lesson in futility. Ralph Waldo Emerson says, "The only right is what is after my constitution; the only wrong what is against it." People who vacillate are often without a constitution. They have vague ideals and a handful of morals and ethics to which they cling. But critical thinkers have so defined their constitution (again and again and again, constantly defining and redefining) that to vacillate is to, as Jim Rohn says, "choke on the dust of your own regret."

Writing a Constitution

. . . .

Let's begin by figuring out what is written on *your* constitution. Please answer the following questions:

What is your favorite color?
How do you like your eggs prepared?
What are your favorite toppings on pizza?
How do you eat spaghetti?
How fast do you drive on the freeway?
How many times a day do you eat?
How do you feel about technology?
What do you think about religion?

How do you feel about Asians?
How do you feel about African-Americans?
How do you feel about Anglo-Americans?
How do you feel about Hispanics?

What are the first words which come to mind when you see or hear each of the following:

Jehovah's Witnesses
Mormons
Muslims
Christians
Catholics
Buddhists
Cannibals
Aborigines
The Unibomber
L.A. Riots
Watts Riots
I.R.S.
Richard Nixon
George Washington
Christopher Columbus
Bill Clinton
The United States of America
Racism

Do you like cats?
What do you value in a friendship, a relationship, a human being?
What brand of automobile do you favor?
Are you musically inclined?
What kind of movies do you like?
Do you want to be rich?

Whether or not you offered a response to each question is immaterial. In order to learn anything about what your constitution reads, you must begin applying one question to each response you offered: why? For example, if you think "deceit" when you see Richard Nixon's name, and if you think "honesty" when you see George Washington's name, you need to question your responses. Why did you respond this way? Did you learn that George Washington "cut down a cherry tree and never told a lie," while Richard Nixon engaged in covert activities to conceal operations in Vietnam and a scandal at the Watergate Hotel? Well, this realization would represent a beginning. However, true dissection involves digging a little deeper. Who taught you these things, and why did you consider this person's opinion credible? And what if someone told you George Washington was a slave owner, a murderer, and a cheat? Oh, what then?

Once you ascertain why you responded the way you did to the aforementioned list of questions, and once you write those responses down, you can begin to take a closer, more critical look at your responses; hopefully, this will bring you closer to understanding exactly what can be found on your constitution. So, your next step is to write your constitution. What do you stand for and why? Please note: the aforementioned questions regarding your favorite color, how you like your eggs scrambled, etc. may not have anything to do with *what* is written on your constitution; however, the answers to the questions do have something to do with *how* your constitution was composed. Just as you may have to reevaluate how *you* like your eggs prepared (because you may have learned that you have simply liked what others told you to like), you may have to reevaluate what *you* stand for (once again, your values may be someone else's—maybe you have never decided *for yourself* what is written on *your* constitution).

Though constitutions will vary in length and content, here are two student examples:

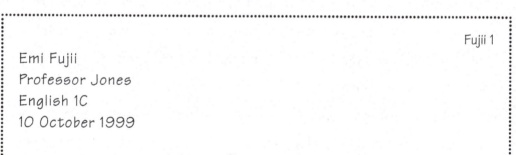

Fujii 1

Emi Fujii
Professor Jones
English 1C
10 October 1999

More Than Religion

As of October 10, 1999, the contents of this document pertain to the beliefs, perceptions, and other variants that affect what I stand for. Currently, I stand for religion, the environment, peace, and greed/selfishness.

Religion

Religion is very important to me. I believe the basis for all religions is essentially the same; people need someone or something to embrace as omniscient. I think religion is a scapegoat for unexplainable phenomena: the afterlife and the meaning of life. Though it is an effective form of creating unity among people, it also creates disunity. Donning a religious label is a façade for most individuals because they fail to reflect what is supposedly preached.

Ironically, I have a strong association to Buddhism due to my father's occupation as a Buddhist minister. The opportunity to see both sides of a minister, which is rare for most, constantly reminds me that my father is only human. I have grown up with such an eminent presence of Buddhism that it has molded many of my beliefs, but it has also allowed me to explore fallacious or unnerving claims. For instance, references to Hell in Christianity constitute an existence of a soul, where in Buddhism a soul is nonexistent. Though I am not well versed in other religions, I have attended morning masses and group discussions; they seem to revolve around the glorification of God. Also, "temple" is supposed to be a place where people worship, yet it houses various organizations, hosts many fund-raisers, and manufactures some of the best gossip around. It becomes a place where people have to watch every step taken. I am, however, a Buddhist. There are more Buddhists than adherents to any other religion, and the Buddhists represent the only major religion which hasn't repeatedly and willingly started large-scale wars. William Golding, in "Thinking as a Hobby," states: ". . . if we were counting heads, the Buddhists were the boys for my money." I was originally a Buddhist as a result of my upbringing. Now I'm a Buddhist because I have scrutinized other religions and made a conscious decision, on my own accord, to be a Buddhist. Buddhism encourages the individual to strive for enlightenment and self-awareness.

Environment

I believe in protecting the environment. I believe that the environment is essential to human existence. It houses all living organisms known to humans, and it supplies nourishment for survival. I feel that many people have neglected to replenish what they have taken from the earth. It seems as though the human race is the only species that destroys its environment, whether through nuclear waste, radiation, smog, water pollution, trash, human discharge, or oil spills. I think many people fail to realize that once this planet is a dump, it will be too late to act; everyone cannot just move to Mars, only to do the same thing.

Again, this belief can be traced back to my father and the Japanese culture. The focus on nature and environment is very important in the Japanese culture; vegetation covers about 70% of Japan's land mass. As a young child, I recall going on family trips. My father's idea of a family trip was to go camping, hiking, or to engage in some rigorous outdoor activity, almost always dealing with nature and appreciating the environment. Through those encounters with nature, I have grown accustomed to not only appreciating but protecting Earth's splendor.

Peace

I believe in promoting peace. I write "peace" at the end of each and every letter I compose. When there is an opportunity to make a wish, I wish for peace. But what is peace? Is it inner peace? World peace? A peace corps? A peace sign? I guess I am hoping that some-day everyone will find and share a single, free state of mind. But realistically that is not possible because people rapidly change their train of thought, and everyone is on a different plane. Peace represents my hope, and that is something I stand for.

My parents are, once again, at the core of my belief. Violence was not promoted in my family; instead, understanding was practiced. And I think the first step to reaching accordance is to understand one another. Taking time to see beyond a mask is to realize everyone is composed in a similar fashion. When people realize this, an appreciation for each other may grow, resulting in a state of peace.

Greed/Selfishness

I believe in not being greedy/selfish, but unfortunately I am very greedy and selfish. Greed and selfishness are characteristics that are bequeathed to everyone and, possibly, every organism. As living creatures there is the instinct to survive, and that behavior reciprocates self-centeredness. Individuals make certain choices over others to enhance their quality of life. As the famous philosopher, Thomas Hobbes, wrote in his book, *Leviathan*, "of the voluntary acts of every man, the object is some good to himself." I think this characteristic mirrors many actions in which people participate. The reasoning why this topic is structured into my constitution is to remind me that I am also a part of this plague. Though I may stand for many things, "the object is some good to [me]."

Once more, my father's presence has influenced this outlook. Earlier I had mentioned that even though my father is a minister, he is only human; hence, he too possesses the traits of greed and selfishness. I, unfortunately, am greedy and selfish. However, becoming conscious of such negative traits marks the first step to understanding oneself.

Note: Emi not only categorizes her constitution (religion, environment, peace, greed/selfishness) but she asks herself *why* she stands for these things and *who* influenced her to feel this way. She also seems honest, for she lets us know she is both selfish and greedy.

Of the three constitutions presented in this chapter, Emi's is the most responsibly written. Unlike the two that follow, Emi's does not read like a first draft but, instead, one over which she pondered and labored. This is apparent when noting her decisive tone. For example, she writes: "Once more, my father's presence has influenced this outlook." Clearly, she does not vacillate but commits, decisively, to the derivation of the beliefs for which she stands.

Joey Gu
Professor Jones
English 1C
15 September 2001

Angst

What is hate? *Merriam Webster's Collegiate Dictionary, Tenth Edition* defines hate as "[an] intense hostility and aversion usually deriving from fear, anger, or sense of injury; extreme dislike or antipathy: (532). But what is hate really? Is it an emotion? Is it a sin? Is it an enemy perhaps? Is it the steam rising from an angry character's head in any given Saturday morning cartoon? Is hate the byproduct of violence and envy, discrimination and injustice, diversity and solitude? Or is hate merely a companion, something or someone a person becomes accustomed to as he or she advances in life?

Growing up, I quickly learned to express myself through anger. I was taught to stand up for myself and to resist "bullies." I would spend my spare time with the neighborhood children throwing rocks at passing vehicles. Every heated argument I had with my parents resulted in bloodshed, for I would violently beat the stucco walls of my house, ending the argument with nothing except for the scars on my hands and, quite possibly, the scars on my character. At times I ask myself why I am so aggressive. And the more I ponder the more I realize just how much sense everything really made. Growing up, I was physically abused. One particular time, for instance, I had injured my right leg falling off a scooter. When I told my parents what had occurred, they did not believe me. My father beat my back with a pole, and he screamed at me to walk. Eventually, he took me to a doctor and it was officially concluded that my right leg was, indeed, broken. But that was not the only thing that was injured. As I grew older, my respect for others diminished. My compassion for my friends and family disappeared. I became, as James Joyce would put it, a "little ball of hate." I hated attending school, I hated eating breakfast, I hated rainy days, and I hated the world. Then I began playing indoor soccer. The thrill of running and slide tackling an opponent made me ecstatic. I absolutely loved the feeling of colliding into an opponent, hearing my bones crack on his body and his bones crack on mine. My coach asked me one day from where I got all of my energy. I told him that I was full of anger and frustration. He then told me that anger is something that everyone has to deal with, but a strong way to deal with anger is to hate anger itself. So what is hate? I believe hate is a companion, indeed, and it is a force that compels me to scrutinize and change my beliefs, my values, and my future.

Note: Joey's constitution has many strong elements. For instance, it focuses on "hate" and attempts to advance the concept by citing anecdotal support in addition to a dictionary definition and a quotation by Joyce. Specifically, Joey's anecdotal support is replete with concrete language like "throwing rocks," "stucco walls," "scars on my hands," and "beat my back with a pole." Such language gives readers the opportunity to enter Joey's "reality," for such language can be seen by the mind's eye; it leaps from the page and affects the reader with a poignant, almost discombobulating embrace.

Challenges, however, are present in Joey's constitution. First, what does he stand for? Through "active inferencing," one might gather that he stands for "hate." But even if that were an accurate extraction, isn't there more to infer? Based on Joey's relationship with his father, where might he stand on "family," "parenting," "abuse," "love," or "relationships?" And since physical release via indoor soccer seemed to appease his appetite for destruction, might one infer that "exercise" or "sport" also composes his constitution? Note this, especially those of you hoping to lose your wool and leave the flock: what Joey has composed is an excellent *first* draft. What he must do now is meditate, reflect, or ruminate on what he has articulated. Then, using Emi Fujii's constitution as a model, he should compartmentalize the "philosophy" for which he stands. This should equip him with a more lucid perception of what he stands for and why.

Shane Johnson
Professor Jones
English 1C
15 September 2001

A Purpose for Everything

First of all, I believe in "telling it like it is." Though I'd like to think this is an original belief, I suspect I value "telling it like it is" because I was often lied to as a child. When I wasn't the product of lies, I was the product of gross embellishments (everything from Columbus and George Washington to Santa Claus, the Tooth Fairy, and my auntie's premature death). I became conscious of my desire to "tell it like it is" when listening to Jim Rohn, a modern-day philosopher and motivational speaker, discuss "straight talk" and how one "shouldn't stretch it, excuse it, or paint it some phony color; instead, one should tell it like it is." This made sense to me. Hence, the number one thing I stand for is "telling it like it is." Some might consider this, simply, being honest.

Second, I believe in making a conscious attempt to listen to others. Several years ago, when I gave my first speech, I noted how refreshing it was to feel like others were actually listening—not just looking my direction—to what I had to say. This made me feel understood and respected. It made me feel human; thus, I began making a conscious attempt to make others feel the same way. I feel like I'm helping make my part of the world a little better by making its inhabitants feel welcome. And why do I embrace such a service-oriented ideal? Probably because I detest the egocentric, and probably because I do what I can to suppress or release the egocentric within me.

Third, along the lines of being service-oriented, I stand for only working in a vocation which directly *benefits* society. Though this is totally relative to how one might define "directly *benefits* society," I still believe that certain people fall under this umbrella: teachers, medical doctors, police officers, fire persons, nurses, and some musicians. I do realize that exceptions exist in each, but I truly believe that the human race exists as a service-oriented network designed to help people succeed, to (as Utopian as this may sound) create some semblance of harmony on this planet. Why do I feel this way? Though I'm not religious (I don't pledge allegiance to any particular religion), I believe there must be a purpose for human beings. We're not just supposed to preoccupy ourselves with money, mortgages, divorces, and senility. There has to be something more. Again, why do I feel this way? Maybe I've read too much Vonnegut. Maybe I've seen my father come home from too many "long days" at work. Maybe I've been given a glimpse of happiness, and maybe I'm hoping for a little bit more.

Note: Shane's constitution is well-organized, and he attempts to explain precisely *why* he stands for "telling it like it is," *why* he stands for "making a conscious attempt to listen to others," and *why* he stands for "working in a vocation which directly benefits society." He also attempts to note *who* influenced him to feel this way.

The challenge, however, with Shane's constitution revolves around the haphazard manner in which he notes the derivation of his beliefs. He writes: "Probably because I detest the egocentric . . . [and] Maybe I've read too much Vonnegut." The challenge is this: the derivation of his beliefs has not been identified. In order for Shane to gain more insight into his beliefs, he must ruminate on *why* he "detests the egocentric" and *why* he thinks his beliefs are linked to "read[ing] too much Vonnegut." Arguably, his constitution would improve by simply organizing it like Emi Fujii's and giving more time to understanding *why* he stands for "telling it like it is," "making a conscious attempt to listen to others," and "working in a vocation which directly benefits society."

Writing a World View

· · · · · · · · · ·

Now that you have defined your constitution, let's see if this awareness can help inform your world view, your opinion of the world. Chances are you believe America is "the greatest country in the world." ("I pledge allegiance to the flag of the United States of America." "My country 'tis of thee, sweet land of liberty.") Again, we are products of our conditioning. But, what is your opinion of the world? What is your current world view? (By the way, there are no wrong answers to this question, as long as you can support your claim.)

Here are what some students have written (the first two world views are, acceptably, short. This is fine, for it is expected that many students know much more about themselves—hence, a lengthy constitution—than they do about the world around them):

Sean Stokes
Professor Jones
English 1C
10 October 1999

Disease

My view of the world is negative. There is disease, famine, poverty, greed, and conflict all over the world. Regarding the environment, there are deforestation problems causing world-wide changes in temperature. There are pollution problems in the air, oceans, and soil. There is unnecessary slaughtering of animals for fur, aphrodisiacs, and novelty items. Generally, problems in the world seem to be increasing rather than being solved.

Note: Sean's world view focuses on specific problems. Now that he is conscious of how he views the world, he can take a more active stance in affecting change and working toward solutions.

Critical thinkers should note how Sean's second assertion, "There is disease, famine, poverty, greed, and conflict all over the world," is not adequately supported. Such an assertion should be coupled with examples from credible sources. Does Sean offer other assertions in need of support?

Michael Juhn
Professor Jones
English 1C
10 October 2001

Too Much Money

The world today is based on money. Every country has some sort of monetary system. Countries trade with one another and buy things from each other. It's like a giant marketplace. In the news there are often stories about other countries' economies. For example, when the economy crashed in Asia, it was all over the news in America. These types of stories seem irrelevant to most people, but they are relevant stories. These stories are important because the American economy is connected to the economies of other countries. In fact, if America were to go into another great depression, there would be many countries that would also be greatly affected. The world revolves around money, and America is leading the way.

Note: Michael offers a focused world view by having his commentary revolve around one entity: money. Critical thinkers should ask this question: What could Michael do to ground his world view's speculative, conjectured tone?

Joey Gu
Professor Jones
English 1C
10 October 2001

The Global Toilet

The world is foul. True, the world and its inhabitants have evolved since the dawn of time, either biologically or technologically, but there are so many things wrong with the world. For example, there is a shortage of food in most third-world countries, and the world's natural resources are diminishing rapidly. 800 million people world-wide are at risk of losing their lives due to a lack of proper nutrition. In Africa, for example, one half of the children die before age ten, and in India, 63% of the children are underweight. 15% of the world's population, approximately 870 million people, earn about 53% of the world's income, while 50% of the world's population earns only 8% of the world's income. Also, in the United States, one out of every eight college female students is a victim of rape. One in every four experiences attempted rape, and 84% of those raped females know the rapist personally. The media have also played a major role in the downward-spiraling of humanity. The MTV show, Jackass, has prompted—and some might argue that it has even encouraged—teenagers nationwide to make their own home-videos of "jackassness." Furthermore, the Jenny Jones show started out as a program that dealt with issues concerning society as a whole, such as abortion and substance abuse. Recently, however, the show has dealt with issues titled "My Daughter's a Whore. Clean Up or Get Out the Door" and "My Mom's Dressin' Way Too Sexy." The world also stinks of greed and betrayal, death and destruction. And many plants and animals on this planet are victims of that destruction. It seems that maybe the world really is a toilet. Too bad there is no handle for one to flush.

Note: Joey's world view adheres to one claim, "The World is foul," and it is well-advanced by the support. More specifically, his argument is well-advanced when citing MTV and Jenny Jones. The challenge with his statistics, unfortunately, is that they are stated without proper attribution. While Joey seems well-intentioned, from what sources did his information derive? How can we accept them without being given the opportunity to investigate their credibility? Also, when Joey writes, "The world also stinks of greed and betrayal, death, and destruction," he must support this by citing examples.

If you read the student responses, chances are *your* "current world view" was influenced, tainted. To further taint your responses, take note of these observations:

- In some countries, slaves are still bought and sold.
- Though we are post-Hitler, post-Stalin, post-Columbus, post-Jackson, genocide still exists.
- If we could shrink the Earth's population to a village of precisely 100 people, with all existing human ratios remaining the same, it would look like this:
  - There would be 57 Asians, 21 Europeans, 14 from the Western Hemisphere, including North and South America, and eight from Africa.
  - Fifty-one would be female, and 49 would be male.
  - Seventy would be non-white, while 30 would be white.

- Sixty-six would be non-Christian and 33 Christian.
- Eighty would live in substandard housing.
- Seventy would be unable to read.
- Half would suffer from malnutrition.
- One would be near death, and one would be near birth.
- Only one would have a college education.
- Half of the entire village's wealth would be in the hands of only six people, and all six would be citizens of the United States.

Also, in order to further contort your perspective, note how drunk drivers are punished in America as opposed to how drunk drivers are punished in other countries.

Australia:
The names of the drivers are sent to the local newspapers and are printed under the heading: "He's Drunk and in Jail."

Malaysia:
The driver is jailed and if married, his wife is jailed too.

South Africa:
A ten-year prison sentence and the equivalent of a $10,000 fine.

Turkey:
Drunk drivers are taken twenty miles outside of town by police and are forced to walk back under escort.

Norway:
Three weeks in jail at hard labor, one year loss of license. Second offense within five years, license revoked for life.

Finland and Sweden:
Automatic jail and one year of hard labor.

Costa Rica:
Police remove plates from car.

Russia:
License revoked for life.

England:
One year suspension, a $25,000 fine, and jail for one year.

France:
Three year loss of license, one year in jail, and a $1,000 fine.

Poland:
Jail, fine, and forced to attend political lectures.

Bulgaria:
A second conviction results in execution.

El Salvador:
Your first offense is your last—execution by firing squad.

*Aspiring critical thinkers should research the aforementioned claims to further inform their world views. Moreover, regarding the penalties for drunk drivers, note how first, second, and third-time offenders are prosecuted in the United States. Also, note the following statistics:

- The NHTSA reports that during the period 1982 through 1999, approximately 349,472 persons lost their lives in alcohol-related traffic crashes.
- The NHTSA reports that more Americans have died in alcohol-related crashes than in all the wars the United States has been involved in since our country was founded.
- The CSAP in 1996 reported that eight people each day die in alcohol-related crashes.
- Approximately 1.4 million drivers were arrested in 1998 for driving under the influence of alcohol.

Such statistics might suggest that a problem exists; perhaps solutions should be found.

If you already committed to offering your "current world view," do you feel inclined to make a new decision based on new information? If so, you have begun thinking critically. Yes, though critical thinkers do take stands, they are intelligent enough to know that they will have to revise their respective stances, constantly looking to redefine their outlook based on an ever-changing society and an ever-emerging consciousness.

Now that you have defined your constitution and your "current world view," it is time for you to learn even more about yourself. It is time for you to begin asking the right questions. First of all, ask yourself this: What did you learn in high school that you found valuable? What didn't you learn? What expectations were fulfilled? As a high school graduate, do you feel rewarded or cheated?

Answer these questions before reading on.

Now, what have you learned in college that will prepare you for life after college? What skills must you still learn? To paraphrase Adrienne Rich, what parts of your college education can you afford to *receive,* and what parts must you *claim?* Answer these questions before reading on.

Remember, as a critical thinker, your job is not to offer right answers, but to ask right questions. In questioning the education you received in high school, you are beginning to define what, specifically, you must learn in college. By questioning what you will need following college, you may identify, specifically, what you must *demand* to learn before you enter the "real world."

Now, take out your pen and begin reading critically. This involves underlining, taking notes in the margin, reading and rereading, and, most importantly, asking questions. Remember, your brain, like a complex filing system, will look for answers (encourage your brain to offer you more than one answer—do not cling desperately to the first answer presented) to any questions you ask; however, you must ask the questions.

The Speech the Graduates Didn't Hear

Jacob Neusner

• •

Jacob Neusner, formerly university professor at Brown University, is Distinguished Professor of Religious Studies at the University of South Florida in Tampa. His speech appeared in Brown's The Daily Herald *on June 12, 1983.*

• • • • • • • • • •

We the faculty take no pride in our educational achievements with you. We have prepared you for a world that does not exist, indeed, that cannot exist. You have spent four years supposing that failure leaves no record. You have learned at Brown that when your work goes poorly, the painless solution is to drop out. But starting now, in the world to which you go, failure marks you. Confronting difficulty by quitting leaves you changed. Outside Brown, quitters are no heroes.

With us you could argue about why your errors were not errors, why mediocre work really was excellent, why you could take pride in routine and slipshod presentation. Most of you, after all, can look back on honor grades for most of what you have done. So, here grades can have meant little in distinguishing the excellent from the ordinary. But tomorrow, in the world to which you go, you had best not defend errors but learn from them. You will be ill-advised to demand praise for what does not deserve it, and abuse those who do not give it.

For four years we created an altogether forgiving world, in which whatever slight effort you gave was all that was demanded. When you did not keep appointments, we made new ones. When your work came in beyond the deadline, we pretended not to care.

Worse still, when you were boring, we acted as if you were saying something important. When you were garrulous and talked to hear yourself talk, we listened as if it mattered. When you tossed on our desks writing upon which you had not labored, we read it and even responded, as though you earned a response. When you were dull, we pretended you were smart. When you were predictable, unimaginative, and routine, we listened as if to new and wonderful things. When you demanded free lunch, we served it. And all this why?

Despite your fantasies, it was not even that we wanted to be liked by you. It was that we did not want to be bothered, and the easy way out was pretense: smiles and easy Bs.

It is conventional to quote in addresses such as these. Let me quote someone you've never heard of: Professor Carter A. Daniel, Rutgers University (*Chronicle of Higher Education*, May 7, 1979):

> *College has spoiled you by reading papers that don't deserve to be read, listening to comments that don't deserve a hearing, paying attention even to the lazy, ill-informed, and rude. We had to do it, for the sake of education. But nobody will ever do it again. College has deprived you of adequate preparation for the last fifty years. It has failed you by being easy, free, forgiving, attentive, comfortable, interesting, unchallenging fun. Good luck tomorrow.*

That is why, on this commencement day, we have nothing in which to take much pride.

Oh, yes, there is one more thing. Try not to act toward your coworkers and bosses as you have acted toward us. I mean, when they give you what you want but have not earned, don't abuse them, insult them, act out with them your parlous relationships with your parents. This too we have tolerated. It was, as I said, not to be liked. Few professors actually care whether or not they are liked by peer-paralyzed adolescents, fools so shallow as to imagine professors care not about education but about popularity. It was, again, to be rid of you. So go, unlearn the lies we taught you. To Life!

• •

Thoughts, Ideas, and Discussion Questions

1. Define *slipshod, garrulous, pretense,* and *parlous.*
2. Articulate Neusner's claim in one sentence.
3. Identify all of the facts in Neusner's article.
4. Neusner writes: "Outside Brown, quitters are no heroes." This implies, of course, that inside Brown quitters *are* heroes. Based on your own experiences in college and out of college, when are quitters considered heroes?
5. Neusner writes: "Worse still, when you were boring, we acted as if you were saying something important." Has this occurred to you in class or out of class while speaking to a faculty member?
6. Does Neusner's article include any sarcasm? If read aloud to a real student body, with what tone might this speech be delivered?
7. Note Neusner's final four sentences. As a student do you agree or disagree with his claims? Are you offended, humbled, or humored?
8. Neusner writes his article with style, choosing his words with tact and precision. Identify sections that you consider well-written.

Applications

1. Mark Twain once wrote, "The time to begin writing an article is when you have finished it to your satisfaction. By that time you begin to clearly and logically perceive what it is that you really want to say." In adherence to this advice, write a response to Neusner, praising or attacking his article. But again, as suggested by Twain, after you finish writing your response, begin creating the response that *really* represents how you feel and what you think about what Neusner wrote.
2. Write a short response to any one of Neusner's accusations.
3. Perform ten interviews, asking college graduates who have now entered the "real world" if Neusner's accusations/assumptions are true.
4. You probably listened to commencement speakers when you graduated from high school. If you remember what they said, are there things you would add or expunge from their addresses? If you were selected to give a commencement address, what would you write?

The Damned Human Race

Mark Twain

• •

Mark Twain, the pseudonym of Samuel Clemens (1835–1910), was a master satirist, journalist, novelist, orator, and steamboat pilot. He grew up in Hannibal, Missouri, a frontier setting which appears in different forms in several of his novels, most notably in his masterpiece The Adventures of Huckleberry Finn *(1869). His satirical eye spared very few American political or social institutions including slavery, and for this reason, as well as because it violated conventional standards of taste,* Huckleberry Finn *created a minor scandal when it was published. Nonetheless, with such books as* The Innocents Abroad *(1869),* Roughing It *(1872),* Old Times on the Mississippi *(1875),* The Adventures of Tom Sawyer *(1876), and* The Prince and the Pauper *(1882), Twain secured himself a position as one of the most popular authors in American history. "The Damned Human Race" comes from* Letters from the Earth *(1938). Twain built his career upon his experiences in the western states and his travels in Europe and the Middle East, but he eventually settled in Hartford, Connecticut. His last years were spent as one of the most celebrated public speakers and social figures in the United States.*

Reflecting upon the experience of writing, Twain once wrote in his notebook, "The time to begin writing an article is when you have finished it to your satisfaction. By that time you begin to clearly and logically perceive what it is that you really want to say."

• • • • • • • • •

I have been studying the traits and dispositions of the "lower animals" (so-called), and contrasting them with the traits and dispositions

---

"The Damned Human Race" by Mark Twain.

of man. I find the result humiliating to me. For it obliges me to renounce my allegiance to the Darwinian* theory of the Ascent of Man from the Lower Animals; since it now seems plain to me that that theory ought to be vacated in favor of a new and truer one, this new and truer one to be named the Descent of Man from the Higher Animals.

In proceeding toward this unpleasant conclusion I have not guessed or speculated or conjectured, but have used what is commonly called the scientific method. That is to say, I have subjected every postulate that presented itself to the crucial test of actual experiment, and have adopted it or rejected it according to the result. Thus I verified and established each step of my course in its turn before advancing to the next. These experiments were made in the London Zoological Gardens, and covered many months of painstaking and fatiguing work.

Before particularizing any of the experiments, I wish to state one or two things which seem to more properly belong in this place than further along. This in the interest of clearness. The massed experiments established to my satisfaction certain generalizations, to wit:

1. That the human race is of one distinct species. It exhibits slight variations—in color, stature, mental caliber, and so on—due to climate, environment, and so forth; but it is a species by itself, and not to be confounded with any other.
2. That the quadrupeds are a distinct family, also. This family exhibits variations—in color, size, food preferences and so on; but it is a family by itself.
3. That the other families—the birds, the fishes, the insects, the reptiles, etc.—are more or less distinct, also. They are in the procession. They are links in the chain which stretches down from the higher animals to man at the bottom.

Some of my experiments were quite curious. In the course of my reading I had come across a case where, many years ago, some hunters on our Great Plains organized a buffalo hunt for the entertainment of an English earl—that, and to provide some fresh meat for his larder. They had charming sport. They killed seventy-two of those

*Charles Darwin (1809–1882) published *The Descent of Man* in 1871, a highly controversial book in which he argued that human kind had descended from "lower" forms of life—Eds.

great animals; and ate part of one of them and left the seventy-one to rot. In order to determine the difference between an anaconda and an earl—if any—I caused seven young calves to be turned into the anaconda's cage. The grateful reptile immediately crushed one of them and swallowed it, then lay back satisfied. It showed no further interest in the calves, and no disposition to harm them. I tried this experiment with other anacondas; always with the same result. The fact stood proven that the difference between an earl and an anaconda is that the earl is cruel and the anaconda isn't; and that the earl wantonly destroys what he has no use for, but the anaconda doesn't. This seemed to suggest that the anaconda was not descended from the earl. It also seemed to suggest that the earl was descended from the anaconda and had lost a good deal in the transition.

I was aware that many men who have accumulated more millions of money than they can ever use have shown a rabid hunger for more, and have not scrupled to cheat the ignorant and the helpless out of their poor servings in order to partially appease that appetite. I furnished a hundred different kinds of wild and tame animals the opportunity to accumulate vast stores of food, but none of them would do it. The squirrels and bees and certain birds made accumulations, but stopped when they had gathered a winter's supply, and could not be persuaded to add to it either honestly or by chicane. In order to bolster up a tottering reputation the ant pretended to store up supplies, but I was not deceived. I know the ant. These experiments convinced me that there is this difference between man and the higher animals: He is avaricious and miserly, they are not.

In the course of my experiments I convinced myself that among the animals man is the only one that harbors insults and injuries, broods over them, waits till a chance offers, then takes revenge. The passion of revenge is unknown to the higher animals.

Roosters keep harems, but it is by consent of their concubines; therefore no wrong is done. Men keep harems, but it is by brute force, privileged by atrocious laws which the other sex were allowed no hand in making. In this matter man occupies a far lower place than the rooster.

Cats are loose in their morals, but not consciously so. Man, in his descent from the cat, has brought the cat's looseness with him but has left the unconsciousness behind—the saving grace which excuses the cat. The cat is innocent, man is not.

Indecency, vulgarity, obscenity—these are strictly confined to man; he invented them. Among the higher animals there is no trace of them. They hide nothing; they are not ashamed. Man, with his soiled mind, covers himself. He will not even enter a drawing room with his breast and back naked, so alive are he and his mates to indecent suggestion. Man is "The Animal that Laughs." But so does the monkey, as Mr. Darwin pointed out; and so does the Australian bird that is called the laughing jackass. No—Man is the Animal that Blushes. He is the only one that does it—or has occasion to.

At the head of this article* we see how "three monks were burnt to death" a few days ago, and a prior "put to death with atrocious cruelty." Do we inquire into the details? No; or we should find out that the prior was subjected to unprintable mutilations. Man—when he is a North American Indian—gouges out his prisoner's eyes; when he is King John, with a nephew to render untroublesome, he uses a red-hot iron; when he is a religious zealot dealing with heretics in the Middle Ages, he skins his captive alive and scatters salt on his back; in the first Richard's time he shuts up a multitude of Jew families in a tower and sets fire to it; in Columbus's time he captures a family of Spanish Jews and—but *that* is not printable; in our day in England a man is fined ten shillings for beating his mother nearly to death with a chair, and another man is fined forty shillings for having four pheasant eggs in his possession without being able to satisfactorily explain how he got them. Of all the animals, man is the only one that is cruel. He is the only one that inflicts pain for the pleasure of doing it. It is a trait that is not known to the higher animals. The cat plays with the frightened mouse; but she has this excuse, that she does not know that the mouse is suffering. The cat is moderate—unhumanly moderate: She only scares the mouse, she does not hurt it; she doesn't dig out its eyes, or tear off its skin, or drive splinters under its nails—manfashion; when she is done playing with it she makes a sudden meal of it and puts it out of its trouble. Man is the Cruel Animal. He is alone in that distinction.

The higher animals engage in individual fights, but never in organized masses. Man is the only animal that deals in that atrocity of atrocities, War. He is the only one that gathers his brethren about him

---

*In his nonfiction Twain often introduced newsclippings as evidence of human atrocity. In this instance the article has been lost, but Twain is most likely referring to the religious persecutions that followed the 1897 Cretan revolt.—Eds.

and goes forth in cold blood and with calm pulse to exterminate his kind. He is the only animal that for sordid wages will march out, as the Hessians did in our Revolution,* and as the boyish Prince Napoleon did in the Zulu war,** and help to slaughter strangers of his own species who have done him no harm and with whom he has no quarrel.

Man is the only animal that robs his helpless fellow of his country—takes possession of it and drives him out of it or destroys him. Man has done this in all the ages. There is not an acre of ground on the globe that is in possession of its rightful owner, or that has not been taken away from owner after owner, cycle after cycle, by force and bloodshed.

Man is the only Slave. And he is the only animal who enslaves. He has always been a slave in one form or another, and has always held other slaves in bondage under him in one way or another. In our day he is always some man's slave for wages, and does that man's work; and this slave has other slaves under him for minor wages, and they do *his* work. The higher animals are the only ones who exclusively do their own work and provide their own living.

Man is the only Patriot. He sets himself apart in his own country, under his own flag, and sneers at the other nations, and keeps multitudinous uniformed assassins on hand at heavy expense to grab slices of other people's countries, and keep *them* from grabbing slices of *his*. And in the intervals between campaigns he washes the blood off his hands and works for "the universal brotherhood of man"—with his mouth.

Man is the Religious Animal. He is the only Religious Animal. He is the only animal that has the True Religion—several of them. He is the only animal that loves his neighbor as himself, and cuts his throat if his theology isn't straight. He has made a graveyard of the globe in trying his honest best to smooth his brother's path to happiness and heaven. He was at it in the time of the Caesars, he was at it in Mahomet's time, he was at it in the time of the Inquisition, he was at it

---

Revolution: Approximately 17,000 mercenaries from Hesse, a part of Germany, fought for the British during the American Revolution.—Eds.

**Zulu war:* Napolean III's son died while fighting for the British during the 1879 Zulu rebellion in what is now the Republic of South Africa. Great Britain annexed the Zulu territory shortly after, and that is the context for Twain's remarks in the next paragraph.—Eds.

in France a couple of centuries, he was at it in England in Mary's day,* he has been at it ever since he first saw the light, he is at it to-day in Crete—as per the telegrams quoted above—he will be at it somewhere else tomorrow. The higher animals have no religion. And we are told that they are going to be left out, in the Hereafter. I wonder why? It seems questionable taste.

Man is the Reasoning Animal. Such is the claim. I think it is open to dispute. Indeed, my experiments have proven to me that he is the Unreasoning Animal. Note his history, as sketched above. It seems plain to me that whatever he is he is *not* a reasoning animal. His record is the fantastic record of a maniac. I consider that the strongest count against his intelligence is the fact that with that record back of him he blandly sets himself up as the head animal of the lot: Whereas by his own standards he is the bottom one.

In truth, man is incurably foolish. Simple things which the other animals easily learn, he is incapable of learning. Among my experiments was this. In an hour I taught a cat and a dog to be friends. I put them in a cage. In another hour I taught them to be friends with a rabbit. In the course of two days I was able to add a fox, a goose, a squirrel and some doves. Finally a monkey. They lived together in peace; even affectionately.

Next, in another cage I confined an Irish Catholic from Tipperary, and as soon as he seemed tame I added a Scotch Presbyterian from Aberdeen. Next a Turk from Constantinople; a Greek Christian from Crete; an Armenian; a Methodist from the wilds of Arkansas; a Buddhist from China; a Brahman from Benares. Finally, a Salvation Army Colonel from Wapping. Then I stayed away two whole days. When I came back to note results, the cage of Higher Animals was all right, but in the other there was but a chaos of gory odds and ends of turbans and fezzes and plaids and bones and flesh—not a specimen left alive. These Reasoning Animals had disagreed on a theological detail and carried the matter to a Higher Court.

One is obliged to concede that in true loftiness of character, Man cannot claim to approach even the meanest of the Higher Animals. It is plain that he is constitutionally incapable of approaching that altitude; that he is constitutionally afflicted with a Defect which must

---

Mary's day: In the time of Mary I, who reigned as Queen of England between 1553 and 1558; her vigorous persecution of Protestants earned her the nickname "Bloody Mary."—Eds.

make such approach forever impossible, for it is manifest that this defect is permanent in him, indestructible, ineradicable.

I find this Defect to be *the* Moral Sense. He is the only animal that has it. It is the secret of his degradation. It is the quality *which enables him to do wrong*. It has no other office. It is incapable of performing any other function. It could never have been intended to perform any other. Without it, man could do no wrong. He would rise at once to the level of the Higher Animals.

Since the Moral Sense has but the one office, the one capacity—to enable man to do wrong—it is plainly without value to him. It is as valueless to him as is disease. In fact, it manifestly is a disease. *Rabies* is bad, but it is not so bad as this disease. Rabies enables a man to do a thing which he could not do when in a healthy state: kill his neighbor with a poisonous bite. No one is the better man for having rabies. The Moral Sense enables a man to do wrong. It enables him to do wrong in a thousand ways. Rabies is an innocent disease, compared to the Moral Sense. No one, then, can be the better man for having the Moral Sense. What, now, do we find the Primal Curse to have been? Plainly what it was in the beginning: the infliction upon man of the Moral Sense; the ability to distinguish good from evil; and with it, necessarily, the ability to *do* evil; for there can be no evil act without the presence of consciousness of it in the doer of it.

And so I find that we have descended and degenerated, from some far ancestor—some microscopic atom wandering at its pleasure between the mighty horizons of a drop of water perchance—insect by insect, animal by animal, reptile by reptile, down the long highway of smirchless innocence, till we have reached the bottom stage of development—namable as the Human Being. Below us—nothing. Nothing but the Frenchman.

There is only one possible stage below the Moral Sense; that is the Immoral Sense. The Frenchman has it. Man is but little lower than the angels. This definitely locates him. He is between the angels and the French.

Man seems to be a rickety poor sort of a thing, any way you take him; a kind of British Museum of infirmities and inferiorities. He is always undergoing repairs. A machine that was as unreliable as he is would have no market. On top of his specialty—the Moral Sense—are piled a multitude of minor infirmities; such a multitude, indeed, that one may broadly call them countless. The higher animals get their teeth without pain or inconvenience. Man gets his through months and months of cruel torture; and at a time of life when he is but ill able to bear it. As soon as he has got them they must all be pulled out again, for they were of no value in the first place, not worth the loss of a night's rest. The second set will answer for a while, by being reinforced occasionally with rubber or plugged up with gold; but he will never get a set which can really be depended on till a dentist makes him one. This set will be called "false" teeth—as if he had ever worn any other kind.

In a wild state—a natural state—the Higher Animals have a few diseases; diseases of little consequence; the main one is old age. But man starts in as a child and lives on diseases till the end, as a regular diet. He has mumps, measles, whooping cough, croup, tonsillitis, diphtheria, scarlet fever, almost as a matter of course. Afterward, as he goes along, his life continues to be threatened at every turn: by colds, coughs, asthma, bronchitis, itch, cholera, cancer, consumption, yellow fever, bilious fever, typhus fevers, hay fever; ague, chilblains, piles, inflammation of the entrails, indigestion, toothache, earache, deafness, dumbness, blindness, influenza, chicken pox, cowpox, smallpox, liver complaint, constipation, bloody flux, warts, pimples, boils, carbuncles, abscesses, bunions, corns, tumors, fistulas, pneumonia, softening of the brain, melancholia and fifteen other kinds of insanity; dysentery, jaundice, diseases of the heart, the bones, the skin, the scalp, the spleen, the kidneys, the nerves, the brain, the blood; scrofula, paralysis, leprosy, neuralgia, palsy, fits, headache, thirteen kinds of rheumatism, forty-six of gout, and a formidable supply of gross and unprintable disorders of one sort and another. Also—but why continue the list? The mere names of the agents appointed to keep this shackly machine out of repair would hide him from sight if printed on his body in the smallest type known to the founder's art. He is but a basket of pestilent corruption provided for the support and entertainment of swarming armies of bacilli—armies commissioned to rot him and destroy him, and each army equipped with a special detail of the work. The process of waylaying him, persecuting him, rotting him, killing him, begins with his first breath, and there is no mercy, no pity, no truce till he draws his last one.

Look at the workmanship of him, in certain of its particulars. What are his tonsils for? They perform no useful function; they have no value. They have no business there. They are but a trap. They have but the one office, the one industry: to provide tonsillitis and quinsy and such things for the possessor of them. And what is the vermiform appendix for? It has no value; it cannot perform any useful service. It is but an ambuscaded enemy whose sole interest in life is to lie in wait for stray grapeseeds and employ them to breed strangulated hernia.

And what are the male's mammals for? For business, they are out of the question; as an ornament, they are a mistake. What is his beard for? It performs no useful function; it is a nuisance and a discomfort; all nations hate it; all nations persecute it with a razor. And because it is a nuisance and a discomfort, Nature never allows the supply of it to fall short, in any man's case, between puberty and the grave. You never see a man bald-headed on his chin. But his hair! It is a graceful ornament, it is a comfort, it is the best of all protections against certain perilous ailments, man prizes it above emeralds and rubies. And because of these things Nature puts it on, half the time, so that it won't stay. Man's sight, smell, hearing, sense of locality—how inferior they are. The condor sees a corpse at five miles; man has no telescope that can do it. The bloodhound follows a scent that is two days old. The robin hears the earthworm burrowing his course under the ground. The cat, deported in a closed basket, finds its way home again through twenty miles of country which it has never seen.

Certain functions lodged in the other sex perform in a lamentably inferior way as compared with the performance of the same functions in the Higher Animals. In the human being, menstruation, gestation and parturition are terms which stand for horrors. In the Higher Animals these things are hardly even inconveniences.

For style, look at the Bengal tiger—that ideal of grace, beauty, physical perfection, majesty. And then look at Man—that poor thing. He is the Animal of the Wig, the Trepanned Skull, the Ear Trumpet, the Glass Eye, the Pasteboard Nose, the Porcelain Teeth, the Silver Windpipe, the Wooden Leg—a creature that is mended and patched all over, from top to bottom. if he can't get renewals of his bric-a-brac in the next world, what will he look like?

He has just one stupendous superiority. In his intellect he is supreme. The Higher Animals cannot touch him there. It is curious, it is noteworthy, that no heaven has ever been offered him wherein his one sole superiority was provided with a chance to enjoy itself. Even when he himself has imagined a heaven, he has never made provision in it for intellectual joys. It is a striking omission. It seems a tacit confession that heavens are provided for the Higher Animals alone. This is matter for thought; and for serious thought. And it is full of a grim suggestion: that we are not as important, perhaps, as we had all along supposed we were.

• •

Thoughts, Ideas, and Discussion Questions

1. Define *quadrupeds, larder, scrupled, appease, chicane, tottering, avaricious, miserly, broods, brethren, fezzes, degradation, lamentably, gestation, parturition.*
2. Articulate Twain's claim in one sentence.
3. Does Twain poke fun at the scientific method, or does he use it as a vehicle to add credibility to his satire?
4. In paragraph 17, Twain writes: "And in the intervals between campaigns he washes the blood off his hands and works for 'the universal brotherhood of man'—with his mouth." What is Twain asserting?
5. In paragraphs 18, 21, and 32, Twain mocks religion. How is this mockery germane to his claim?
6. According to Twain, Man suffers from a defect: the Moral Sense. Do you agree with Twain that the Moral Sense "has but the one office, the one capacity—to enable man to do wrong"?
7. What groups of people is Twain making fun of in his essay?
8. What flaws exist in Twain's essay?

Applications

1. Write "The Damned Human Race II," using examples from current issues, problems, wars, or "skirmishes" to support your claim.
2. Invert Twain's claim, and write an essay supporting Man as the evolutionary by-product of the Lower Animals. Simply put, support Darwin's theory, and disprove Twain's.

The Uncritical American; or, Nobody's from Missouri Any More

Wayne C. Booth

• •

Wayne C. Booth, the George M. Pullman Distinguished Service Professor of English at the University of Chicago, is the author of many widely acclaimed books, including The Rhetoric of Fiction *and* The Rhetoric of Irony. *"The Uncritical American; or, Nobody's From Missouri Anymore," is an article adapted from a chapter in Mr. Booth's* Now Don't Try to Reason with Me: Essays and Ironies for a Credulous Age, *which was published in Fall, 1970. The original audience for this article was an annual conference of English Teachers at Asilower in California.*

• • • • • • • • •

1

My family were almost all passionately committed to "education." They were schoolteachers, most of them, and they believed in the righteousness of collecting academic degrees. Their church had taught them that man cannot be saved in ignorance, that the glory of God is intelligence, and that any right-living man can become a god of his own world by learning—over aeons—how to do it. Yet they were deeply suspicious of that chief product of genuine education, the critical intelligence. The very words "criticism" and "critical" were anathema throughout my adolescence, when I was first discovering the pleasures of critical probing. "Anybody can criticize," my mother would say to me, in rebuke, even as she struggled toward her

From *Now Don't Try to Reason with Me: Essays and Ironies for a Credulous Age* by Wayne C. Booth, 1970. Reprinted by permission of University of Chicago Press, publisher.

bachelor's degree, won at age forty-five, and her master's degree at fifty. "If you only wouldn't stir things up so much," she would say, while encouraging me in what she liked to call my progress toward the Ph.D. There was never the slightest doubt in anyone's mind that to move toward higher and higher degrees was to *progress*; yet whenever I tried to apply anything important that I learned from my best teachers—whenever, that is, I tried really to think about everyday matters like politics or church belief or the Boy Scout movement, it was, "There you go, criticizing again!"

I don't suppose anyone will be surprised when I say that in this ambivalence toward education and its fruits my family was very much like the whole of this nation today. Never before has a country spent so much of its substance on education; everyone pursues degrees like merit badges, and it is quite clear that the kingdom of heaven is closed to dropouts, no matter what we heretics may say. And yet few of us seem willing to accept the educated behavior that ought to result from formal education. Few graduates of our high schools or colleges seem able to apply their minds in an educated way to the world around them; few of them threaten anyone with a genuinely critical judgment. I don't know whether we are a more credulous generation than our fathers, but it surely must be true that in proportion to the amount of time and money we spend ostensibly educating each other we are the most credulous, gullible, superstitious people of all time.

Since if this is true it is a pretty serious indictment of all of us teachers, I'll want to give some documentation about it as we go along. But first I should make clear that I am not simply repeating that old charge men often make against those who believe what to them are foolish or outlandish beliefs. It is easy to whip together a collection of all of the nonsense *other* men believe, label it something like *The Anatomy of Nonsense,* or *The Prevalence of Nonsense,* or *Scientific Fads and Fallacies,* or *Science Is a Sacred Cow,* or *Strange Beliefs of Mankind,* or *The Age of Credulity,* or *Bouvard et Pecuchet,* or *This Believing World*—and you've got a very amusing book. Such collections of stupidities, such *sottisiers,* usually say more about the collector than about those he describes. Every such book I have seen has succumbed to the temptation of making the beliefs seem more outlandish than they ever were in their original form, in order to make the collection more amusing or startling. But when I describe our time as a credulous time, I am not thinking of our many crazy beliefs so much as of the *way* we believe them; not what we believe but how. Even if all of us knew the ten most insidious errors of our time, and set out to spend the rest of our lives correcting them, we could not hope to make an appreciable difference in the Total Error Count, our TEC, before we die: ten errors will spring up for every one we kill, and what is more, we will ourselves manufacture errors even as we try to communicate our beautiful list of truths. But if you and I could learn to think for ourselves, and if in our lifetimes we helped a few of our fellows to do the same, our troubled country might someday notice the difference.

The test is, then: What process has been gone through by the believer before he has made up his mind? An educated man in this sense is one who requires of himself certain kinds of mental activity before he will accept an idea, follow a leader, embrace a plan of action, or embark on a way of life. He will certainly make use in his cogitations of promptings from the heart and gut, but knowing as he does that these organs are the devil's favorites, he will reserve a special scrutiny for all beliefs that carry with them slogans like "In your heart you know he's right." He will never forget that like all other men, he lives in error. There is no way to avoid it, in any society, and especially in one like ours that employs a huge corps of professional deceivers who work full time to maximize, as it were, our TEC quotient. But knowing how inescapably he shares the common lot, he will know one thing that is not common: how to match the degree of his conviction to the quality of his reasons. He will labor to believe only when belief is warranted and to doubt only when doubt is warranted, and he will thus labor to master the processes of thought that yield warrantable belief or doubt.

2

When we shift our concern in this way from *what* is believed to *how* it is believed, it is easy to see that our problem is not simply one of a too easy affirmation. We do have many round-heeled folk whose minds are easily seduced, and we have polite old-fashioned words for them: they are credulous or they are gullible or they are superstitious. The words for those who fail in the opposite direction are not so clear. Some of them we call cynical, or skeptical; we might coin a word *substitious*. Young people often try to simulate education by moving from superstition to substition. After all, if I don't commit myself to anything or anybody, nobody can accuse me of naive commitment. But once they have found some sort of commitment, they accuse those who refuse to follow them of being "overly analytical," of spoiling the world by intellectualizing it. College students often accuse faculty and administrators of using reason to postpone commitment and action, or substituting study and scholarship for the truths of the heart.

As soon as we look behind the epithets used by believers and doubters against each other, I think it becomes clear that to be genuinely critical—to judge on the basis of thought—is to have no easily predictable relationship with belief or doubt, with yes or no, with joining or splitting. The critical mind does not know in advance which side it will come out on, and the surest sign that a man has given up thinking is to find that the yeses and nos flow in predictable, general patterns. Someone said that the trouble with President Johnson was that you couldn't even rely on the *opposite* of what he said. The joke was intended initially against Johnson. But it bounced back finally against the teller. Like the rest of us, he wanted a neat formula for belief: my enemy is *for* it, so I know where *I* stand.

It is clear then that it will do no good to indict a "nation of sheep" and try to turn them into a nation of mules. A blind confidence in negation is as credulous, as uncritical, as a blind confidence in affirmation. In fact the two forms of blindness are very closely related, and easily lead into each other: mankind cannot endure very much uncritical doubt for long, and it is not surprising that men who have learned that nothing can be proved soon feel licensed to believe anything they damn please. If no convictions can be finally supported by reason, then why not succumb to the will to believe something—anything—rather than operate in a belief vacuum?

It is scarcely surprising, then, that all about us we see social and religious solutions being invented and embraced as lightly as one might choose a breakfast food. For some it is the John Birch Society—a group whose works are clearly going to affect our lives with increasingly disastrous results in the next few years. For others it is left-wing groups showing equal carelessness about fact and an open contempt for any attempt to think things through. For some it is new religions whose claims are embraced without even a pretence at thought; for others it is one or another of the pseudo-psycho-religions, claiming to cure the soul with nudity or vegetables or group therapy sessions or orgone boxes or omphalic worship or standing on your head. Nothing has surprised me more than the recent revival, among would-be intellectuals, of interest in astrology. Astrology has always had its believers, but now one finds adherents cropping up everywhere—

not just in reactionary bastions like the Living Theater but among students in major colleges and universities. I don't have time to give here my neat little refutation of the claims of astrology, but needless to say they are not decisive for anyone who has already decided to believe. What is interesting—for those of us who are interested in that sort of thing—is the comic flimsiness of the evidence offered *for* astrology— or for astroprojection or for flying-saucerism or whatever. No doubt each of these and innumerable other beliefs *work,* as we say, for some believers. Miraculous cures occur in most new religions, and they are not to be scoffed at, especially when they are performed by the devil himself. Even those curious half-religions that spring up around academic subjects have the power to heal loneliness or boredom: if Bacon or Marlow really wrote Shakespeare's plays, life may be interesting after all. And if you ask me for evidence, you are at best a spoil-sport and more likely an enemy of the Light.

We seem to be approaching a glorious age when everyman will be entitled to his own cult, as a birthright. Can we wonder that a man as intelligent as Malcolm X should require decades to see through Fard's myth of Yacob when his white brothers, with university degrees, were preaching Velikovsky's myth of the earth's history or Egyptian numerology or what not? I know men who talk as if they would give their lives for this or that totally conjectural theory about who killed Kennedy or King or Kennedy, or about a currency standard that will save the world, or about how the Jews are conspiring for world mastery. Most of us seem convinced that commitment is so valuable that even a commitment to madness is better than apathy. Somehow we have failed to teach those who have passed through our schools—and all of these credulous folk have done so—that commitment is admirable only when it is to admirable causes. When a member of the California state board of education, George A. Brown, commits himself to a pernicious campaign of censorship, his commitment is a pathetic thing because it is uncritical. No doubt he has the best of intentions, as we say. He believes that he is serving truth and virtue (or so one can assume). But even the most elementary critical ability—what one would hope for from an average eighth grader—would have shown him that truth and virtue are not served by cutting swear words out of short stories. Mr. Brown wants Hugh Hefner's story deleted from a text because Hefner's Playboy philosophy is objectionable. I happen to think the Playboy philosophy one of the silliest bits of intellectual pretension ever to catch the American mind and heart, and its popularity illustrates my theses about uncritical Americans. But did none of us teachers ever try to teach Mr. Brown that this method of combatting Hefner's story is first undemocratic, second irrelevant, third fatally ineffective, and fourth unnecessary? Mr. Brown is, I'm afraid, closer than he would think to the current mood of many college students who believe, or seem to, not only that truth can be discovered intuitively (and it can be) but that it is tested that way as well. The motto seems to be, If you feel it's true, it's true. Well, I was brought up with this notion, which was used by every religious denomination, including my own, to demonstrate its superior truth. One man who lived not far from my home *felt* in his heart that God had commanded him to kill his wife, and he did. Last spring two other men acted, apparently, on the truths of the self-righteous heart and assassinated what they took to be enemies of our country.

I have been coming dangerously close to the very error I warned against—listing "foolish beliefs" as if in themselves they provided proof of our uncritical habits. But they do not. For all I really *know,* some of these beliefs may turn back against me ultimately, by proving to be true. I do think that our eagerness to embrace any belief that happens along points to our mass credulity, but a much more convincing kind of evidence is found when we look at how men proceed when they attempt to persuade each other.

3

Every argument (whether openly argumentative or disguised as journalism or literature) will betray the author's picture of the educational level of his readers, and it will do so far more profoundly than in the simple choice of vocabulary that is sometimes tested by the news media when they want to discover whether they are writing over everyone's heads. The picture of the reader will be made most revealingly at those many points at which the writer ceases to push his argument, believing that he has found an assertion which the reader will take either as self-evident fact or as self-evident principle or assumption. If an author tells me that I should vote for Wallace because the Supreme Court has gone too far too fast in its decisions on race relations, he has told me not only something about himself but something about his picture of me; if another author tells me I should vote for Wallace because it is good to get the racists out into the open—period—he has told me something of his picture of my natural assumptions and natural critical expectations. And I submit that the reader implicitly portrayed by what gets addressed to the American public these days, in general journals of left, right, and center, is one that ought to scare us all.

Take as an example an article on "The Good Things in America Today" in *U.S. News & World Report*. It was published just after the Democratic convention of 1968, when perhaps more people than ever before were calling America "sick," and though it was thinly disguised as a "report," it argued quite openly, from the title on, that "the nation's strengths are . . . great and varied," that "the United States today is not the 'sick giant' so often portrayed by critics—but a strong and powerful nation, one that continues to be the envy of the world at large." Now I think a case might be made for this position, but it would not be an *easy* case. If it were made with care, by someone who took the trouble to look first at the arguments for our being a sick society, it would induce thought on both sides, and it might even lead to some ideas about how to capitalize on our strengths and reduce our weaknesses. But how do you suppose *U.S. News & World Report* handles the case?

The article reveals in every detail that the anonymous author assumes a reader fat for the kill—not only already in agreement, or very nearly so, but unaware of any possible counterarguments and totally indifferent to all demands for coherence of argument or precision and relevance of factual evidence. The editors of *U.S. News & World Report* see their readers as prosperous, white businessmen—and there's nothing *especially* wrong in that. But that they should see them as ignorant, uncritical, complacent white businessmen is disturbing, since it seems likely that most of the readers are formally educated, as we say—not just high school graduates but college trained.

The first three arguments for the thesis of health appear under the boldface heading "So much for so many": (1) "Never, in the past, has a society offered so much prosperity to so many of its people." The reader presumably can be counted on to remind himself that he shares in this prosperity, and he needs no proof that his material prosperity is a sign of national health. Yet it takes only a moment's thought to show that nobody who has claimed that the nation is sick has denied our material prosperity—not in this sense. (2) "Far from being a sick society, Americans in the majority are showing themselves to be strong and morally responsible." It feels good to be told that you are strong and morally responsible, especially when others have been nagging at you about how peaked you look. The only evidence given, therefore, at this point, is that Americans "are spending billions to erase poverty in the nation—and more billions to help other nations." Again this would not be denied, as a bare fact, by the critics, and the reader is expected to say to himself, "Actually I'm generous to a fault—all that money down the drain, and all we get for it is criticism." The evidence for strength is our "nuclear defense system . . . that is providing security for much of the world. American troops drove Communist invaders out of South Korea, kept the peace in Lebanon and staved off a Communist take-over in South Vietnam." Again it is revealing that the author stops at this point; these are thought to be self-evidently good things, as signs of our strength. The reader is postulated as someone so uncritical that he will not know or will forget that for most of those who call the country sick, the undeclared war in Vietnam is one symptom of the disease. (3) Next we turn to culture, and we learn that "the 'American way of life' is turning up everywhere"—the two pieces of evidence offered are that young people in Communist countries "are playing 'rock' music" and that in France the "light luncheon favored by American businessmen is making heavy inroads on the Parisian cuisine"!

And so we go on through this cheerful, mindless landscape. There are, of course, some arguments in the piece that might be taken seriously by critics as well as by the presold: for example, professors might be impressed by the assertion that "university presses, alone, have multiplied sales five times since 1948." But the interesting revelations come from all those arguments that will seem absurd, or at best incomplete, from *any* other point of view except that of the "uncritical American." Some arguments are so curious that it is hard not to suspect that the editors are joking: "Similarly, a French philosopher noted: 'To make life simpler in an increasingly complicated world is an American art.' That art is making it possible, as one instance, for Americans to dial a number on the telephone and hear a prayer, a short sermon, the latest baseball scores, a lecture on alcoholism, or argument against committing suicide." One can imagine exactly the same list used by proponents of the view that America is sick, since Americans cannot distinguish the important from the trivial, and do not see the difference between "dialing a prayer" and praying. But such imaginings are not assumed to be within the capacity of the reader of this piece.

One good way, then, to discern the reader whose uncritical biases are being played to, is to ask, "Where do the arguments stop? What is thought to need no proof?" Another way is to look at what lines of argument are most heavily emphasized and what played down or ignored. In this piece, economic power abroad and prosperity at home ("for the majority") are dwelt on lovingly: "America's economic power, far from declining, is pushing ahead to even more dominance in the world." "Predictions are heard that U.S. industry on that continent [Europe] soon will become the world's third-largest economic power—after America itself and Soviet Russia." When poverty is mentioned, it is "what passes for poverty," and it is "seen by many foreigners as an acceptable standard of living." There is no mention of reports of widespread starvation and malnutrition in America. When black America is discussed, it is almost entirely in terms of the increased prosperity of those above the poverty line: "Since 1960, the number of Negro families earning more than $7,000 a year has more than doubled. Median income of the Negro family has gone up from $3,233 in 1960 to $4,900."

Even when the article finally returns for a second try at cultural matters like education, books, and music, the emphasis is statistical and economic. It is assumed that there is no reason to meet arguments against the *quality* of education, so long as we have more people in college and high school than other nations. Nothing need be said about the *quality* of the books we produce, so long as the "dollar volume" of book sales has doubled in ten years. When religion is mentioned, again statistics are decisive: "45 percent of all Americans" attend church during a typical week; "97 percent of adult Americans" believe in the existence of God.

No such analysis as we are undertaking here can tell us whether the conclusions of the writer are true; all we can say is that the reasons offered could be persuasive only for a reader with certain very strong and very obvious prejudgments and certain very dangerous habits of mind. He believes in economic and military power as ends in themselves; he is impressed by quantities rather than qualities; he enjoys personal prosperity and power and does not want to think about them; he wants to feel that he and his country are moral and generous and "cultured" (but he doesn't care too much about the details); and he is terribly eager to be convinced that things are getting better all the time. The boldface headings of the sections taken by themselves reveal these biases almost in schematic form: "So much for so many; Succor to world, Story of progress; Rise from poverty; Production miracle; A rugged dollar; America's head start; Passion for education; Europe surpassed; Book-buying people; Wide map for culture; How Americans really feel; Steady, undramatic lives; Money ignored; Courage rewarded." (The evidence about the praise-worthy indifference to money—"college youngsters" work in slums and in camps for underprivileged children—is especially interesting in view of the contrasting evidence throughout the article that the readers of this magazine are not the least inclined to ignore money.)

Lest I overpersuade you, I must repeat that no analysis of this kind, even if prolonged indefinitely, can establish the falsehood either of the general case or of the particular claims used to support it. All it can lead to is an assessment of the adequacy of the *case made* to the *conclusions*. And when the case made is as feeble as this one, we can only infer that the assumed reader is by no conceivable stretch of our definition an educated man. It is hard to deduce whether the author is consciously playing down to a least common critical denominator or is himself unaware of how shoddy his case is. If he is aware—and there is plenty of evidence that the writers of such articles in the weekly media frequently are—then we have proof of a moral as well as an intellectual problem; his cynicism is a direct threat to us all. If he is unaware, then we have just one more uneducated man on our collective conscience: if he, or any of his presumed readers, ever studied under any of us, and we tell him now that he is pathetically unqualified for making his way in the world, can we English teachers honestly claim to have done all that might have been done for him, before it was too late?

Anyone who once starts thinking about these matters will find examples in almost every journal, left, right, and center. I could have spent time, for example, on an incredibly empty piece in *Ramparts,* a panegyric on District Attorney Garrison in which the evidence supporting him and his conspiracy theory is chiefly assertions about the stupidity and wickedness of Garrison's enemies and about his own courage and liberality of viewpoint. Or I could have used examples from SDS literature, in which unproved assumptions about depraved America and its revolutionary situation are offered fully as uncritically as anything else I have quoted. I could have used the opening pages of Mark Lane's *Rush to Judgment* or the lines of so-called argument in any one of dozens of pieces of literary criticism *in my files* (as the other McCarthy used to say). Or I could have used the advertisements of intellectual journals. I especially like the ad of a new journal, the Marshall McLuhan Newsletter, which will cost fifty dollars a year and which promises to get itself into my hands in as "little as 72 hours after Mr. McLuhan has written it." Its service will include, the ad says, not only detecting changes in American society "the minute they occur—but following them, monitoring them, checking their feedback to evaluation potential and consequences at every stage. This is not (like a book) merely a snapshot of the present; it is a radar-fix on its every movement." Here is prophecy, hot off the mountaintop, available for only fifty dollars a year, and cheap at the price. The only reasons for subscribing, stated or implied, are that the stuff will be new, up to date, hot off the mind, and that it will thus put you ahead of other men if you read it. I tremble as I wonder whether any of my former students will fall for that ad.

4

None of this gets us very far in the positive task of deciding how we should think and how we should act. What are the *valid* processes by which an educated man tests whether he should believe or doubt? Where *does* truth come from? Doesn't it often come intuitively, and are we not all dependent, as Pascal said, on truths of the heart that reason does not recognize? And if that is so, aren't we right back where we started?

Well, I hope not, not if we can become aware of the temptations and make it a major task of our lives to learn how to combat them. I certainly cannot claim to know any simple formulas for the processes of heart and mind that will carry us through fraud and greed and folly to sound beliefs and effective action. But I am convinced both that the task of becoming educated is more difficult than ever before and that, in spite of what some people are saying, it is still both possible and relevant. We cannot solve all of life's problems by learning to think, but we can't solve any of them without it. We can't avoid mistakes by determining to combat the new credulity, but we will make many more if we simply swim with the tide. Thinking for oneself of course gets one into kinds of trouble that simply accepting slogans and cliches often avoids. It may, in fact, lead to imprisonment and even death if our society should finally, like many societies past and present, corrupt itself to the point of denying us the right to free thought.

In the next few years the uncritical Americans are going to come out of the woodwork in battle array, and in increasing numbers. In their very existence they are an indictment of American education and, by implication, of the English teachers who have failed to educate them. In their attack on us, however, they may show us more clearly than some of us have seen what the nature of our vocation is. We are committed to the awakening of minds, to the sharpening of the critical intelligence, to the creation of critical Americans. There is no profession nobler than this—if we practice it honestly and well. And there is no profession which so clearly has the future of America in its hands. If that frightens us a little, it ought to, even as we remember for our comfort Socrates' discovery that it is better for a man to die than to stop thinking.

• •

Thoughts, Ideas, and Discussion Questions

1. Define *anathema, ambivalence, credulous, epithets, pretense, affirmation, bastions, pernicious, peaked, postulated, discern, schematic, panegyric, depraved.*
2. Articulate Booth's claim in one sentence. (You may find it helpful to summarize each section; then, see if the four summaries support one particular claim.)
3. Booth is not as bothered by "our many crazy beliefs," but he is bothered by "the way we believe them." Identify this "way" we believe.
4. Why must a critical thinker, according to Booth, not vacillate but commit to one side of an issue?
5. According to Booth, is a commitment to madness better than apathy?
6. How are "prejudgments and certain very dangerous habits of mind" related to lacking critical thought when reading or listening to an argument?
7. To support his claim, Booth writes, "I could have used the advertisements of intellectual journals," and then he proceeds *to use* one of the advertisements for support. He uses this "I could have used" technique several times. Is it effective? Is it more effective than what he could have achieved by adhering to traditional argumentative form?

Applications

1. Take a stand arguing for or against Booth's claim. Use examples from advertising, magazines, newspapers, and journals for support.
2. Scrutinize between five and ten newspaper or magazine articles. Assign a numerical evaluation (1–10) to each article; this evaluation should reflect how educated the writer of the article thinks her reader is. Then, offer a written evaluation of each article to support the assigned numerical evaluations.

If you're still reading, you are probably strong-willed or simply embracing a subservient role as a student in a required course. This first chapter is steeped in negativity, what some might consider pessimism, but it probably succeeded in doing one thing: increasing your awareness. If so, you're taking the road less traveled, and hopefully you're beginning to deviate from the herd mentality. Hopefully, you'll be presented with the staff; you can be a shepherd (or at least a sheep dog).

What is now important, especially in a chapter titled "What is Critical Thinking?", is to address argumentative etiquette. There is an etiquette to just about everything, and there are definitely things that anybody who is studying critical thinking and argumentation should know. Thus, what follows are six lessons in critical thinking (with a title inspired by Wayne Booth):

Lessons in Critical Thinking; or, an Argument Is Only Pointless if We Have The Experience But Miss The Meaning

argument = a discussion (an argument is not a quarrel).
thinking critically = this does not mean thinking negatively. Critical thinking can be completely positive, completely negative or, more responsibly, an amalgamation of both.

1. **If you ask a question and do not get the answer you desired, ask the same question differently.** This strategy can be found when people take polls. For instance, one pollster might compose the following question: Do you support programs that provide money to people living below the defined poverty level? Now, if the percentage of people answering "yes" were 79%, and if the pollster needed a much lower number to satisfy his administration's needs, he might ask the same question differently. For instance, he might write: Do you support welfare programs? Since it is the same question, but it is just being asked differently, perhaps the percentage should still be the same. Unfortunately, words have an awful tendency to frame perceptions and, hence, that might explain why when this question was asked after the initial question, a much lower percentage of people answered "yes." Still, by asking the same question differently, the pollster attained his goal. This strategy is also evidenced in sales. Essentially, whether the salesperson is selling houses, automobiles, office buildings, airplanes, or businesses, the answer he is looking for is "yes." However, you may notice that when a salesperson asks you, "So, would you like to get this car today?" and you say "no," the salesperson does not pack up his proverbial bags and leave. Instead, he

attempts to address your objection, identify with it, and refute it. His refutation, of course, will probably end with the same question being asked differently: "So, based on that new information, would you like to drive away in this car today?" Similarly, when engaged in an argument, if you ask a question and do not get the answer you desired, ask the same question differently. Offer new information. Offer hypothetical examples. Of course, you may never get the person to change his mind. You may, however, get the person to make a new decision based on new information. And that new decision may be the answer you were looking for.

2. **If you offer an assertion, you must have an example to support it.** By definition, an assertion is "a statement or declaration, often without support or reason." Hence, if you asserted that the school systems in Europe are better than those in America, then you'd best be equipped with the requisite examples, even though Wayne Booth suggests that "nobody's from Missouri anymore," we know that some people do desire evidence. Some people do desire proof. These people might be deemed "critical thinkers." Regardless, when arguing with someone who possesses such desires, the proof ought to be there. Further, if you deem yourself a "critical thinker," then DO NOT offer an assertion unless you have an example to advance it.

3. **When arguing, if you must raise your voice, do it quickly, and do it for emphasis.** Employ such vocal inflexion like a writer would employ italics. On occasion it may be necessary, but be conscious of it. Those on the receiving end of your amplified voice may only tolerate it for so long. Remember to lower it, take a deep breath, and remember that if people think you are about to explode, they might be more concerned with the results of the explosion than they are with the argument you're attempting to advance.

4. **Try to control your argument.** While "control" is an illusion or a state of mind, and while we human beings find ourselves steeped in our own subjectivity, it is still advisable to attempt control or restraint, especially when you find that your appeals are far more emotionally-driven than they should be. Emotional appeals, of course, may be a component of any argument, but they become lofty unless they are grounded by logical appeals. Similarly, ethical appeals, if relied upon too heavily, can find themselves floating among the unwarranted and unsubstantiated. This is a problem with such appeals. While logical appeals may seem dry, academic, or simply boring, if delivered responsibly, they should seem more credible and reliable than emotional and ethical appeals. Further, emotional appeals often flirt with bias, prejudice, fallacies, blind assertions, and sweeping overgeneralizations. An example of this can be found when a student argues to his professor that he should have earned a higher grade on an assignment. The argument may begin in a responsible manner, for the student may cite logical appeals to

advance his contention. If, however, the professor is able to combat each appeal and the student becomes frustrated, the student might blurt, "You're unfair. You're mean. You're outrageous." In this situation, the student has just articulated three assertions, and as a critical thinker or a person who values the formal constructs of argumentation, he should be prepared to offer an example for each one. Unfortunately, these assertions were (most likely) emotionally-driven. They are steeped in anger, immaturity, and bias. So again, try to control your argument by remaining conscious of the appeals you have chosen to employ. Use emotion, for it is attractive, and it can advance an argument. But do not forget to mix it up. And if you find yourself becoming too emotive (relying too heavily on emotional appeals), make a decision immediately to correct your current course of action.

5. **You are not your argument.** Remember that while you may feel passionately about your argument, *you are not your argument.* This might best be supported by Jim Rohn, a motivational speaker, when he discusses how difficult this is, yet how essential it is to continued growth. The example he cites is biblical. Rohn cites this about Jesus: "Jesus could say, 'I love you but I hate your sinful ways.'" Now, how is it possible to love and hate in the same sentence? If you hate a person's actions, do you have to hate the person? Or is it possible to love a person (for instance, your mother, father, brother, sister, grandfather, grandmother, significant other) but hate what he does to himself? An example suggesting the viability of a love/hate relationship can be found in the granddaughter's love for her alcoholic grandfather. She loves her grandfather. She has undying love for her grandfather. But she cannot stand what he's doing to himself. In fact, she hates it! Still, she has learned to distinguish the two. She loves him, but she hates his sinful ways. Such separation is a sign of emotional and intellectual maturity. Some critical thinkers would argue that the ability to separate or delineate the two is ESSENTIAL. Consider examining another scenario. The trial attorney may argue many cases over the course of a year. In each case, he may present his opening argument. If he were his argument, then we should diagnose him with schizophrenia or multiple-personality disorder because he has become the following: "George Pearson should not have to pay this increase in child support," "Martha Bivinsdorf was not legally sane when she killed her husband," "Ms. Jodstone did, in fact, violate the contract," "Robert Ash is entitled to this insurance settlement," etc. See, in certain arenas, this ability to delineate or separate a person and his argument is developed and honed. For this writer, the arena consisted of three classes: "Philosophy of Law," "Business Law," and "Constitutional Law II." In "Constitutional Law II," I was asked to argue *for* "Brown vs. The Board of Education." After doing so for approximately five minutes, I was given approximately ten seconds to

collect my thoughts, and then I was asked to argue *against* "Brown vs. The Board of Education." There are many things to learn from such an exercise. First, when studying both sides of a case, we are often able to see the motivations for people's arguments. We also become familiar with the facts, and we become familiar with the opposition's claims. Second, and something "critical thinkers" may wish to examine, being expected to argue both sides of an argument convincingly and passionately helps absolve a person of the emotional connection he may have at one time thought necessary when constructing an argument. Notice, the passion can still be present, for passion can be created simply from a desire to win or to emerge victorious. And hence, hopefully you can still find the passion to argue, even if you do not agree with the claim you're attempting to advance. But know this: you are not your argument. Just as a person can delineate love and hate, just as an attorney can delineate his many arguments, and just as a student of law can delineate both sides of an argument, you must separate yourself from your argument. When people attack you, they should focus on your political views, religious views, marital status, sexual orientation, physical appearance, mental ineptitude, etc. Note, however, that you are, indeed, not your argument.

6. **Listen with the intention of listening, not with the intention of offering your retort.** One way people telegraph the intention to offer a retort as opposed to genuinely listen is when they interrupt. Such people are so excited about what *they* have to say that what you are saying is no longer important and, frankly, it's probably not being heard. Of course, some would argue that they do listen, but they simply have a terrible habit of interrupting. In that case, note this: those who interrupt are often perceived as pushy, rude, disrespectful, overbearing, and egotistical; they are also often perceived as bad listeners. Thus, if you are guilty of interrupting, even if you do not think you are guilty of the aforementioned "charges," realize that this is often the perception of such people. If you want to dodge this perception, and if you want to escape this stigma, exhibit the patience required to listen. And if you're on the receiving end of a "pauser," a person who pauses often while speaking, then simply ask the question: "Are you finished?" If the person is not, he'll tell you. Of course, if he is, then the soapbox is yours.

Observations

Before you begin reading the next chapter, take some time to reflect on what you learned in Chapter 1. Specifically, note what you think about what you learned, for in the spirit of promoting consciousness, it is essential that you not only become aware of your observations but that you commit them to paper. Use these observations like one would use a journal: as a tool for measuring growth and insight.

Preliminary Observations

_____

_____

_____

_____

_____

_____

_____

_____

_____

_____

_____

_____

_____

_____

_____

_____

_____

_____

_____

Refined Observations

_____

_____

_____

_____

_____

_____

_____

_____

_____

_____

_____

_____

_____

_____

_____

_____

_____

New Observations

_____

_____

_____

_____

_____

Methodologies for Critical Thinkers

Jon St. Amant

If you have ever studied for a test, you may have created a methodology to which you adhere. Possibly, you research or question what will be on the test, what format it will be presented in (true/false, multiple choice, fill in the blank, short response, essay, oral), and you ruminate on what you must do to pass it. Then, you might begin preparing by using 3 × 5 cards, working individually, with a friend, or with a group. Conversely, maybe you embrace a different methodology. Maybe you crack open your book, flip blindly through the pages for several minutes, and then watch television for several hours, assuring yourself that you'll either stay up late and "cram," or you'll wake up early the next morning. This, too, is a methodology.

Chances are you have created some methodology for test preparation, whether or not you are conscious of it. Likewise, you have a methodology for washing a car, making pasta, taking a shower, and going to the bathroom. These methodologies exist despite your conscious acknowledgment of them. Hence, when you *think,* you may adhere to some sort of methodology. And there isn't, necessarily, one methodology approved by The Critical Thinking Core of America's Literate (a company which, unfortunately, does not formally exist). But, just as adhering to certain test-taking methodologies can help a person succeed in academia, adhering to certain critical thinking methodologies will make it easier for you to read critically, argue effectively, and think responsibly.

Activities of Thinking

· · · · · · · · · ·

1. *Investigation:* Search for evidence. Hunt for any data that will answer the key question about the issue. The evidence must be both relevant and sufficient.
2. *Interpretation:* Decide what the evidence means.
3. *Judgment:* Reach a conclusion about the issue. The conclusion must meet the test of logic.

Unfortunately, in an image-centered society, one eager to stigmatize and persecute, it is uncommon to find people who pledge strict adherence to the aforementioned activities of thinking. Many people investigate, interpret, and judge, just not in that order. Often times, people either expedite the process, as in the fifteen second "snap judgment" found in the first impression ("He's smart," "She's ugly," "I'll vote for him"), or people judge first, interpret second (as they side step or backpedal due to faulty judgment), and finally investigate. This isn't good. The sine

qua non to thinking responsibly is postponing judgment until thoroughly investigating (gathering data/evidence/support), and then interpreting the evidence germane to an issue, person, problem, etc.

Types of evidence include anecdotal (your everyday experiences, news stories, case literature), experimental (based on controlled studies in a laboratory), statistical (any information that can be qualified), and testimonial (the expressed views of authorities, i.e., "expert testimony").

Evidence, of course, must be scrutinized, for it is often manipulated and abused.

Applications

Apply the activities of thinking to one of the following ideas:

1. Polygamy should be legalized.
2. Money should be taken from the military budget and put toward K–12 public schools.
3. Prayer should be encouraged in public schools.

4. The allocation of funds which support the prison system should be siphoned to provide money for families in America living below the poverty level.

Component Parts

. . . .

Another methodology many find useful is breaking an argument into component parts. Ostensibly, an argument has three component parts: the stated premise, the hidden premise, and the conclusion. If you can identify these three parts, then you can address, refute, or support the argument *because* you have identified the hidden premise. The argument will not hold water if the hidden premise is corrupt.

Here is an example:

I should never have taken that trip to Mexico. It didn't provide me with any relaxation.

Stated premise: It didn't provide me with any relaxation.

Hidden premise: Relaxation is the only basis for taking a trip to Mexico.

Conclusion: I should never have taken that trip to Mexico.

In dissecting the component parts, question the validity of the stated premise: "It didn't provide me with any relaxation." Is this statement completely accurate? Could this person have been provided with an inkling of relaxation, as infinitesimal (and, according to him, nonexistent) as it may have seemed? Second, in ruminating on the hidden premise, is relaxation the only basis for taking a trip to Mexico? What about sightseeing? What about culture? What about perspective shifts? What about xenophilia?

Finally, note the conclusion. Is it reasonable? Do the premises lead inescapably to this conclusion and no other?

Applications

Identify each argument's component parts:

1. I've gained seventeen pounds in three months. They must be a result of all the steak I've been eating. I'd better stop eating steak.

2. It's perfectly clear why he's not a good baseball player. He's overweight.
3. *The Adventures of Huckleberry Finn* should be banned because in many places Twain used the word "nigger."
4. *The Catcher in the Rye* should be banned because in many places Salinger used the word "goddamn."
5. Eighteen-year-olds can join the military and, ostensibly, kill people in combat. Hence, they should be allowed to buy alcohol.

Your Reality or Mine?

• • • • • • • • • •

Another methodology writers can employ when endeavoring to think critically is to identify the "reality." "Your reality or mine?" is a popular question asked by people interested in first defining the terms and, second, debating an issue. For instance, if someone says, "TV shows no longer represent Christian values and Christian beliefs," you would do well to define "Christian values and Christian beliefs" before you offered your retort.

Note this example:

Irene says to Bob, "Ya' know, Edward is a real idiot."
"What?" Bob queries. "Edward is one of the brightest guys I know."
"Are you kidding?" says Irene. "He said all women belong in the home. That makes him a male chauvinist."
Bob responds, "But he was the valedictorian in his high school class. He's made the Dean's List in college for the past three semesters. Surely he can't be an idiot."
Irene, clenching her teeth, offers an almost inaudible "He's definitely an idiot."

ENTER THE CRITICAL THINKER (C.T.) AS MEDIATOR.

C.T. says, "Ah, Irene and Bob. Could it be, Irene, that you define an idiot as a male chauvinist, one with a gender bias?"
"Yes," Irene agrees.
C.T. continues, "And could it be, Bob, that you define an idiot as one who does not do well academically?"
"Yes," says Bob.

"Bob, would you agree that Edward's comment about women was indicative of a chauvinist?" queries C.T.

"Yes," says Bob.

C.T. continues, "Moreover, would you consider his comment rude and inappropriate?"

"Yes," says Bob.

"Isn't his acknowledgment of Edward's insensitivity toward women what you were looking for, Irene?" asks C.T.

"Yes," says Irene.

C.T. finishes, "Can you both see how you agree with each other regarding the inappropriateness of Edward's comment and how you simply have differing definitions of 'idiot?'"

The sky opens up, the seas part, and Bob and Irene say, "Yes."

In the aforementioned example, Bob and Irene could have mitigated their argument by simply defining their realities.

Applications

What terms must be defined before the argument can commence?

1. Drugs are eroding our society.
2. Receiving an education will make criminals reform.
3. Kids today are without good morals and values.
4. John is so intelligent.

Another methodology critical thinkers can employ is induction. Induction is a type of reasoning by which a general statement is reached on the basis of particular examples. For instance, if you go to the X movie theater four times and notice that each time a baby's cry disrupts your movie experience, you may conclude that a baby's cry will disrupt your movie experience whenever you go to X movie theater. Here is another example: If you turn on ESPN and notice that the first three golfers you see are wearing tanktops, you may conclude that the PGA has embraced a more lenient dress code.

However, can you depend on these conclusions? Can you depend on the *quality* and *quantity* of your observations which led to your conclusions? Regarding the movie theater, should we ask what movies were viewed and what rating they were assigned? Should we determine at what time the movies were watched? Are there other variables to consider? And what about the golfers? Could the golfers have been caddies? Could what you were viewing have been a non-PGA sanctioned tournament? See, if you do not take time to increase the quality and quantity of your samples, you might make an inductive leap, reasoning from what you have learned about a few examples to what you think is true of a whole class of things.

The Toulmin Model vs. Aristotle's Deductive Syllogism

• • • • • • • • • •

Two other methodologies include deduction and the Toulmin model. The classic deductive syllogism was created by the Greek philosopher Aristotle. In essence, it comprises three parts: major premise, minor premise, conclusion. Here is an example:

Major premise: People over sixty years old drive slowly on the freeway.
Minor premise: My grandmother is over sixty years old and drives on the freeway.
Conclusion: Therefore, my grandmother drives slowly on the freeway.

While the deductive argument looks well-reasoned, it is only sufficient if the premises are true. Now note the differences between Aristotle's deductive syllogism and the Toulmin model developed by Stephen Toulmin, a modern British philosopher, which comprises a claim, support, and a warrant. Here is a comparison:

Aristotle's Deductive Syllogism

Major premise: The deterrence of crime is an important function of the legal system.
Minor premise: The death penalty would help deter crime.
Conclusion: Therefore, the death penalty should be implemented in the United States as a crime deterrent.

The Toulmin Model

Claim: The death penalty should be implemented in the United States as a crime deterrent.
Support (evidence): In a recent case in New Jersey, a man named Richard Biegenwald was freed from prison after serving 18 years for murder; since his release he has been convicted of committing four murders.
Warrant: Capital punishment helps deter crime.

Note that in adhering to the Toulmin model, you would state your claim and proceed to support it. You would not, however, state your warrant, for the warrant is a general assumption you have made, one which links the support to the claim. It is also important to note that in the Toulmin model, the claim and support will not jibe if the audience does not share the same assumption (warrant) made by the person delivering the argument. For instance, in the following example, pay close attention to the significance of the warrant. If the audience does not assume the same definition of "cruel," the claim and support will not advance the argument, for the fundamental assumption is not shared. This example comes from Mark Twain's "The Damned Human Race," an essay found in Chapter 1. Please note: the syllogism and model which follow address *one* of Twain's many claims.

Aristotle's Deductive Syllogism

Major premise: When someone or something is wasteful, he/it can be considered cruel.

Minor premise: The English earl (and others) killed seventy-two buffaloes, eating part of one, leaving the other seventy-one to rot. Conversely, when given an opportunity to kill seven young calves, the anaconda immediately swallowed one, then lay back satisfied, not harming the other six calves.

Conclusion: Therefore, the English earl is cruel, and the anaconda is not.

The Toulmin Model

Claim: The English earl is cruel, and the anaconda is not.

Support (evidence): He (and others) killed seventy-two buffaloes, eating part of one, leaving the other seventy-one to rot. Conversely, when given an opportunity to kill seven young calves, the anaconda immediately swallowed one, then lay back satisfied, not harming the other six calves.

Warrant: If one is wasteful, one is cruel.

This textbook teaches students how to compose arguments adhering to the Toulmin model; hence, it is really important to begin understanding the significance of the claim, support, and warrant.

Applications

1. Create an example which illustrates Aristotle's deductive argument.
2. Create an example which illustrates the Toulmin model.

For more information on methodologies for critical thinkers, read William Golding's "Thinking as a Hobby," and then respond to the Thoughts, Ideas, and Discussion Questions below. (Unfortunately, Sir William Golding's estate is not granting any publishing company permission to use his famous essay, "Thinking as a Hobby." Thus, until his estate begins granting permission, please simply utilize your skills in research so that you might procure a copy of his work.)

Thoughts, Ideas, and Discussion Questions

1. Define *penal, writhe, opaquely, mused, depravity, pious, gregarious, heady, exalted, oratory, draughts, impediments, nape, inscrutable, veriest, vehemently, revered, irreverent, amiability, skittles, sects, flagged, indignant, libertine, hallowed.*
2. Articulate Golding's claim in one sentence.
3. Offer a definition for the Grade One Thinker, Grade Two Thinker, and Grade Three Thinker.
4. Golding, in two separate instances, makes a distinction between thinking and feeling. How are the two actions different?
5. Golding writes: "She was a Methodist—or at least, her parents were, and Ruth had to follow suit." What are some of the underlying implications behind this claim?
6. When have you been a Grade Three Thinker, Grade Two Thinker, or Grade One Thinker?
7. Ralph Waldo Emerson once wrote: "For nonconformity the world whips you with its displeasure." Relate this quotation to the last sentence in Golding's essay.

Applications

1. Assign yourself one of Golding's labels: Grade One Thinker, Grade Two Thinker, or Grade Three Thinker. Explain why you consider yourself such a "thinker," and explain what you'd deem necessary to evolve or devolve to the next level.

2. Interview five people. Create your own questions. These questions should be designed for one purpose: to find out what type of "thinkers" these five people are.

Observations

Before you begin reading the next chapter, take some time to reflect on what you learned in Chapter 2. Specifically, note what you think about what you learned, for in the spirit of promoting consciousness, it is essential that you not only become aware of your observations but that you commit them to paper. Use these observations like one would use a journal: as a tool for measuring growth and insight.

Preliminary Observations

_____

_____

_____

_____

_____

_____

_____

_____

_____

_____

_____

_____

_____

_____

_____

_____

_____

_____

Refined Observations

_____

_____

_____

_____

_____

_____

_____

_____

_____

_____

_____

_____

_____

_____

_____

_____

_____

New Observations

_____

_____

_____

_____

_____

_____

Identifying Claims

In *The Catcher in the Rye,* Holden Caulfield flunks his speech class because he too often digresses. Instead of adhering to his subject, his topic, or his claim, he moves from one focus to another. While this may be acceptable in certain arenas, it should not be tolerated in formal argumentation. When arguing, or when listening to an argument, it is essential that you hone in on the person's claim. The claim will let you know precisely what the person desires to prove.

There are three types of claims:

Claims of Value

· · · · · · · · · ·

Claims of value make a judgment expressing approval or disapproval.

Claim: In baseball the center fielder is much more important than the shortstop.
Claim: Abortion is wrong.
Claim: Experimenting on animals is wrong.

Here is an example of an essay illustrating a claim of value:

Burn, Baby, Burn!

The Tuesday after Labor Day, 1998, my telephone rang with an odd, urgent peal. It was an old college friend who had just returned from Burning Man. Excited, impassioned, she could hardly stop rambling, yakking on and on, blabbing all about her recent cosmic revelations. Her descriptions of drug-popping-post-modern-hippies

"Burn, Baby, Burn!" was written by Jay Rubin in Spring, 2000. Mr. Rubin is currently a professor of English at College of Alameda.

mingling with neo-nudist-techno-geeks made the week-long Burning Man festival sound like a modern day Sodom and Gomorrah. "Next year!" she insisted emphatically. "You're going!" Sure enough, I attended Burning Man '99. Without a doubt, it was the most awesome, ineffable, mind-boggling experience ever.

Burning Man occurs once a year, in a remote northwest corner of Nevada called the Black Rock Desert. There's no water, no vegetation, and throughout the year, no inhabitants on the sun-scorched terrain. But during the week leading up to Labor Day, twenty-five thousand Internet-connected city-dwelling urbanites wheel their way up a two-lane county road, set up camp on the parched desert floor, and create an interactive, spontaneous city. Many citizens of temporary Black Rock City are Bay Area artists, some who rent moving vans and giant cranes to set up their huge, elaborate art installations, all of which are set aflame on the final night of the festival.

The eponymous Burning Man is a forty-foot-tall wood and neon structure situated out in the center of the playa—playa being the Spanish word for beach, which festival participants call the dusty, desert-ancient, Black Rock lake bed. The Man, standing in the center of a mile-wide circle, is surrounded by sporadic art installations—some as wacky as a twelve-foot pyramid of smashed microwave ovens, others as elegant as huge red ribbons on ten foot poles, shimmying like fish in the hot desert wind. On the perimeter of this mile-wide circle, festival participants set up their camps, some with elaborate themes: Body Painting Camp, Shampoo Camp, even Elvis Yoga Camp. During the days, participants hop on their bikes and cruise out onto the playa to visit the art installations. At one point, while cruising around on my little girl's bike, I spotted a solitary man walking alone across the playa. Approaching him, I asked if he could please explain the significance of the Man. "It's not about the Man," the solo stroller told me. "It's more about the people." He was right. There's one main tenet at Burning Man: "Participate—Don't Spectate." As participants of an art festival, people freely express their inner selves. Of course, not everyone has the means to drag a two-ton iron cube out to the desert, but everyone can dress up in crazy clothes and crafted costumes. There are hairy men in high heels and slinky lingerie and women on stilts wearing flaming mohawk helmets. On Saturday afternoon, more than a thousand women remove their tops, decorate their breasts with paint and glitter, then mount their bikes for a wild ride all through Black Rock City. People deck their bikes with strips of foil and colored cloth. Some build elaborate motorized vehicles, some resembling insects; others build cocktail bars on the back of flatbed trucks, then cruise around the playa. In a phrase, it's a post-apocalyptic, gender-bending fashion show.

At first, these visual images are quite shocking, repellent even, but the unconditional kindness of strangers helps quell the nerves of even the most terrified first-time "newbie." Everywhere on the playa, people are forgivingly affable, polite and friendly in their everyday dealings. They barter rather than vend. They smile, they hug, and they even kiss strangers—even while waiting in the porta-potty line. Some participants prepare elaborate gourmet meals, complete with wine and crème brulee; and what they don't consume themselves, they simply give away, offering up a potluck potlatch to the costumed citizens cruising by.

When the sun sets, the drumming begins. Reverberations are felt across the playa, from miles away, from neighbors next door. Techno-raves pop up on the desert and people dance for hours, some elucidating on Ecstasy, wandering on LSD beneath the Milky Way. At Biancas, a theme camp dedicated to love and sensual pleasure, participants lounge on beat-up couches, legs and arms and lips intermingled, tongues making friends with the smiling mouths of strangers. It's a Hellenistic, Dionysian lovefest.

For one week, day follows night and night follows day till dusk arrives on Saturday. In one tacit, communal procession, the twenty-five thousand festival participants gather in a ring around the forty-foot neon Man, who, to the beat of banging drums, is ritualistically set ablaze. Whoops and hollers echo off the nearby mountains as revelers circle the burning embers, chanting, drumming, reverting to their pagan, primordial past. Eventually, after the sun rises, participants begrudgingly return to their camps, strike their temporary desert homes, pack their cars, their moving vans. A long trail of white dust rises from the playa as festival participants make their exodus back to reality—back to their quiet homes, to their isolated office cubicles, to a place where people are less kind, less open, less aware of the common simplicity and overall benevolence of a spontaneous human culture.

Thoughts, Ideas, and Discussion Questions

1. Define *ineffable, eponymous, quell, affable, potlatch, elucidation, tacit,* and *communal.*
2. Articulate Rubin's claim in one sentence.
3. Does Rubin tend to rely more on abstract or concrete language? How does this help or hinder his argument?
4. Identify the areas where Rubin uses colloquial language. What is his purpose for deviating from academic prose?
5. Does Rubin adequately support his claim?
6. How does Rubin organize his essay?

Claims of Fact

· · · · · · · · · ·

Claims of fact attempt to prove that a condition has existed, currently exists, or will exist in the future. Claims of fact are supported by statistics and examples which can be verified.

Claim: Though women are making their presence felt in the workplace, men still outnumber them in upper-managerial positions.

Claim: Documentaries and news programs are fun to watch, but by looking at the Nielson ratings, one can see that talk shows and sitcoms are what the American people prefer.

Claim: Children who were read to at a young age tend to do better than those who were not.

Here is an example of an essay illustrating a claim of fact:

The Mistake of the Millennium

Amidst chilled champagne and perennial parties, the world will approach midnight on December 31, 1999, with just a little more anticipation than usual. Part of the suspense no doubt revolves around concerns over Y2K and whether every other computer system in the world is going to crash. But it's not just fear in the air New Year's Eve, 1999; it's the excitement and energy of a new beginning that only comes once every one thousand years. If New Year's Day is a time for changes and resolutions, for putting the past behind and looking to the future ahead, then surely a new century and a new *millennium* usher in an even more dramatic shift in eras, a clearer new chapter in our lives and potential mark in history. This is why countless groups have booked the grandest ballrooms and are throwing the biggest celebrations within their means. It's because when the ball drops in Times Square and the world counts down in

Paul O'Brien, a professor of English at Mt. San Antonio College, wrote "The Mistake of the Millennium" in Spring, 2000.

1999, it is more than a new year everyone will be waiting for; it will be the 21st century, the dawning of a new millennium—and, unfortunately, a significant mistake. As a matter of fact, despite popular opinion and common sense, the new millennium will not start until one year later, midnight, January 1, 2001.

It is a forgivable mistake, though, when one considers it mathematically. After all, the assumption is that our Christian era chronology *anno Domini* begins at ground zero—call it time zero—with the birth of Jesus of Nazareth. Presumably, when little baby Jesus became a one-year old, all of Western civilization turned one right along with him. Before that one year's time, however, one would assume that the year was 0 A.D. for just a little while, strange as it looks. By the time Jesus turned one, he was merely completing his first year of life and simultaneously beginning his second one. As a result, with every birthday and with every new year, the year's number represented that many years under time's belt, so to speak, so that when one turns twenty, for instance, one has literally lived twenty years, or two decades. The year 10 A.D. would therefore mathematically mark Western Civilization's first completed decade; the year 100 A.D. would in turn represent the end of our first century; 1000 our first millennium; and 2000 the end of our second millennium and the beginning of the third. What could be clearer?

The culprit isn't our math, however, but a sixth century monk named Denys le Petit, a.k.a. Dennis the Short. If the truth be told, the year was not marked by Jesus's birth for over five hundred years;

it was little Dennis who hatched the plan to make the change to *anno Domini* as we know it. Instead of marking the first day of the year with Jesus's birthday, he calculated the day Jesus was circumcised—roughly one week later—and started the timer from there. But Dennis didn't start time with a zero like a stopwatch or odometer would; he started with the number one, namely because as a Latin scholar he didn't have a numeral to represent the number zero (MacFayden 90). Consequently, the difference in time really is that simple; just take the more intuitive, initial calculations about new decades, centuries, and millennia, and add one year. It wasn't until 11 A.D. that one decade was completed, 101 for the first century, 1001 for the first millennium, and closer to home, 2001 until the second millennium is over.

That won't cancel any parties, naturally. Ultimately, it matters little to most whether a new millennium is one year or the next because it is more the spirit of the time that matters. After all, the numbers are ultimately very arbitrary. No one complains that Dennis the Short was four years off in his centuries-old calculations about Jesus's birth, for example. And no party-hearty millennialist is disheartened upon discovering that our year 2000 will mark 5760 for Hebrews and 1377 for Moslems. A year by any other digit still looks the same, and only the cultic and the anal among us will probably give it a second thought. Most people will stand next to their loved ones on New Year's Eve, 1999, heaving a champagne glass to the heavens and singing "Auld Lang Syne" as usual, relishing the novelty of a warm "Happy New

Millennium!" When the true millennium actually rolls around one year later, it probably won't bother anyone at all; in fact, it will probably only give us one more reason to celebrate a new millennium all over again.

Works Cited

MacFayden, Janet. "Zero." *The Atlantic Monthly* 280.1 (July 1997): 88–94.

Thoughts, Ideas, and Discussion Questions

1. Define *perennial* and any terms which may have been unclear.
2. Articulate O'Brien's claim in one sentence.
3. Notice how O'Brien implements sentence variety. How does this strengthen his essay?
4. Does O'Brien adequately support his claim?
5. Note where O'Brien addresses his opposition. How does this advance his argument?

Claims of Policy

· · · · · · · · · ·

Claims of policy usually house the words *should, ought to,* or *must.* Claims of policy assert that certain conditions exist that call for a solution.

Claim: ESL courses should be taught in all public high schools.

Claim: School uniforms ought to be considered at Beaumont Elementary School.

Claim: The president of the United States must call for a decrease in the military budget and an increase in the budget for public education.

Here is an example of an essay illustrating a claim of policy:

We Make Money by Making You Feel Ugly

In supermarkets it is not uncommon to hear this question posed by an ignorant male: "Honey, why can't you look as good as the women on these magazine covers?" The female either offers a witty retort (her method for saving face), or she hangs her head low, secretly wondering why she can't look as good as those women, *those supermodels, those goddesses* cut from perfection's mold. Unfortunately, what she or most females, for that matter, never hear is that it is impossible to look as good as those supermodels do. In fact, it is impossible for the supermodels to look that good. They only achieve such a level of perfection by relying on one essential resource: the graphic artist. The graphic artist manipulates the supermodel's image, making her more aesthetically appealing and making her appearance impossible to imitate. Yet, because of ignorant males, and because females are ignorant enough to be duped by both their male counterparts and the false images they see before

"We Make Money by Making You Feel Ugly" was written by Estelle Hartson in Spring, 2000. Miss Hartson is a former professor of English and a recovering bulimic. She currently resides in Maine.

them, females are dieting excessively, starving themselves incessantly, and purging themselves until they attain the "impossible look" or deliver themselves to the morgue. Since it can be assumed that males will continue making ignorant comments, and since it can be assumed that women will continue being affected by them, the beauty magazines must begin exhibiting some social responsibility. Just as the tobacco industry has been forced to label each package of cigarettes with a Surgeon General's Warning, it should be mandated that beauty magazines adorn each page featuring the doctored image of a woman with the following Editor-in-Chief's Warning: THE IMAGE OF THE WOMAN ON THIS PAGE HAS UNDERGONE MASSIVE AIRBRUSHING AND RESTRUCTURING (GRAPHICALLY AND/OR SURGICALLY). IT IS NOT POSSIBLE TO LOOK LIKE THIS.

The warning will serve two purposes. First, it provides viewers, female and male, with some incredibly valuable intellectual property. The viewers will know that the photographs they see before them are like movies which are "based on a true story." Yes, the photograph is of a female, and she probably exists. But in *real life*, she cannot look nearly as good as she does on the cover of *Cosmopolitan*. The photograph is "based on a real woman," but the photograph which finds itself on the newsstand or in the check-out line is often as unrealistic as Buzz Lightyear, Woody, or any other Disney character. In essence, these photographs, or advertisements, promote a false ideal, creating a societal dichotomy between fact and fiction. In *Hunger Pains*, a book on the modern woman's tragic quest for thinness, Mary Pipher states:

Sometimes the images are not even of real women. Instead, the photos in the ads are composites that combine the head of an adult woman, the torso of a young girl, and the legs of a boy. Women compare these images with their own bodies and feel anxious and inadequate. None of us has a body like these—they are not found in nature. (20)

This is the grossest form of false advertising. Oliver Stone argues that the cutting and pasting of Lee Harvey Oswald's image on *Time* lead to his arrest and, had he not been killed, his eventual imprisonment. The cutting and pasting of supermodels, however, is far worse, for it is constructing an impossible reality, killing females through bulimia and anorexia and mentally imprisoning others through the same vehicles. Hence, simply mandating that an Editor-in-Chief's Warning be used to inform viewers is a very good idea. But the warning also serves another purpose.

Just as the tobacco industry has admitted that cigarettes can cause cancer, the fashion industry must show some responsibility to the society which supports it by admitting that people buy fantasy, so that's what they sell. Though it's popular to hear spokespersons for beauty magazines say "Our art simply imitates life," the converse is true. Life imitates art, for how can magazines imitate that which does not exist? The fashion industry must admit that the fantasies they peddle are making healthy females an endangered species. It should not be so anomalous to find a woman who is not preoccupied with her weight, a woman who is secure, a woman with a healthy self-image. In a song by Jill Sobule called "Supermodel," the following lyrics are found: "I don't care what my teachers say / I'm gonna be a supermodel / Everyone will want to dress like me / wait and see when I'm a supermodel." The problem is that many think it is actually possible to attain the supermodel look, without help from a surgeon and a graphic artist. Maybe people, however, should pay more attention to the rest of the lyrics in "Supermodel": "I did it yesterday / I'm not gonna eat today / And I'm not gonna eat tomorrow / 'Cause I'm gonna be a supermodel."

It is not a secret that anorexia and bulimia are on the rise. Mary Pipher states: "In fact, over the last 10 years the main change has been that girls are getting eating disorders at younger ages. At this point, even fifth and sixth graders are turning up as clients" (VII). She later states: "The cause of these disorders does not lie primarily within individual women. Rather, the pathology is in our media and wherever else the image of an ideal female body is propagated" (5). But getting the fashion industry to take responsibility for any of this may be a fantasy. Beauty magazines have one job: to make people feel ugly. If a female feels ugly, it is highly likely that she will attempt to remedy her condition. She will need makeup, diet pills, new clothes, and plethoric tips for weight loss. But where will she find these remedies for her manufactured ailments? In beauty magazines, of course.

Works Cited

Pipher, Mary. *Hunger Pains.* New York: Random House, 1995.

Thoughts, Ideas, and Discussion Questions

1. Define *dichotomy, pathology, plethoric,* and any terms which may have been unclear.
2. Articulate Hartson's claim in one sentence.
3. Does Hartson's argument adhere to a linear or lateral structure?
4. Does Hartson spend more time identifying a problem or proposing a solution? Is this effective?
5. What do you think of Hartson's proposed Editor-in-Chief's Warning?

Applications

1. Do other products other than beauty magazines and cigarettes need to post warnings? If so, show how these warnings would help create a more informed populace.
2. Write a response to Estelle Hartson which supports or refutes her claim.

Controlling an Argument
· · · · · · · · · · ·

If you wish to control a spoken argument, make sure the people engaged in the argument adhere to one claim. When people begin digressing, simply ask, "What is your claim?" If you keep people focused on one claim, then supporting or refuting it will be that much easier. And, of course, unless you can present a potential solution, a way in which to persuade the opposition, then you may find yourself involved in a circuitous discussion that sounds more like a quarrel than an argument.

Controlling a Written Argument

. . . .

When writing an argument, it is your responsibility to focus on one claim, be it a claim of policy, a claim of value, or a claim of fact. Remember, the claim is to the argument what the thesis statement is to an essay, or what a topic sentence is to a paragraph. It is the navigational beacon which guides your words and your thoughts. And because a well-constructed argument can help dictate how your readers think, you must make sure your claim is a sound one.

"I told you we need a claim!"

Observations

Before you begin reading the next chapter, take some time to reflect on what you learned in Chapter 3. Specifically, note what you think about what you learned, for in the spirit of promoting consciousness, it is essential that you not only become aware of your observations but that you commit them to paper. Use these observations like one would use a journal: as a tool for measuring growth and insight.

Preliminary Observations

_____

_____

_____

_____

_____

_____

_____

_____

_____

_____

_____

_____

_____

_____

_____

_____

_____

_____

_____

Refined Observations

_____

_____

_____

_____

_____

_____

_____

_____

_____

_____

_____

_____

_____

_____

_____

_____

_____

_____

_____

New Observations

_____

_____

_____

_____

_____

Issue/Problem Papers

One way to begin implementing what you have learned about claims, fallacies, and activities of thinking is through the creation of Issue/Problem Papers. Originally developed by Paul Neumann, a professor of English at Modesto Junior College, Issue/Problem Papers are short (one to two well-developed paragraphs), so the writer is forced to design a cogent, succinct argument. Unfortunately, this shorter, expedited form of argument invites fallacies, so be careful.

Problems are best expressed in the "How can . . .?" or "What . . .?" form.

Here is an example:

Problem: What legal sanctions would decrease gun ownership?

The question form most useful for expressing issues is the "Is . . .?" or "Should . . .?" form.

Here is an example:

Issue: Should people have the right to own guns?

In your Issue/Problem Papers, identify and present either an issue or a problem in the appropriate question format. Then, discuss the issue or problem in terms of your response to it. Your response might be a solution to the problem or a reasonable viewpoint on the issue. The issue or problem should be stated in a single interrogative sentence. The response should be *at least* one fully developed paragraph in length; however, the response should not exceed one page. All papers should be typed and double-spaced.

Format for I/P Papers

• • • • • • • • • • •

Here is the conventional format for an Issue/Problem Paper:

I. Claim

Point 1
Example

Point 2
Example

Point 3
Example

Point 4
Example

II. Address the Opposition

Identify with the Opposition

Refute the Opposition

Offer a Solution

Make a Final Observation

How to Refute the Opposition

• • • • • • • • • • •

We deliver written or spoken arguments for three reasons: to communicate ideas, to discover ideas, and to persuade others. The purpose of a well-constructed argument is not to delight or entertain those who are already of the same opinion or belief regarding a particular issue or problem. No, the purpose is to create awareness among the nay-sayers and, eventually, to persuade these people. Hence, the opposition must not only be addressed and identified with but refuted.

The first thing most writers of arguments do is create a +/– list. This is something Benjamin Franklin would do to identify the positive and negative forces hovering around an issue or problem. Specifically, this list helps one identify the proponents and the opponents of a particular issue or problem.

Here is an example:

Issue: Should beauty pageants and talent competitions for children be banned?

+	–
Make children too dependant on appearance	Encourage healthy competition
Encourage egocentrism	Give children an opportunity to showcase their talents
Emphasize image instead of intellect	Give children much-needed attention
Discourage teamwork	
Children become puppets for obsessive/compulsive parents.	Strengthen parent/child relationships
The objective isn't to have fun; the objective is to win.	Should be looked at like any other individual competition: golf, tennis, swimming, etc.

Once the ideas for and against an issue are organized via a +/– list, the writer can now begin articulating his thoughts and creating a strategy to refute the opposition.

Here is one way to refute the opposition:

I.   Address the Opposition
II. Identify with the Opposition
III. Refute the Opposition

The aforementioned issue, "Should beauty pageants and talent competitions for children be banned?", can be refuted in this manner. Say, for instance, your claim supported banning beauty pageants and talent competitions: "Beauty pageants and talent competitions should be banned." In adhering to a textbook approach, the opposition can be refuted in this manner (this would be the format for refuting the opposition in a body paragraph):

Some people argue that beauty pageants and talent competitions give children much-needed attention. This is reasonable. Children do receive attention. However, it is tough to classify this attention as "much-needed." The type of attention children receive from beauty pageants and talent competitions comes from photographers, agents, publicists, and reporters. This is the basest form of attention, for this attention subverts a child's self-image, teaching the child to praise physical appearance and embrace egocentrism. (*The writer should continue this paragraph, spending the rest of her*

Note: The writer begins by addressing the opposition ("Some people argue . . ."), identifying with the opposition ("This is, in a sense, true. Children do receive attention."), and then refuting the opposition ("However, it is tough to classify this attention as 'much-needed.'")

Another way to refute the opposition is to show why the opposition's claims are irrelevant. This can be done by pointing out the flaws in a faulty argument, largely by identifying logical fallacies (these will be covered in Chapter 9). Essentially, when the opposition is basing its argument on an assumption that is *not* shared, the argument may be corrupt.

Successfully refuting the opposition is analogous to cooking a frog.

When you think about how to prepare a strong argument, think about how one might cook a frog. If a person simply tosses a frog into a pot of boiling water, the frog will jump out, virtually unscathed. But, if a person places a frog in a pot of lukewarm water, the frog will remain in the pot, content. Gradually, the person

Jon St.Amant

turns up the heat, and gradually the water gets warmer and warmer until, finally, the frog is cooked.

Here's the point: refuting the opposition should be done with care and great tact, for your reader, like the frog, needs to be coaxed into the heat; otherwise he will leave the pot. And once your reader has put down your text, left the crowd, or taken himself out of the game, you cannot deliver a successful argument, for you have lost your audience and, hence, have nobody left to convince.

Notice, in the following I/P Papers written by college students, how the paper itself is organized and how the opposition is addressed, identified, and refuted. Specifically, in the first two I/P Papers, note how the writers adhere to the point/example approach (on pg. 93) when offering a response to whether or not Wayne Booth is a Grade One, Two, or Three Thinker. (Grade One Thinkers, according to William Golding in "Thinking as a Hobby," offer solutions. Grade Two Thinkers detect contradictions. Grade Three Thinkers feel as opposed to think.)

Harwood 1

Susan Harwood
Professor Jones
English 1C
10 October 2000

Booth Gets Graded

Based upon his essay, "The Uncritical American, or Nobody's From Missouri Anymore," Wayne Booth is a Grade One Thinker. Throughout his essay, Booth offers many solutions to his readers. One example is this: "But if you and I could learn to think for ourselves . . . our troubled country might someday notice the difference" (Booth 24). In this quotation, Booth proclaims critical thought as a way to diminish the world's existence as ". . . the most credulous, gullible, and superstitious people of all time" (Booth 24). Another solution can be found when Booth states this: "We cannot solve all of life's problems by learning to think, but we can't solve any of them without it" (Booth 30). Booth explains to the readers that although critical thought may not bring about world peace, one must utilize it to effectively solve any of life's delemmas.

Many would argue that based upon his essay, Booth is merely a Grade Two Thinker. This is understandable, for Booth's writing does possess many characteristics of Grade Two Thought. An example is this: "In their very existence, [uncritical Americans] are an indictment of American education and, by implication, of the English teachers who have failed to educate them" (Booth 30). Booth clearly recognizes the contradiction between what America claims to be an "education" and what a real education is. However, one must identify a problem before offering a solution, and that is exactly what Booth is doing as he then offers this solution: "We are committed to the awakening of minds . . . the creation of critical Americans" (Booth 30). Booth not only persuades others but also commits himself to knocking down the walls of bias, hypocrisy, and ignorance that hinder one from pure, critical thought.

Note: Susan does an excellent job of addressing the prompt in a very methodical manner. She begins, of course, by articulating her claim. Then, just as stipulated in the "Format for I/P Papers," she offers a point (her first assertion) followed by an example. After offering her example, she employs a sentence of "commentary." Such a sentence should advance the argument by linking the example to her point.

Conscientious writers, like Susan, do this to avoid relying on the assumption that the reader will make the requisite connection between the point and the example. Another strength in Susan's paper is her second paragraph. In it she does a fine job of refuting the opposition, making sure to end her paper with an affirming, argument-advancing, final observation.

Joey Gu
Professor Jones
English 1C
10 October 2000

Grade-Two Thinking

Wayne Booth is a Grade Two Thinker. According to William Golding, "Grade-two thinking is the detection of contradictions . . . a withdrawal, with eyes and ears open" (Golding 4). In his essay, Booth complements Golding's description of a Grade Two Thinker by stating: ". . . everyone pursues degrees like merit badges, and it is quite clear that the kingdom of heaven is closed to dropouts . . ." (Booth 23). From this excerpt, it is evident that individuals attempt to achieve a certain educational status, not for the knowledge but for the accolades of earning a scholarly education. Booth also writes: "Few graduates of our high schools or colleges seem able to apply their minds in an educated way to the world around them; few of them threaten anyone with a genuinely critical judgment" (Booth 23). According to this, a majority of individuals do not question what they are taught, and to a certain extent, they are hindering their intellectual growth by being so critically naïve. From both examples, it can be concluded that Grade-two thinking is achieved because there are contradictions being detected.

One might argue that Booth is exclusively a Grade One Thinker, and to a certain degree, he is. Booth ". . . points out contradictions" (Golding 4) and offers a solution by stating: "We can't avoid mistakes by determining to combat the new credulity, but we will make many more if we simply swim with the tide" (Booth 30). However, according to Golding, Grade-one thinking should offer a direct solution, and Booth's solutions are more implied than directly stated. Therefore, Booth must offer clear and exact solutions to the contradictions he detects. Until he does so, he will remain a Grade Two Thinker.

Note: Joey, in hopes of persuading his audience that Booth (contrary to Susan's contention) is a Grade Two Thinker, writes in a very responsible manner. Not only does he adhere to his claim but he seems intent on using every bit of space on the page to advance it as well. Remember, because I/P Papers cannot exceed one page, a writer is forced to evaluate his supporting elements, discern which are strongest, and use them to, hopefully, persuade the reader. Joey relies on two well-chosen contradictions and one solution. Cementing those examples are points and commentary which, altogether, contribute to the creation of a poignant, well-composed argument.

Amalia Galvez
Professor Jones
English 1C
10 October 2000

Reasons to War

We war for several different reasons. The settlers waged war against the Indians because of their selfish needs. When the settlers arrived, they fought against the Indians because "they wanted them out of the way; they wanted their land" (Zinn 14). Land was very important to the settlers. According to Zinn, land was "a real human need. Behind the English invasion of North America, behind their massacre of Indians, their deception, their brutality, was that special powerful drive born in civilizations based on private property" (16). This is one of the reasons why the settlers fought the Indians so vigorously for their land. Greed, however, is not the only reason to make war. Often, people make war on other nations or people as a scapegoat to other problems. When Hitler made war against the Jewish people, he told his followers that they were the ones causing the problems in their nation. Several months ago, the nightly news stated that there are people here in the United States, such as Pete Wilson, who blame illegal immigrants for our economic problems.

There are times when the abused make war to fight injustices or to fight for what they believe in. Angry, oppressed people often make war in order to fight their oppressors. Zinn believes that the reason why the Indians fought against the English was because the English were the oppressors: "The Indians certainly did not want war, but they matched atrocity with atrocity" (Zinn 16). This is reasonable. However, many times the Indians ran and hid from the settlers because they did not want to fight. Some believe people war to fight against what they believe are injustices. This is also reasonable. Many times, though, selfish people make war for selfish reasons, as implied in Zinn's interpretation of history.

Works Cited

Zinn, Howard. A People's History of the United States. New York, New York: Harper Collins, 1995.

Note: Amalia addresses and refutes the opposition in her final paragraph. Also, she lets her reader know in the final sentence that the support used to advance this argument derived from someone's *interpretation of* history.

Emi Fujii
Professor Jones
English 1C
10 October 2000

Savages?

When one thinks of a savage, an Indian is depicted; but, in actuality, the savages were the male Europeans who immigrated into North America. Since the first day of school, the fundamentals of America were tainted glorifications of Columbus's and the Founding Fathers' accomplishments. It was they who tried to tame the uncivilized Indians, assimilating them into American culture. As Western culture crossed over into unexplored land, it clashed with the Native Americans' way of life. Edmund Morgan wrote in his book American Slavery, American Freedom:

> If you were a colonist, you know your technology was superior to the Indians. You knew that you were civilized, and they were savages . . . but your superior technology had proved insufficient to extract anything . . . so you killed the Indians, tortured them, burned their villages, burned their cornfields. It proved your superiority, in spite of your failures. . . . (Zinn 25)

Many might depict Indians as savages because of media-enforced stereotypes. Just as the 1934 Encyclopedia Britannica argues that African-Americans have smaller, inferior brains than the Anglo, the TV has portrayed the Indian stealthily hiding behind cacti or rose-colored boulders, waiting to scalp a cowboy. This, unfortunately, paints the Indian as predator when, in reality, the opposite is true. The Indians simply began mirroring the actions of the "civilized" colonists. One "savage," an Indian, stated: ". . . you are here strangers, and come into our Country, you should rather conform yourselves to the Customs, than to impose yours upon us" (Zinn 21). Male European ethnocentricity that manifests itself within the American culture can vial the colors of a savage.

Works Cited

Zinn, Howard. A People's History of the United States. New York, New York: Harper Collins, 1995.

Note: Emi's claim is stated in the first sentence of her I/P Paper. Notice that she uses quotations to advance her argument, and notice that she only uses the quotations to solidify something for which she is arguing. Most of Emi's focus is on analysis and argumentation. The quotations simply tie the argumentative knot, offering her paper credibility. Also notice how she ends her essay with a final, poignant observation.

I/P Paper Topics

• • • • • • • • • •

Now that you have the comprehension, it is time for the realization. Write an Issue/Problem Paper. If you have trouble finding an issue or problem to dissect, you may use one of the following topics:

Gays in the military
Affirmative action
Euthanasia
Capital punishment
Animal experimentation
Legalizing marijuana
Presenting U.S. history from the people's perspective
Preservation of rain forests or endangered species
Why we war
Violence in the media
Immigration
Freedom of speech

Observations

Before you begin reading the next chapter, take some time to reflect on what you learned in Chapter 4. Specifically, note what you think about what you learned, for in the spirit of promoting consciousness, it is essential that you not only become aware of your observations but that you commit them to paper. Use these observations like one would use a journal: as a tool for measuring growth and insight.

Preliminary Observations

_____

_____

_____

_____

_____

_____

_____

_____

_____

_____

_____

_____

_____

_____

_____

_____

_____

_____

Refined Observations

_____

_____

_____

_____

_____

_____

_____

_____

_____

_____

_____

_____

_____

_____

_____

_____

_____

New Observations

_____

_____

_____

_____

_____

Writing Argument Papers

The purpose of writing argument papers is not to win; instead, the purpose of writing argument papers is to influence others. You may not persuade your audience, but you can cause your audience to think and respect the reasonableness of your views. Remember, aim not for victory but for inquiry and dialogue, seeking truth or some respectful common ground.

Argumentation is needed to preserve a free society. By definition, an argument is not a quarrel, but a discussion proffering a statement or statements which support a claim. The goal is to present carefully reasoned support for the claim, taking into account opposing points of view.

How to Write an Argument Paper

• • • • • • • • • •

1. After you choose your topic and before starting your reading and research on it, write what you know about the controversy, both the pro and con arguments. See what you need to find out, and read for that information (support) as well as new ideas. Be sure that you document all notes taken—author, source, date of source, page of information or quotation, total pages of the magazine or newspaper article, and if taking notes from a book, document the publisher and date of publication.

2. Think about the people who share your position and especially those who oppose it. You're writing to try to gain receptiveness from your opponents. They are your primary audience. How do they define the issues? What basic values or assumptions do you both share? What value appeals may you need to argue if they don't share them? What kinds of evidence are they likely to find convincing? Are there any terms that may need to be "defined" or explained because you and your opponents may not understand them in the same way?

3. Claims of fact, value, or policy need to be:
   - Arguable
   - Clearly and exactly stated
   - Appropriately qualified

4. Key concepts may need to be defined.

5. Claims also need to be supported by evidence and motivational appeals.

6. After gathering evidence (facts, anecdotes, statistics, experimental facts, knowledgeable opinion or testimony, reasoned interpretation of facts, textual evidence, cases), question its reliability:
    - Is the evidence up-to-date?
    - Is the evidence sufficient?
    - Is the evidence relevant?
    - Are the examples representative?
    - Are the examples consistent with the experience of the audience?
    - Are the statistics representative?
    - Are the statistics consistent with the experience of the audience?
    - Do the statistics come from trustworthy sources?
    - Are the terms clearly defined?
    - Are the comparisons between comparable things?
    - Has any significant information been omitted?
    - Are the opinions from sources qualified and up-to-date on the subject?
    - Are the opinions from sources biased or swayed by vested interest?
    - Has the source defended the claim with sufficient and appropriate information?

7. Appeals to needs and values in the audience are especially important in value and policy claims.
    - Needs: physiological needs, safety, belongingness and love, esteem, self-actualization.
    - Values: the principles by which we judge what is good or bad, beautiful or ugly, worthwhile or undesirable.

8. Be conscious of the warrant or warrants employed in your argument. Warrants are the assumptions, beliefs, or general principles we often take for granted. These beliefs or values underlie our position and perspective. The audience must share our warrants if our claims are to be accepted. Thus, we often have to defend or argue our warrants. One reason we resist certain arguments is that accepting them would entail changing a part of our value or belief system (constitution, world view).

9. Take into account the opposing views:
    - Address objections and questions
    - Identify with the objections
    - Refute the objections

10. Argue using a reasonable and appropriate tone, and maintain credibility. Most people are persuaded as much by a person's credibility as they are by his or her reasoning. Exhibiting credibility involves being knowledgeable, truthful, morally upright, dependable, and well-intentioned; it also involves caring about others' needs. Here's how to demonstrate credibility:
   - Show evidence of careful, well-documented research, using information from the best authorities.
   - Use an appropriate tone that shows fairness toward the audience and the subject.
   - Produce a clean, thoughtful, well-organized, carefully written and proofread paper.

Outline for Position and Proposal Papers

There are two basic kinds of argument papers: positions and proposals.

A. Position Papers: Outline
   1. Identify the issue and state the thesis.
   2. Introduce counter arguments and acknowledge, accommodate, or refute them one by one using adequate evidence. Simply stated, "Here's what they say; here's what I say to their ideas."
   3. Argue your reasons, concluding with your most persuasive.

B. Proposal Papers (Problem-Solution): Outline
   1. Present the problem. You may need to argue why it is serious enough to merit consideration: if we don't solve it, there will be bad consequences. You may also need to discuss what you regard are the causes, and even argue that one or some causes are more significant than others. Solutions are tailored to causes.
   2. Present your solution (your thesis). You may need to explain or describe it and how it might be implemented.
   3. Deal with objections to your solution, which might include your opponents' view that another or other solutions are preferable to yours. Other generic objections are the following:
      - Things aren't that bad. Why change them?
      - It won't solve the problem.

- We can't afford it.
- It will take too long.
- People won't do it.
- I don't see how to get started.
- It's already been tried, with unsatisfactory results.
- You're making this proposal because it will benefit you personally.
- There's a better solution.

4. Brainstorm for Proposal Papers: possible solutions, advantages, disadvantages. Identify your solution, and offer two alternate solutions.

Note: Like the Issue/Problem Paper, it is essential that you refute the opposition. In traditional argument papers, each body paragraph begins by addressing the opposition, identifying with the opposition, and refuting the opposition. Ideally, 1/3 of each body paragraph should address and identify with the opposition, and 2/3 of each body paragraph should be spent refuting the opposition.

When you end your papers, do it with tact. Summarizing your main ideas works sometimes, but often it's unnecessary and merely repetitive. Instead, use your ending to advance your argument with your most persuasive and important point. Craft your last few sentences so that they're memorable.

Here are some examples of well-written argument papers:

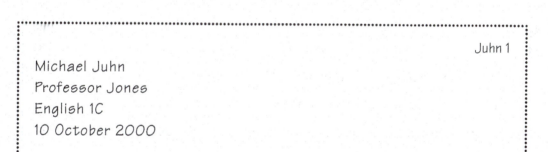

Juhn 1

Michael Juhn
Professor Jones
English 1C
10 October 2000

Class, Not Race

One of the most debated topics of today is affirmative action. Among other things, people debate whether the action is fair or not, or whether or not the action works. Some people also debate whether affirmative action is racist or not; they debate whether or not the action is reverse discrimination. Many people argue over what they think are problems with the program, and they argue over different solutions. It seems as if there is an endless supply of topics to debate when it comes to affirmative action. Although many people are debating over affirmative action, there are many people who do not fully understand it. To fully understand an issue, one must start at the origin of the issue. In <u>Elements of Argument</u> Annette Rottenberg states: "The original objective of these actions was elimination of the barriers to employment and schooling for women and members of minority groups . . . The earliest policies were designed to protect traditionally disadvantaged groups against discrimination" (435). Affirmative action has done well in eliminating many barriers for these disadvantaged groups, but with the introduction of quotas in the 1970s, affirmative action has made a turn for the worse. Affirmative action helps women and members of minority groups whether they need it or not. To say that only women and members of minority groups need special assistance is wrong and unfair. Therefore, instead of affirmative action being ethnicity and gender based, it would be more effective if the action were based on class. Affirmative action has deviated from what it was originally and has become something that is wrong, unfair, and something that does not work the way it was intended to.

Some people think that affirmative action is helping those who need help. This argument does have some validity. Affirmative action has been in effect for some time now, and many improvements have been made for the minority groups. For instance, there is more diversity at schools and in the professional world. However, the length of time something has been in effect does not make it any more right. It is almost impossible to ignore the problems at the universities and colleges. In many universities and colleges, students are passed up for admission because there is not enough space for them. Students of minority groups who might have lower test scores or lower grade point averages take some of this space. The problem with this is that some of these students do not deserve this break. These are the students who come from middle-class suburbia, who have not experienced racial injustices, and come from good schools, but are ultimately accepted because of their ethnicity. This is not fair to the white students who live in lower-class neighborhoods and go to inner-city schools. Although they might have the same or higher potential to do well in college, they are passed up because of the color of their skin. In the interview "Affirmative Action: A Tale of Two Women," Mandalit del Barco says, "Students who come from a school that was economically disadvantaged, and lack opportunities available to others, need that extra help." Linda Chavez replies:

I do not disagree with that, that is what affirmative action was initially. But kids of middle-class families, whose parents are sometimes college-educated, are given a preference at Berkeley or Stanford based solely on their ethnic background . . . That is the core of the problem: programs do not reach out to the kids who are disadvantaged and who come from inner-city schools. (448)

This is a problem indeed. Accepting students of color just for the sake of diversity is wrong. Not all students of minority groups need the special assistance, and not all white students come from well-off homes and good schools. Those that look at the applications must stop looking at the ethnicity of the applicants and start looking for qualities that actually matter, such as income, ability, and potential of the students.

There are also those who believe that affirmative action based on ethnicity is the most logical way that the action should work. This belief does seem true. Affirmative action has opened doors for many people of minority groups. Students of different ethnicities are being accepted to top universities, and people of different colors now hold many respectable jobs. However, hiring employees and accepting students based on ethnicity is not only wrong but very insulting to the minority groups. In "Affirmative Action: A Tale of Two Women,"

Linda Chavez states: "Racial preferences are also patronizing, and ultimately, a very racist concept. They imply that, somehow, you cannot apply the same standards to blacks and Hispanics as you do to whites, because minorities will not be able to meet them"(447–448). People of minority groups should be taken seriously for their abilities and not just simply accepted because of their skin color. The problems with ethnicity-based affirmative action can also be seen when checking the statistics. Nathan Glazer writes: ". . . blacks are to be found disproportionately among the poor (they form 12 percent of the population, but 30 percent or more of the population in poverty) . . ." (444). Shelby Steele also writes:

> Had America worked from the 1960s on to educate blacks to the same standard as whites, had it truly labored to eradicate discrimination, there would be more virtue and power on both sides of the racial divide today. The disingenuousness of affirmative action—born of the black struggle for freedom—can be seen in two remarkable facts: Middle-class white women have benefited from it far more than any other group, and 46 percent of all black children live in poverty. (442)

These statistics show the failure of ethnicity-based affirmative action. If ethnicity-based affirmative action is so successful and has helped so many people of different colors, then why are so many blacks still living in poverty? The answer is, because the current affirmative action programs do not work. Affirmative action opens doors for some minorities and allows for some minorities to attend universities, but it does not train the minority groups as a whole to be able to obtain these accomplishments on their own.

These problems in affirmative action show that a change is needed in the system. The best thing to do would be to have class-based affirmative action instead of ethnicity-based affirmative action. This system would help those who really need the help. Students in poor neighborhoods, who attend poor schools, would be given the training needed starting at a young age, possibly middle school. Then those students having the ability, and showing the potential, would be given the opportunity to attend a college or university. Financial aid would be provided, and ethnicity would not be an issue. This would help students who come from poor schools compete at the college level. This form of affirmative action would train and help those who actually need help, and it would help people of all ethnicities.

Works Cited

Del Barco, Mandalit. "Affirmative Action: A Tale of Two Women." Elements of Argument. Ed. Annette Rottenberg. Boston: St. Martin's, 1997.

Glazer, Nathan. "Race, Not Class." <u>Elements of Argument</u>. Ed. Annette Rottenberg. Boston: St. Martin's, 1997.

Rottenberg, Annette. <u>Elements of Argument</u>. Boston: St. Martin's, 1997.

Steele, Shelby. "Affirmative Action Must Go." <u>Elements of Argument</u>. Ed. Annette Rottenberg. Boston: St. Martin's, 1997.

Note: Michael adheres to the traditional method for addressing, identifying, and refuting the opposition. Additionally, he offers a solution-oriented conclusion which is indicative of William Golding's Grade One Thinker. Finally, he restates his claim frequently, almost forcing the reader to focus on the argument without deviation or invitation of day-dream-like digression.

Dirk Ellington
Professor Jones
English 1C
10 October 2000

Affirmative Action? No!

Just after the Civil Rights movement of the mid-sixties, the American job market was dominated primarily by whites. In an attempt to promote ethnic variety in the job market, a program was created. This program, known as affirmative action, was believed to be a solution to discrimination against women and ethnic minorities. It is designed to give preferential treatment toward these groups in education and job placement. However, if one would take the time to look over the statistics while considering America's future, he would come to realize that affirmative action is wrong.

Originally created to help African-Americans and women be more successful by eliminating the barriers of segregation and discrimination, affirmative action hasn't served its purpose. "The disingenuousness of affirmative action—born of the black struggle for freedom—can be seen in two remarkable facts: Middle-class white women have benefited from it far more than any other group, and 46 percent of all black children live in poverty" (Steele 442). Although affirmative action has helped middle-class white women, it hasn't done much to improve the livelihood of so many African-Americans.

Those in support of affirmative action claim that it helps minorities and gives them a chance that they normally wouldn't have gotten. They're absolutely correct. Affirmative action does give opportunity to minorities, often at the expense of individuals from the majority. It favors minorities and sometimes lowers standards, which allows someone having less skill or knowledge to get the same job as another person who is capable of performing the job without any trouble. It gives minorities a chance that they normally wouldn't have gotten, but the question is, are they skilled and motivated enough to deserve that chance? No, they probably aren't, because if they were, we wouldn't have affirmative action in the first place. It also stigmatizes them as "affirmative action babies." They are looked down upon as people who can't "stand up" by themselves. In the long run, a lot of minorities may feel inadequate. In "Affirmative Action: A Tale of Two Women," Linda Chavez states:

I have been chosen for jobs on the basis of being a Mexican-American woman. Each time, it has been an unmitigated disaster. There was a presumption that I thought in a certain way, and that I was going to serve a certain function. When it turned out I was not interested in being the token Hispanic, things did not work out well. There have been other times when the affirmative action prejudice stigmatized me. I had to constantly demonstrate that I have earned my position. (449)

Linda felt that her preferential treatment was degrading. She also said, "Racial preferences are also patronizing, and ultimately, a very racist concept. They imply that, somehow, you cannot apply the same standards to blacks and Hispanics as you do to whites, because minorities will not be able to meet them. This is a misguided notion promoted by many liberals" (448). More importantly, giving preference to less-qualified people because of their last name, gender, or skin color hurts the job market. What if affirmative action were applied to professional sports? Let's imagine a basketball team that had to edit its roster of players because of this new system. Since African-Americans make up most of the players in the league, they're considered the majority. The coach would only be able to select a few of the qualified players (most being of African-American descent) before moving on and choosing other less qualified players of minority ethnicities. Imagine how basketball and other sports would change! Since skill level wouldn't be as important as ethnicity, the level of competition would drastically decrease. Games wouldn't be as exciting to watch, and companies would stop advertising on sports stations. An entire dissertation could be written on the problems that this would cause.

Another thing that advocates of affirmative action say is, because America is a "melting pot" of different ethnicities, we should promote variety in the job market. This idea is naturally becoming a reality. Because our society admires other cultures, we are very open to variety. However, excluding members of the ethnic majority in order to bring variety into the job market is wrong. A "wrong" can't be fixed with another "wrong." In other words, we can't attempt to fix the problems caused by racism in the past by creating a new racist technique now. There was an incident at a Target store in Ontario, California where the management decided to fire one hundred and fifty-one qualified white people, only to diversify the ethnic makeup of the employees by hiring seventy-five ethnic minorities. Most of the newly hired people were interviewed on the spot, while most of the white applicants were rejected and turned away. They were denied an opportunity to work at Target because they were white. Is this right?

Proponents of affirmative action also bring up history and contend that in the past, white males were given priority to education and jobs. Because of this, white men tend to be more successful in the job market than women and people of minority groups. I agree. White people (specifically males) hold higher positions because a lot of them come from wealthier families and are able to afford better educations than the families of immigrants and ethnic minorities. As the population is becoming more diverse, some of the minority ethnicities are establishing concentrated areas in which one ethnicity dominates the surrounding business. Take the city of Rowland Heights, California, for example. The people of this city consist mostly of Chinese and Koreans. A Korean person helps out her ethnicity by giving business to places owned by fellow Koreans. Although it borders on ethnocentrism, it is essential for minority ethnicities to achieve equality. With populations such as this sprouting up in more and more places, why do we need to have programs that implement reverse discrimination to make the job market more "diverse?" In other words, why must employers discriminate against a well-qualified Caucasian man only to hire a woman of "color" who is not as qualified? Will the job she does be as good as the job he could have done because an employer managed to fill a quota based on the hiring of minorities? The answer is, obviously, "no!"

Works Cited

Del Barco, Mandalit. "Affirmative Action: A Tale of Two Women." <u>Elements of Argument</u>. Ed. Annette Rottenberg. Boston: St. Martin's, 1997.
Steele, Shelby. "Affirmative Action Must Go." <u>Elements of Argument</u>. Ed. Annette Rottenberg. Boston: St. Martin's, 1997.

Note: Attempt to trace Dirk's organization, specifically how he chose to address, identify, and refute the opposition. You'll notice that instead of adhering to the traditional method, he chose to apply this process in a lateral, as opposed to linear, manner. Also, note where Dirk borders on offending the reader with overtly egregious and, arguably, irresponsible assertions. How might these assertions fare with the typical reader? How did they fare with you?

The following essay, by Susan Harwood, was written in response to the "Who Should Survive?" prompt (found in the Appendix under "Additional Exercises").

Susan Harwood
Professor Jones
English 1C
10 October 2000

Who Should Survive?

Assuming there are only eleven people left on Earth and four must be chosen based upon their ability to procreate, these four should survive: Mr. Newton, Mary Evans, Dr. Dane, and Mrs. Clark.

The first person chosen to survive is Mr. Newton. It is reasonable to infer that Mr. Newton can procreate because he is twenty-five years old. This is further supported by Mr. Newton's hobby in physical fitness. While this does not prove he is in good shape, perhaps he is, and this may increase his chances of successful procreation. Some may argue that Mr. Newton's suspected homosexual activity would impede his ability to procreate. This, however, is illogical, for regardless of Mr. Newton's sexual preference, as long as he is physically capable, he can procreate. Others may criticize Mr. Newton's black-power advocacy. This is reasonable; however, it has nothing to do with his ability to procreate.

The second survivor chosen is Mary Evans. Mary is eighteen years old, so it is quite possible that Ms. Evans may be able to procreate, and if so, she probably has many fertile years ahead of her. Some may argue that Mary should not be chosen because she wears glasses; therefore, she is genetically flawed. This, however, is irrelevant because the criterion is to possess simply the ability to create another human being, not necessarily a genetically perfect one.

The third person chosen to survive is Dr. Dane. At thirty-seven years of age, it is reasonable to assume that Dr. Dane may be able to procreate. This is further substantiated by the fact that Dr. Dane already has one child. While this does not guarantee that Dr. Dane is still capable of reproduction, perhaps he is. Dr. Dane's ability to procreate may be enhanced by the fact that he is in good health and jogs daily. Some may argue that Dr. Dane should not be chosen because his only child, Bobby, is mentally retarded. This is a reasonable argument; however, as long as Dr. Dane is physically capable, he can procreate and, therefore, meets the criterion. Furthermore, it is possible that any future offspring of Dr. Dane may be genetically normal.

The last person chosen to survive is Mrs. Clark. Mrs. Clark is twenty-eight years old, so as long as she is physically capable, she probably has the ability to procreate. Some may object to Mrs. Clark's membership to the Zero Population Growth. This is quite reasonable because such a belief may hinder rapid growth of the human race. However, Mrs. Clark is a college graduate, and while this does not mean she is intelligent, perhaps she is. Perhaps she may realize, under the circumstances, that she may play a vital role in the survival of the human race, and her belief in Zero Population Growth may become obsolete.

One of the seven not chosen to survive is Mrs. Dane. Being rather obese may greatly increase Mrs. Dane's chances of having problems with infertility because it is more than likely that Mrs. Dane may not be in good health. Being diabetic may also increase Mrs. Dane's chances of being infertile because diabetes may cause hormonal imbalances and may possibly weaken all body systems, including the reproductive system. Some may say that Mrs. Dane should be chosen because she does have one child already, so it is reasonable to assume that she may be able to procreate again. This is understandable; however, Mrs. Dane is thirty-seven, and it is possible that she may soon be going through menopause. Hence, Mrs. Dane is not the best choice to save the future of the human race.

Secondly, Bobby Dane was not chosen to survive. Bobby is only ten years old, so he probably does not yet possess the ability to procreate. Some may argue that he may be able to reproduce in a few years because he is healthy and strong for his age, but his potential abilities in the future do not help save the human race today. Hence, Bobby does not pass the test to survive.

Mrs. Garcia was another who was not chosen to survive. Mrs. Garcia worked as a prostitute and was married at the seemingly young age of sixteen. As a result of these potentially risky sexual behaviors, Mrs. Garcia may have possibly contracted a sexually-transmitted disease. If Mrs. Garcia was infected, the disease may contribute to problems that may hinder Mrs. Garcia's ability to procreate including infertility or miscarriage. Some would reason that because Mrs. Garcia is twenty-three, it is logical to infer that she can procreate, but one cannot logically dismiss the potential problems that may stem from her sexual behavior. Hence, Mrs. Garcia does not accurately meet the criterion for survival.

Jean Garcia also did not fulfill the criterion for survival. Jean is only three-months old, so it is quite reasonable to assume that he or she may be unable to procreate at this stage in life. Some may say that Jean may be able to procreate later in life, which may be reasonable; however, Jean's potential for the distant future will not effectively help the human species survive today. Therefore, Jean Garcia was not chosen to survive.

Another person not chosen to survive is Mr. Blake. Mr. Blake is fifty-one, and being an older man may increase his chances of possibly experiencing a sexual dysfunction such as impotence or other erectile dysfunctions that may, perhaps, hinder his ability to breed successfully. Some may dispute this judgment because Mr. Blake does have four children; however, he may have possibly had these children when he was younger and more fertile. Furthermore, it is not known whether or not these children are, in fact, Mr.

Blake's biological children. Thus, Mr. Blake was not chosen to be on the list of survivors.

Father Frans was another who was not chosen to survive. Father Frans is a Catholic priest, so he is more than likely sworn to an oath of celibacy. If Father Frans kept true to his word, this could possibly hinder procreation. Some would argue that because he was often criticized for having liberal views, it is possible that Father Frans may abandon his oath and try to procreate. This is not reasonable, however, for it is not known for sure that Father Frans' liberal views were ever present in the realm of sexuality.

Finally, Dr. Gonzales was also not chosen to survive. Unfortunately, the gender of Dr. Gonzales is unknown. If a female, at the age of sixty-six, Dr. Gonzales would more than likely have gone through menopause and, therefore, would probably not be able to procreate. If a male, Dr. Gonzales may potentially experience some kind of sexual dysfunction due to his age, as chances of experiencing dysfunction tend to increase with age. Some may argue that because Dr. Gonzales is, in fact, a doctor, he or she may be of use to the other survivors; however, this is irrelevant to the criterion.

Out of the eleven people left on Earth, only four will survive. These four have been chosen through the process of critical thought and reason because their ability to procreate is, ostensibly, more reliable than the others. While many of the candidates possessed admirable characteristics, unless pertaining to their ability to procreate, such characteristics were not entertained. It stands to reason, then, that Mr. Newton, Mary Evans, Dr. Dane, and Mrs. Clark should be chosen to survive.

Note: Susan has composed a relatively responsibly-written argument. "Relatively" is used, for even though Susan is a talented writer, she fell victim to some of the pitfalls that regularly plague "Who Should Survive?" essays. First, however, let's look at what she did exceptionally well. This begins in her introductory paragraph. In it, she identifies her criterion, "ability to procreate," and makes it clear that four people have been chosen to survive based on that criterion. Why, future sheep herders, is this smart? It is smart because it provides her with a scapegoat, a reason to disqualify the others. Because this is offered in the beginning, she has defined her reality and, hence, made an attempt at composing an essay devoid of the usual prejudice and bias that can find themselves lurking among disqualified candidates.

Susan also does an exceptional job of qualifying her assertions. In paragraph two, for instance, she employs language like "It is reasonable to infer," ". . . perhaps he is, and this may increase . . .", "Some may argue," and "Others may criticize." She does not write in a definitive manner, and this helps keep her from making fallacious assertions.

Susan also adheres specifically to her claim. In paragraph two, she does not even mention that Mr. Newton is finishing his last year of medical school. Justifiably, she does not mention this, for it is not relevant to her criterion. Her criterion is "ability to procreate." Unless finishing the last year of medical school has something to do with "ability to procreate," then it need not be mentioned.

Susan also does a fine job of refuting the opposition. Not only does she state why each person was chosen, but she attempts to hone in on, primarily, what the audience might deem a fault or reason not to select the candidate. She, of course, does this by following the format: address the opposition, identify with the opposition, and refute the opposition. Overall, she has composed a decent argument.

Her argument, however, does house some weaknesses, and they must be addressed. First, when choosing Mrs. Clark (fifth paragraph), Susan attempts to refute the opposition by deducing that, based on possessing a college degree, Mrs.

Clark may be intelligent and, hence, may rescind her membership in Zero Population Growth. This suggests that another criterion exists. Unfortunately, Susan has now suggested that "willingness to procreate" also plays a role in choosing people to survive. Had she focused simply on "ability to procreate," she could have refuted the opposition just as she did in paragraphs two, three, and four. Because of this single error, the reader is led to believe that, perhaps, a separate agenda exists. Perhaps she has criteria as opposed to a criterion.

Something similar occurs in paragraph six when attempting to disqualify Mrs. Dane. Susan ends the paragraph with this: "Hence, Mrs. Dane is not the best choice to save the future of the human race." This, unfortunately, is new language that is being introduced to the reader. More importantly, it is not germane to the criterion. Remember, support is introduced into an essay to advance the claim. In this case, the last sentence should not read "Mrs. Dane is not the best choice to save the future of the human race" but, rather, "Mrs. Dane is not the best choice, for she may have trouble procreating due to her obesity and diabetes."

Next, in paragraph ten, Susan disqualifies Mr. Blake, and until she makes her second-to-last assertion, her paragraph is relatively sound because her argument hinges on Mr. Blake's age and its relationship to his potential inability to procreate. This is good. Unfortunately, she proceeds to transcend age and state this: "Furthermore, it is not known whether or not these children are, in fact, Mr. Blake's biological children." Why does this raise a red flag? A red flag now waves for this reason: Susan helped support choosing Dr. Dane by citing the fact that Dane already has a son, Bobby. Unfortunately, nowhere does it state whether or not Bobby is Dane's biological child; as a result, Susan has just, perhaps unconsciously, introduced a new quasi-criterion into the mix.

Finally, in paragraph eleven, Father Frans is disqualified because of an "oath of celibacy" as opposed to his "[in]ability to procreate." For the discerning reader, it should be plainly evident that such a disqualification mirrors the discrepancy in paragraph five surrounding Mrs. Clark. Both, unfortunately, suggest that "willingness to procreate" has something to do with the criterion.

Susan has clearly constructed a decent argument. To improve it, however, what might she do? Should she simply remedy the discrepancies housed by various paragraphs? Should she add another criterion? Should she revise the current criterion? Should she choose different survivors? Ruminate on these questions, for they are definitely pertinent to producing a responsibly-written "Who Should Survive?" essay.

What follows are three in-class essays. Students should note that in-class essays encourage the adoption of a slightly different strategy than what is employed when writing take-home essays. In the following three in-class essays, the students were provided with the prompt(s) one week ahead of time. During those painstaking 168 hours, students could engage in pre-writing activities, the creation of preliminary drafts, and a search for ten quotations (the ten quotations were, eventually, committed to a 5 × 8 card. Students were encouraged to use the quotations to support their assertions and make their arguments more credible). Students were given two hours to compose their arguments. Their only aids were copies of the prompt(s), a dictionary, and the aforementioned 5 × 8 card. It is worth noting that prewriting (at the least, creating an outline) and proofreading are still germane to the creation of a responsibly-written argument. At a minimum, students should expect to budget their time in the following manner: allot fifteen minutes to prewriting, one hour and thirty minutes to composing the argument, and fifteen minutes to proofreading, making sure to double space in order to leave ample room for added sentences, transitions, and qualifiers.

The following example of an in-class essay was written in response to the following prompt:

Compare two whistleblowers to Jeffrey Wigand or Lowell Bergman of <u>The Insider</u>. Then, show how "The Reward Is?", "Allegory of the Cave," "Self-reliance," and/or "Civil Disobedience" relate to whistleblowing. Finally, discuss whether you think whistleblowing is an act representative of critical thinkers.

Thuy Nguyen
Professor Jones
English 1C
10 October 2000

Critical Whistleblowers

In defining the term "whistleblowers," different definitions may be provided depending on each individual's perspective. Generally speaking, a whistleblower is a person who tells the truth. However, this definition is too broad to form a detailed concept of "whistleblowers." What kind of truth will make the teller a whistleblower?

Would a boy who cut down a tree and later admitted his act be considered a whistleblower? Definitely not. A whistleblower has something that makes him or her different from an honest person; although, honesty is an important characteristic of a whistleblower. To be more specific for the sake of argument, a whistleblower is a person who stands for truth and justice while others may choose to conform to false perceptions or injustice. The causes of false perceptions and injustice must be great and must unfavorably affect society's interests. Many whistleblowers act on the consciousness of knowing the consequences that may occur from their just actions. They must investigate and collect enough evidence before deciding to blow the whistle. The act of investigating, analyzing, and considering solutions is, in fact, the activity of critical thinking. Whistleblowing is, therefore, an act representative of critical thinkers.

Being considered "trouble-makers" in most cases, whistleblowers face a tremendous pressure from the opposing side. There is Dr. Jeffrey Wigand, whose story was made into the movie The Insider. As the head of Research and Development for Brown and Williamson, a tobacco company, Dr. Wigand blew the whistle on the tobacco industry's conduct of using ammonia with nicotine to increase addiction. There is Dr. Paul Michelson, who filed a lawsuit against Scripps Clinic and Research Foundation and a colleague for deceivingly billing Medicare. There is Robert Wityczak, who chose to stand up against

Rockwell for mischarging the government for construction materials. All three of them either got fired or were physically harassed on the job. Still, they acted on behalf of society and risked their careers to expose the unethical conduct of their employers. How, in their acts of blowing the whistle, do they show their critical thinking skills?

Following the definition mentioned earlier, whistleblowers are critical thinkers when they examine the problems. In the case of Dr. Wigand, after being fired for disagreeing with the company's C.E.O. on the use of ammonia in tobacco, he was forced to make a choice between keeping the company's secret and retaining the medical benefits for his family or reporting the company's unethical conduct and losing his medical benefits. As a critical thinker, Dr. Wigand had to consider the solutions and weigh the importance of each decision. As shown in the movie, there are many times when Dr. Wigand argues with Lowell Bergman, the journalist, about how his decision will affect his children and his future. His consideration and the decision to expose the truth are exactly the acts of critical thinking.

Similar to Dr. Wigand, Dr. Paul Michelson also faced a problem that was contradictory to his professional ethic. Upon discovering a colleague's misconduct of performing unnecessary surgeries and mischarging Medicare for surgeries that were never performed, Dr. Michelson had to decide whether to keep silent to protect his job or report the problem to protect the patients (investigating, analyzing, and considering solutions). In a report to a subcommittee in 1986, Dr. Michelson said: "I was certain that I, too, would expose myself to a potentially ruinous defamation or restraint of trade in the event the authorities failed to act conclusively and expeditiously." Clearly a critical thinker, Dr. Michelson filed a lawsuit and won the case. What he did perfectly fits the definition of a whistleblower, a person who stands for truth and, hence, shows how whistleblowing is an act representative of critical thinkers. This is also supported when examining Robert Wityczak.

Robert Wityczak, a defense contractor for Rockwell, was forced to sign timecards to bill the government for the time he worked on other projects. He also discovered many material requisitions that were filed for personal use (investigating and analyzing). He conformed to the others but constantly felt conflicted. He told a subcommittee before Congress decided to amend the False Claims Act: "Yet I was still facing a tremendous conflict inside between my loyalty to the company and my loyalty to my country" (considering solutions). Facing the contradiction forced Mr. Wityczak to take action by reporting the mischarging to the F.B.I. as opposed to the subcommittee. Similar to the two whistleblowers mentioned earlier, Mr. Wityczak was physically harassed on the job and, later, fired. He also must have known the consequences of going against his company, the majority in this case. However, he decided to blow the whistle for the "loyalty to [his] country." Standing up for his constitution is an act of a critical thinker. Furthermore, by investigating, analyzing, and considering solutions, Wityczak cements the notion that whistleblowing is an act representative of critical thinkers.

By examining the whistleblowers, it is quite obvious that each of them committed to his own constitution, telling the truth. Each decided to blow the whistle not only because the problems contradicted their constitutions but also affected the society: public health in the case of Dr. Wigand, and the government's budget in the case of Dr. Michelson and Mr. Wityczak. All three of them stood for the truth after carefully considering the problems and solutions. They perfectly demonstrate critical thinking.

In discussing the definition of "whistleblowers" and "critical thinkers," it seems that "critical thinkers" and "whistleblowers" are synonymous. Thoreau, in "Civil Disobedience," asserts: "A wise man will not leave the right to the mercy of chance, nor wish it to prevail through the power of the majority." This is exactly what a whistleblower will do. He will stand for "the right" even if the whole society is against him. The power of the whistleblower is the power of the truth being presented. He, the whistleblower, stands alone but holds the power. As Thoreau states, "A minority is powerless while it conforms to the majority; it is not even a minority then; but it is irresistible when it clogs by its whole weight." How can a whistleblower expose the truth if he or she does not commit to the activity of critical thinking, which means analyzing, investigating, and considering solutions? This, again, proves that a whistleblower is a critical thinker.

In "Allegory of the Cave," Plato believes that the person who has seen the "light"—the Truth—". . . must be made to descend again among the prisoners in the den, and partake of their labors and honors, whether they are worth having or not." This is an implied image of a whistleblower. A whistleblower is a person who sees the "light" and makes others aware of it. Again, he or she must also be a critical thinker in order to understand the truth and hold it in his or her constitution, for in order to see the "light," he or she must investigate and analyze before reaching the solution which, most likely, will involve making others aware of the "light" or the truth.

Upon examining these examples of whistleblowers and comparing them to the act of critical thinking, it seems clear that whistleblowing is an act representative of critical thinkers. The person who chooses to blow the whistle must investigate and analyze the issue or problem until he or she uncovers the truth. After doing so, he or she has to consider and weigh the solutions. A whistleblower is a critical thinker because he or she holds the truth and fights for it. As Plato states in "Allegory of the Cave," "Yes . . . he would rather suffer anything than entertain these false notions and live in this miserable manner."

Note: Thuy offers a fine argument. First, she is aware of the potential ambiguity inherent in two terms: "whistleblowers" and "critical thinking." Hence, she defines both in her first paragraph. By doing this, she has defined her perception or "reality" and, in essence, made sure not to allow the reader's definition of "whistleblower" and "critical thinking" to act as an impediment when evaluating whether or not her support advances her claim.

Thuy also does a fine job of establishing that Wigand, Michelson, and Wityczak are, indeed, whistleblowers; responsibly, she does this before showing how what they did is representative of critical thinkers. Hence, in paragraph two, she directly addresses the first component of the prompt. In paragraphs three, four, five, and six, she shows how the actions of Wigand, Michelson, and Wityczak support her claim. (Thuy could strengthen paragraphs three, four, five, and six by offering examples of the solutions under consideration or examples of the importance/repercussions of each decision. She can do this by, for instance, in paragraph four, linking Michelson's actions to the definition of "critical thinking," as provided in paragraph one. Furthermore, in paragraph five, she could more explicitly link each activity (investigating, analyzing, and considering solutions) to each component of Wityczak's plight by simply writing this: "When Wityczak said to a subcommittee, 'Yet I was still facing a tremendous conflict inside between my loyalty to the company and my loyalty to my country,' he is obviously engaging in the third activity of critical thinking: considering solutions.")

In paragraph seven, Thuy does something very skillful: she addresses the prompt and advances her claim. Many would do this in two paragraphs, but she is able to, in a succinct, cohesive manner, attain the goal in one. She, masterfully, does the same thing in the following paragraph, and then she brings her argument to a close. (To strengthen her closing paragraph, Thuy could further develop her response to the prompt's final tier. She could do this by citing other sources, for instance, Emerson's "Self-reliance" or dialogue from *The Insider.*

The following in-class essay was written in response to this prompt:

As you probably know, even professional writers fail to define their terms when composing arguments. Choosing three essays on "sex and violence in popular culture," identify the terms employed by each essayist and his/her definitions of the terms. Next, note the similarities and differences between each essayist's definitions. Then, note whether or not the essays would have been more responsibly written had the essayists first defined their "realities." Finally, identify the essay whose views most accurately reflect your stance on sex and violence in popular culture. Explain why the essay most accurately reflects your stance by citing examples from the essay and from other sources.

David Lemus
Professor Jones
English 1C
10 October 2000

Defining Violence

Sometimes authors of essays employ similar terms, especially when arguing on topics such as sex and violence in popular culture. Three authors that did so are Paul Klite, author of "TV News and the Culture of Violence," Holman W. Jenkins Jr., author of "Violence Never Solved Anything, But It's Entertaining," and Mike Oppenheim, author of "TV Isn't Violent Enough."

The term that all three authors use throughout their essays is "violence." Klite uses the term a total of twenty-three times. Klite defines "violence" with this argument: "violence" _is_ "TV news." He states: "The seventy-five percent of Americans who watch TV news regularly are subjected to a substantial nightly dose of catastrophe." This is to imply that the news on TV broadcasts images of violence on a regular basis. Next, Jenkins uses the term "violence" a total of seventeen times. He defines violence with this argument: "violence" _is_ "TV entertainment." Jenkins Jr. writes: "Cable, especially premium cable, has become the violence medium. . . ." What he means is this: violence has become a major part of television entertainment. Lastly, Mike Oppenheim uses the term much less than the other writers. He uses the word "violence" eight times in his essay. He defines "violence" with this argument: "television violence" <u>is</u> nothing like "real-life violence," for "TV violence" is "unreal," and "real-life violence" is very much "real." Oppenheim writes this: ". . . quiet corpses left by TV's good guys, bad guys, and assorted ill-tempered gun owners is ridiculously unreal." This analysis is very important. Obviously, violent shows on TV, such as <u>Jag</u> or <u>Walker, Texas Ranger</u>, are fake; they are an "act." Real violence is not an act. In addition, the definitions the authors provide for the reader have similar characteristics but also have very distinct differences.

Indeed, there are some similarities between each author's definition of violence. For instance, Klite and Jenkins Jr. both agree that violence on TV has an influence on people. Klite states in his essay: "Television's power to influence behavior and belief attracts. . . ." Similarly, Jenkins states this: ". . . teenagers swarm to horror flicks as the boys can demonstrate their manly unflappability and girls can demonstrate their vulnerable desirability." What the authors are implying is that "violence" can affect people. Also, all three authors' definitions of violence share one thing in common. They all recognize that violence is on TV. Klite, by recognizing that the news broadcasts violence, is stating that violence is on TV. Jenkins, by noting that cable is the medium for violence, is stating that violence is on TV. Like the other two authors, Oppenheim claims the same, yet he offers a detailed example of violence. Oppenheim writes: "On a recent episode, Matt Houston is at a fancy resort, on the trail of a vicious killer who specializes in knifing beautiful women. . . ." Since Klite states that the TV news is violent, Jenkins claims that TV entertainment is violent, and Oppenheim offers an example of violence on TV, all definitions state that "TV is violent."

Along with those similarities come the differences which, in fact, are more distinguishable. One difference is that Klite uses the news to address violence, and the others do not. Klite writes: ". . . broadcast images have enormous power . . . Yet, the news industry has no ethical guidelines for airing violent images." This means that the news airs too much violence. On the other hand, Jenkins Jr. claims that most violence on TV is spawned by "entertainment." He writes: "Ted Turner, who can often be heard denouncing television violence from a podium, has given us Saturday Night Nitro on TNT—whole evenings of delicious violence. . . ." Unlike Klite, who uses real news violence, Jenkins points out that "TV entertainment" is violent. Then there is Oppenheim. He claims that "TV violence" is nothing like "real-life violence." Along with the examples of TV violence, he offers the reader an example of "real-life violence." He states: "I've sewn up many. A real-life, no-nonsense criminal with a blackjack . . . has a much better success rate [of causing damage]. The result is a large number of deaths and permanent damage from brain hemorrhage."

He writes this after stating that one punch to the human skull is not as effective as TV makes it appear. Klite's definition is that violence is on the "TV news." Next, Jenkins defines violence by way of "TV entertainment." Finally, Oppenheim contradicts both authors by writing: "TV isn't violent enough."

Jenkins uses entertainment on television to advance his claim that television is violent. What he doesn't do is use detailed examples of violence on television. He would have been more responsible had he stated more examples of violence on TV, like Oppenheim.

Next, there is Paul Klite. Klite mentions forms of violence on the news. He writes: "Events on television have generated copycat crimes, including mass murder, terrorism, . . . and suicide." By using these words, such as "murder," "terrorism," and "suicide," the reader can relate to what kind of violence the author is writing about. The reader, perhaps, can visualize what violence is after reading such terms. This is very responsible of him.

Finally, Oppenheim comes up with the most responsible definition of "violence." Not only does he use examples of real violence but TV violence too. In the previous examples from his essay, he uses terms such as "killer," "knifing," "death," and even "brain hemorrhage." He gives the readers examples such as this: "The next day he shows up with this cute little Band-Aid over his eyebrow [after being beaten by a number of mafia men]. We can't pass that. You'll have to add one eye swollen shut, three missing front teeth, at least twenty stitches over the lips and eyes, and a wired jaw." This is obviously an attempt by the writer to have his audience visualize what true violence is. Hence, Mike Oppenheim is very responsible, for he offers many examples of violence on TV, and, in reality, he uses very descriptive terms.

Clearly, violence is an issue that needs to be reduced and, if possible, ceased. Jenkins, author of "Violence Never Solved Anything, But It's Entertaining," writes it best when he states: ". . . but making the television the issue only avoids the question of how we could be doing a better job of identifying the homicidally mentally ill before someone gets hurt." Indeed, that is the issue. How can we, society, fight against violence? Is it by censoring TV, music, and any other form of entertainment? It can seem that way, but "TV violence" is not the issue; "real-life" violence is the issue. TV and music are major aspects of popular culture. Claiming that those are the only causes of violence is fallacious, for it cannot be proven. Leave entertainment as an aspect that may contain images of violence, and let's focus on fighting "real" violence in popular culture.

Note: David has composed a clear, well-organized, well-focused argument. He does a fine job of identifying the term under scrutiny ("violence") and delineating between Klite's, Jenkins', and Oppenheim's definitions. David also employs nice transitional language to link sentences and paragraphs. For instance, in paragraph two, he uses "Next" and "Lastly" to note shifts in focus from Klite to Jenkins to

Oppenheim. Later in paragraph two, he articulates the following sentence: "In addition, the definitions the authors provide for the reader have similar characteristics but also have very distinct differences." This is smart, for he has adequately primed the reader for the discourse that awaits in the next two body paragraphs.

To strengthen his argument, David should address "realities," for this is a term found in the prompt. Also, he needs to further develop his stance on sex and violence in popular culture by citing additional sources. Finally, while his claim is adequate, could it be strengthened by including his stance on sex and violence in popular culture?

The following in-class essay was written in response to this prompt:

Choosing three essays on "sex and violence in popular culture," classify each as "reasonable" or "unreasonable" based on the detection of contradictions, bias, fallacies, or irresponsible language. Then, explain why one of the three essays is the most responsibly written. Finally, state whether or not you agree with the argument posed in the most responsibly-written essay. Make sure to define your stance on sex and violence in popular culture, and support it by citing examples from the responsibly-written essay and from other sources.

Susan Harwood
Professor Jones
English 1C
10 October 2000

It's Not Just The Television

The effects of sex and violence on television remains a controversial issue in the American society. Many articles have been written expressing different opinions regarding the influence of violent content on television upon children. After examining "The Myth of Television Depravity," "Hollywood's Children," and "TV Causes Violence? Try Again," it is clear that only one essay is reasonable; furthermore, the most responsibly-written essay is "TV Causes

Violence? Try Again," for it expresses what the American society should accept: the increasing amount of violence seen in young people stems not from the contents of television but from other deeply-rooted societal problems.

The first essay, "The Myth of Television Depravity," by Michael Hirschorn, is unreasonable because it contains many contradictions and fallacies. One fallacy can be found when Hirschorn states this: ". . . to accuse television of subverting family values without considering this mainstream programming means someone is either not doing his homework or just doesn't care." This statement is clearly a false dilemma because the critics Hirschorn is addressing could have a number of reasons for accusing television of being too violent and sexual besides the two he allowed in his statement. Therefore, the essay is unreasonable because it clearly contains a fallacy. The essay also contains a number of contradictions. One example can be found when the author proclaims: "It is remarkable, in fact, how consistently prime-time television dwells on the very issues the conservatives complain are being ignored by Hollywood." Hirschorn is seemingly implying that the content on television is not as "inappropriate" as some believe. However, Hirschorn contradicts this statement when he cites examples from television shows that clearly contradict his proclamation. One example is found when a character on Ellen exclaims: "Could one of you please introduce me to the girl without the bra?" The "conservatives," as Hirschorn labels them, would probably view this statement as inappropriate for children; therefore, Hirschorn contradicts himself. Another contradiction to Hirschorn's proclamation can be found in an episode of <u>Roseanne</u> that he cites in his essay. As the episode ends, Roseanne talks of different ways to describe an erection, as stated by Hirschorn: " 'raising the flag' and 'standing up for democracy.' Then, pretending not to know the camera is on, the producer exclaims, 'Is that on? Aw shit!'" Obviously the critics would deem this use of foul language and talk of erections as inappropriate for children; therefore, Hirschorn's essay is unreasonable because it contains contradictions.

The next essay, "Hollywood's Children," by Diane Lynn, is also unreasonable, for it contains bias and numerous fallacies. First of all, the author shows a bias against television ("Hollywood"). Lynn never once addresses her opposition or makes any reference to television shows that do not contain the negative influence that she proclaims all shows have on society. The article is unreasonable because the author's opinion clearly houses bias. Secondly, the essay contains various types of fallacies. One example can be found when Lynn states: "<u>The Amos 'n Andy Show</u> spread its own share of racial stereotypes but America didn't care because producers have long known that they can preach just about anything as long as they can elicit a good laugh. . . ." This is clearly an example of <u>Post Hoc</u> or "Doubtful Cause." America not caring about the content of the show has absolutely nothing to do with the knowledge of the producers about what they can "preach." The essay is unreasonable because it contains this fallacy. Another fallacy, an example of a Slippery Slope, can be found in this quotation: "The Lessons of life 'As seen on TV' are regurgitated in the form of catty soap-opera-like behavior, sexual harassment, crime, and a personal life that resembles an episode of <u>Jerry Springer</u>." It is clear that Lynn is implying, rather absurdly, that if one watches television, he will incorporate all he observes into his own life. This is obviously a fallacy, for most people watch television for entertainment purposes. Many other influences and circumstances must be present before one acts out what he sees on television, and even then, such an instance is based only on epidemiologic research; there is no causal connection. Another fallacy can be found in the essay as Lynn states: "Like a kid who swears there is a monster under his bed after watching a late-night horror flick, many of us are prone to view human nature in an increasingly distrustful and cynical manner after filling the space between our ears with the sight and sound of bickering talk-show guests." This is clearly a False Analogy because the over-active imagination of a child creating monsters cannot be compared to the influence of television upon an adult's perception of the world, for one should hope they are not like entities; therefore, Lynn has committed yet another fallacy. This essay is clearly unreasonable because it contains bias and many fallacies.

The last essay, "TV Causes Violence? Try Again," by Ira Glasser, is the only reasonable essay examined, for it contains no bias, contradictions, or fallacies that were not part of the author's strategy. First of all, Glasser's essay acts as a rebuttal to another essay that blames television for the violence of America's youth; therefore, Glasser uses care not to portray a bias-loaded opinion toward television but to, instead, focus on logic and reason to convey his message. In his strategy to prove the other essay wrong, Glasser actually uses fallacies to his advantage. One example of this can be seen when Glasser states: "Some early epidemiologic research showed a statistical association between heart disease and the number of television sets a person owned." The reader can clearly detect an example of the Post Hoc fallacy, for the number of television sets one owns is obviously not a cause of heart disease. However, Glasser goes on to shed light on the fact that this is a fallacy to advance his claims, for he then states: "Clinical trials demonstrated that cholesterol, not the number of television sets one owned, was causally related." Glasser uses this fallacy to show that just as television sets do not cause heart disease, television does not cause violence. It is evident that this essay is reasonable because the only fallacy found is one that was purposely placed to advance Glasser's claim, and there is no bias or contradictions in the essay.

Not only is "TV Causes Violence? Try Again" a reasonably-written essay but also the most responsibly-written essay, for it alerts society to the fact that there is not one cause for increasing violence but, instead, many influences. The other essays examined are blindly one-sided arguments that leave room for error because they are based upon emotion. Glasser's essay is one of critical thought and logic, for Glasser shows that society's problem with violence cannot be blamed on television; the real cause is deeply rooted, but as Glasser states, "We don't want to address those intractable problems." Society is quick to find a scapegoat to blame its inefficiencies on, for it would be inconvenient to examine other problems such as broken homes, decreasing parental guidance, and the desensitization of society to sex and violence. Glasser's essay is responsible because he blows the whistle on society's lazy and irresponsible reaction to violence. This is evident when he states: "Finding scapegoats and diverting our attention from real and difficult problems is not new." Glasser proclaims here that throughout history, society has ignored the real problems and, instead, placed the blame on scapegoats that are easier to deal with. Glasser's essay is the most responsible because he uses reason and critical thought to alert the world that society itself, not television, is to blame for increasing violence in young people.

Glasser's claim is one that more people should be aware of. Television is but a reflection of the society that creates it. As the American society has become increasingly desensitized to sex and violence, so reflects the contents of popular television shows. The societal problems with violence and promiscuous sexuality will not end with the censorship of television; it may, however, make the situation worse. If television is censored, the youth may not be entertained and may turn to other sources of entertainment which may very possibly include violence and/or sex. Increasing violence is a tremendous problem in the American society, for it reflects the morals of the young; however, there is no easy solution, and nothing is solely to blame. Television is an easy scapegoat only to those who are in denial about the internal breakdown of society. These societal problems will only get worse and more painful unless the community works together to heal the pain and find the roots of the problems that are the real cause of the outrageous amount of violence that fills the lives of young people.

Note: Susan's argument is exceptionally poignant for many reasons. First, Susan does a fine job of not only addressing the prompt in her introductory paragraph but articulating an argument-encompassing claim as well. To compose a claim that adequately reflects what will be argued and what should be proven is essential. This, however, is often difficult, but Susan makes it look really simple. Susan also does a fine job (in paragraphs two and three) of identifying fallacies in essays written by Hirschorn and Lynn. Notice, however, that she does not simply assign a fallacy to each essay; instead, she explains specifically *why* what she excerpted is fallacious. Next, after showing why Glasser's essay is reasonable, she proceeds to show why it is also the most responsibly-written essay of the three under examination. Finally, she makes it clear that she supports Glasser's claim, for it simply mirrors her stance on sex and violence in popular culture. (It is clearly evident that Susan has followed the prompt diligently, addressing each of the prompt's components in the appropriate order.) To strengthen her argument, she could further develop her stance on sex and violence in popular culture by citing sources in addition to Glasser. This would provide her argument with more depth and, ostensibly, more credibility.

Observations

Before you begin reading the next chapter, take some time to reflect on what you learned in Chapter 5. Specifically, note what you think about what you learned, for in the spirit of promoting consciousness, it is essential that you not only become aware of your observations but that you commit them to paper. Use these observations like one would use a journal: as a tool for measuring growth and insight.

Preliminary Observations

_____

_____

_____

_____

_____

_____

_____

_____

_____

_____

_____

_____

_____

_____

_____

_____

_____

_____

_____

_____

Refined Observations

_____

_____

_____

_____

_____

_____

_____

_____

_____

_____

_____

_____

_____

_____

_____

_____

_____

_____

_____

_____

New Observations

_____

_____

_____

_____

_____

_____

Whistle Blowers

In grade school, whistle blowers are stigmatized as tattletales, talebearers, or informers. They are "rats" or "sell-outs," and they are definitely disloyal to "the code." They represent the antithesis of machismo or being a "macho." But is this what we really think, or is this a belief Big Brother has helped us construct?

Americans love rooting for the underdog; just look at *Rocky, Hoosiers,* and *Apollo 13,* or note popular responses to *The Adventures of Huckleberry Finn, The Catcher in the Rye,* and *I Know Why the Caged Bird Sings.* And what about *Serpico, Brubaker, Marie, Silkwood,* and *The Insider?* These stories revolve around an underdog, an "unfortunate soul," a whistle blower. So why have we been conditioned not to root for the whistle blower? Is it because the "powers that be" would prefer to discredit the whistle blower, so that the proletariat does not ever turn on the aristocracy?

Interestingly enough, the U.S. government has attempted to protect whistle blowers under the False Claims Act; this Act stipulates that "if a company does business with the federal government or with any company or organization receiving federal funds, any of its employees, customers, vendors, competitors, subcontractors, etc. can receive a contingency-fee recovery plus attorney fees for 'blowing the whistle' on any 'false claim' submitted by the company for government funds." This is excellent for those who fall under the government's umbrella. However, what about company employees who are not protected by the False Claims Act? What are they to do?

In Tallahassee, Florida, the Office of the Governor has sponsored a Whistle Blower's Act. It offers a state employees' hotline for reporting gross mismanagement, illegal or fraudulent conduct, gross waste of funds, and gross neglect of duty. The hotline assures the whistle blower that his or her identity will be kept confidential. Again, this is terrific, but what about those not classified as state employees?

Some companies have clauses in their employee/employer contracts which protect employees who choose to blow the whistle. Phoenix Business Group's HMO/Health Insurer Honesty and Accountability Act, for instance, protects patients and employees by stating: "[We] further prohibit the denial of benefits by unqualified persons, unreasonable delay in payment to providers . . . [and] punishment of 'whistle blowers.'"

But how many employees and/or patients know their rights? How many are willing to risk their livelihood by taking on Goliath? And how many are not protected via "whistle blower clauses" in their contracts?

As a critical thinker, you need to make a conscious decision whether or not you think it is one's duty, as a thinking being, to blow the whistle after witnessing injustices. Because in such a world of conflict, a world of victims and executioners, some believe it is the job of thinking people, as Albert Camus suggested, not to be on the side of the executioners.

The ACMFO (Audit Commission on Multi-national Finance Organizations) defines whistle blowing as "calling the attention of a manager or person in the immediate line of command, to something which does not fit within stated institutional goals, does not follow organizational procedures, is against the law, is a public hazard, fails to satisfy professional and/or ethical standards of behavior, involves criminal behavior." But the question isn't whether or not you can define it. The question is, would you do it? You have defined your constitution and, hence, you have a well-informed idea of the principles for which you stand. But if you found yourself in a seemingly powerless situation, one which offered serious repercussions, one which put you and your family at risk, would you blow the whistle simply because you'd witnessed an injustice?

Scenarios for Whistle Blowers

• • • • • • • • • • •

Examine the following scenarios:

Scenario 1

You work in a hospital. You notice that one of the patients you've been assigned to has had his prescribed amount of morphine doubled due to increasing pain, yet he is still being given his original dosage as per doctor's orders. You notify your supervisor. She tells you not to worry about it. "It's being taken care of," she says.

A week passes, however, and nothing has changed. You decide to do some investigating. You learn that the hospital is receiving money for the "extra" morphine from the patient's HMO, but the hospital is keeping the money, apparently funneling the money into patient programs, hospital beautification, and administrator salaries. You also learn that your patient's situation is not unique. In fact, it seems that every patient in the hospital is being cheated of something his or her HMO is paying the hospital to administer.

Now that you have sufficient evidence to support your claim, you speak to your supervisor again. She, however, has this to say: "You had no business snooping through patients' personal files and hospital records. Furthermore, you should be fired for such actions, but this time I'll go easy on you. Just forget about all of this nonsense, and do your job." She begins to walk away, but then stops, turns around, and says, "If you mention this to anyone, you'll lose your job, and you'll never work in a hospital again."

Do you blow the whistle?

What if you were married, had two children, and depended on your income from this job to stay afloat financially? Would you blow the whistle?

Scenario 2

You find out that a member of your immediate family is pedaling child pornography on the Internet. You are vehemently against the exploitation of children through pornography. Everyone in the family thinks this family member simply makes his or her money as a photographer. You find out about his or her real vocation, however, and he or she offers to pay for your entire college education or give you $60,000 over four years if you don't say anything. Do you blow the whistle?

Many people witness injustices on a daily basis. While some are excused or painted a phony color, others must be addressed, and critical thinkers need to feel compelled to pick up a whistle and blow it. The question, however, is this: What is the protocol for blowing a whistle?

While Frank Serpico told his superiors (and eventually the *New York Times*), and while Jeffrey Weigand told a reporter who eventually aired his findings on television, students of critical thinking should simply articulate their thoughts in a formally-written letter. Here are two "real-life" examples. Both come from former students of the author, and both letters were very effective. (The names of the whistle blowers and their targets have been changed for fear of issues regarding libel and defamation of character.)

20 March 2000
Edward Smith
Global Com, L.A.
1000 Abby Street
Los Angeles, CA

Dear Edward:

I am writing you regarding some events that have transpired here, at the Irvine facility, within the last month. These events involve Mr. Bob Jones engaging in some inappropriate acts that I view as uncalled for in a business environment. This past month has been very awkward for me. I feel very uncomfortable around Mr. Jones and feel somewhat hesitant to approach him regarding work-related issues, thus making it very hard to be as productive and efficient in the workplace. I also believe that Mr. Jones has purposely segregated himself from me, to avoid any confrontation in this matter of Sexual Harassment.

On March 5th of this year I received a phone call from Mr. Jones when he was at the Burbank facility. He called me at the Irvine facility and asked me, "Did you get it?" I replied, "Get what?" He responded, "The email—check your email!" I then proceeded to tell him that I was on the phone with a client and that I would call him back. I returned his phone call shortly, but he was busy so I left him a message. I then recalled that he mentioned an email, so I checked my emails, and I had an email from him. I opened up the email, and it in-cluded a pornographic picture. I was very upset and called Mr. Jones back at the Burbank facility, and he was not available once again. I asked Steve Rogers, the person who answered the phone, to relay to Mr. Jones that I did not appreciate what he had sent me in the email.

Steve noticed that I was upset and asked me what was wrong. I said that I was alright and asked him to have Mr. Jones call me. Steve then called me back and asked me, "Why did he send you that?" It seems that Mr. Jones had shown him the email that he sent me. I replied, "I don't know, Steve, but I am pretty upset about it." He re-sponded by saying, "Do you send him stuff like that too?" I replied by saying, "Of course not!" It also seems that Mr. Jones found the email humorous, yet when showing it to other employees, they apparently looked perplexed. According to Steve, when he questioned Mr. Jones as to the reason he sent the email, he responded with, "You should see what she sends me." This, unfortunately, represents the basest form of defamation, for I have not sent him anything with sexual con-notations or denotations. I confronted Mr. Jones two different times regarding this situation. I confronted him on the afternoon of February 25th and at noon on March 2nd. He seemed indifferent. He acknowledged that his act was inappropriate, but he never apolo-gized for his actions.

In another event that happened on February 22nd (President's Day), I have reason to believe that Mr. Jones spent over two hours viewing pornographic sights on the computer I use. The next day after the holiday, I returned to work, logged on to the Internet, and noticed that someone had logged on under my name and password. I was very upset when I reviewed the history of the web pages visited because there were over five pornographic sights visited. I confronted Mr. Jones and asked him if he knew of anyone using my computer or if he himself had used it. He denied ever having used it and declined to question anyone on the issue.

I still felt very uncomfortable about the whole situation; hence, when Robert Evans (Computer Technician) visited the Irvine facility, I asked him if he could find out at what time someone logged onto the computer. He confirmed the date and time of President's Day, when most of the employees had the day off. I checked to see who was in the office that day at that specific time of nine to eleven in the morning, and the only person who had access to the computer I use would have been Mr. Jones. I never confronted Mr. Jones about this because Robert Evans insinuated that he would address the situation. I never heard anything from either Mr. Jones or Robert Evans.

Edward, I would like to state that the purpose of this letter is NOT to get Mr. Jones or anyone else, for that matter, in trouble.

Mr. Jones is a very hard worker who is very dedicated to his job. He is also a very understanding boss who has demonstrated strong character and good judgment in the past, hence, the reason I was very conflicted about writing this letter to you. But I do believe that he acted in a very irresponsible manner this past month, and some type of action should be taken to acknowledge that this should have never happened and, furthermore, will never happen again.

I am, in fact, requesting a written apology from Mr. Jones for the email he sent and for lying to me about not viewing pornographic sights on the computer I use. I would also like a memo to be sent out to the several staff members who were present when he claimed I sent him pornographic emails. In this memo, he should address his wrongful act, and he should withdraw his claim that I ever sent him inappropriate emails. My reasoning for this is that Mr. Jones has made me look very unprofessional, and he has defamed my character by making this comment. Though I am only asking for a written apology and an inter-company memo to the respective staff members, Mr. Jones should also attend a sexual-harassment sensitivity course.

I would like to reiterate that I do not wish to get anyone into any trouble. All I am asking for is an apology and the assurance that a situation of this kind will never present itself again. I have sought legal counsel and am aware of other options. But once again, at this time I am only seeking the aforementioned restitution.

Lastly, I have attached a file of the email sent by Mr. Jones. I must warn you that this file is very explicit, and under no circumstances do I wish to offend anyone. I, however, feel it is essential for you to view this file to fully understand my request to further investigate this incident.

Thank you for your time and patience. I expect to hear from you soon.

Eva Gonzalez

Cc: Bernard Emel, Harold Douglas, and Michael Moreno

Note: When Eva first composed this letter, she was nervous *and* anxious, for she had never done anything like this before. Fortunately, she did not have to wait long for a conclusion to her workplace trials. The letter, addressed to Mr. Jones' superior, was emailed, so Eva didn't have to wait for a postal carrier to hand deliver it. Within twenty minutes of sending the email, she was contacted by the company President/ CEO (who called her from his cell phone as he sat in a company jet in Europe). He attempted to reassure her, and he offered her his personal number, encouraging her to call him anytime. He also advised her that the President of Human Resources would be contacting her immediately. (Of course, the President/CEO and the President of Human Resources received this email via the "Cc," located at the end of the letter.) After one week of interviewing and investigating Eva's claims, the President of Human Resources suspended Mr. Jones for one month, without pay. Next, Mr. Jones was required to write Eva a formal letter of apology. Next, he was told to attend a sexual-harassment sensitivity course. Next, he was demoted. In addition to disciplining Mr. Jones, the letter also sparked the creation of new company bi-laws, ones including an entire section on what *is* and what *is not* appropriate when sending emails. What students should note, however, is the way in which this letter was written and organized. Note Eva's attention to precise diction, and notice the presence of a legal reference. It seems that whenever the issue of corporate responsibility arises, the companies involved only take action if they are somehow legally bound.

27 March 2000
Maverick's Restaurants Inc.
8 Grossmont Center Ste. 270
Atlanta, Georgia 30305

Dear Robert Tervalon:

On Sunday, the 26th of March, I was fired from Maverick's by Mike Kardon. While admitting to the oversight of ringing a 16oz. Panna in favor of the 32oz. size, an error on my part, I refuse to take blame for any devious or intentional acts of deception. The following is my account of the exact events in question.

While running a four-table station at 9:00 p.m., table 38 of my station was sat with Hayden, Nicole, and Justin, three fellow employees. While attending to an earlier table, I was also sat another table on 33. I immediately greeted 38 as Hayden ordered a 16oz. Panna, with two glasses, and Justin ordered a water. I then took the first round on 33 while dropping change on 32. I proceeded to drop off both first rounds, and upon receiving an appetizer order from Hayden, I was handed an empty bottle and told he wanted a larger bottle. I was then sat a fourth table on 34, took their first round, took the order on 33, and while manicuring several plates in my vicinity, I walked over to the bar and told Billy I needed a large Panna for Hayden.

After "hobarting" my dishes, I rang a first round for 34 and grabbed their drinks and the Panna on my way out. Although completely capable of handling my station, I was definitely working at a higher pace due to the rapid turnover of tables. Additionally, the fact that much of the team was immersed in side-work left me with much responsibility. I proceeded to drop the bottle at 38 and take the order at 34. I then stopped at 38 where I received several different requests from the table, including an entrée order. I also noticed a 16oz. soda/beer glass and red wine glass. At that time I noticed 32 had been sat again. I greeted them, and they proceeded to give me their <u>entire</u> order. This took several minutes, and now I felt even more hurried because I had to get an entire entrée order in from 38 and a complete order, drinks and appetizers included, in from 32.

I tried to solicit some help, and while "ringing," asked if I could get the first round run by Bryan, a neighbor. At this time, Billy had called out to mention to 86 the drink ring for the glass of Ferrari and the glass of Coke. I rang in the wine 86; however, I did not ring in the Coke, for I did not think we charged employees for soda. I based this on the fact that I had never been charged for a soda while eating at Maverick's, only for juices, lemonade, etc. I continued to work my tables while getting the dessert order for 38. I dropped their dessert, reviewed my check briefly with its respective 50% employee discount, and gave them their bill. Then, while attending my other tables, I was approached by Mike Kardon and asked to sit down with him.

I was promptly told that Maverick's does not hire "thieves" or dishonest people. Then I was told that I was being fired. End of story. Nothing I said or could say was going to be heard by Mike, and before I could even respond, he had left the building. To simply terminate someone without the facts or without even listening to an explanation leads me to believe this was malicious and premeditated. I believe Mike's actions stem from an isolated incident involving a disagreement between myself and his girlfriend, a fellow employee. I have no previous friendships with any of the employees other than working occasionally with them and would not benefit at all by not ringing in their entire order. In fact, I would lose check average, liquor sales, and tip percentage. I did not receive any written drink order, did not get their drinks for them, and did not knowingly forget anything. What I heard from Billy was 86 Ferrari and a Coke. Whether the many other distractions at that particular time or the fact that I heard "and Coke," instead of "Jack Coke," caused this debacle, I do not know. All I know is that I've done nothing but work hard at Maverick's for the last six months, with the only setbacks stemming from a car accident, my vehicle being impounded, and two tardy issues; nonetheless, in each case I had phoned ahead. Moreover, when I was told to change anything, I quickly adhered to the prescription, and a remedy immediately followed.

I have always been a courteous team-player at Maverick's and have ameliorated any miscommunications I've had with Maverick's employees. It would be ample punishment, if not excessive, for me to pay for this oversight. I will gladly pay for a Jack 'n Coke and sixteen ounces of water. But to pay for the mistake with my livelihood constitutes unlawful and unwarranted termination.

There are many mistakes made during the daily course of operations. I am not excluded from these. I believe, however, that there were several mistakes made during the evening in question. I believe if the guests/employees are going to leave their seats to get drinks in the bar, <u>the drinks should be paid for in the bar</u>. I believe I should receive a bar transfer on a busy zone instead of spoken words, ambiguous and said amidst the music and "noise" of the restaurant. I believe if it is not standard to "call" drinks, I should not receive them. I believe if it is not policy to have four-table stations, <u>there shouldn't be four-table stations</u>. (This is, in fact, company policy.) I believe if sodas are not free, then we have *all* been thieves. Lastly, I believe the termination of my job was handled in haste, with lack of professionalism and a severely biased opinion of the truth.

I have sought legal counsel. I have been apprised of employer/employee rights; Maverick's does not need to suffer any legal redress because of a simple misunderstanding. I simply want to be given my job back.

Sincerely,
Sam Baldwin
Cc: Frank W. Evans

Note: Before Sam was encouraged to write this letter (by a one-hour lecture on whistleblowers), he was planning to accept his fate and begin looking for a new job. Fortunately, he realized that when crimes against one's constitution are committed, options do exist. After presenting this letter to the General Manager (Maverick's has five managers on staff at each restaurant, and the G.M. is the highest ranking manager), Sam was relieved, for the G.M. was eager to offer him his job back. What really made the difference was the fact that Sam had a four-table station (which is against company policy). Also, he claimed to have sought legal counsel, and he included a "Cc" to the corporation President/CEO. (Sam, however, never sought legal counsel, and he never sent a copy of this letter to Frank W. Evans. He would have, but after meeting with the G.M., it wasn't necessary.) Sam was invited back to Maverick's, and he was given the opportunity to create his own schedule, affording him the opportunity to pick the "good shifts." Also, Mike, the manager who fired Sam, was required to offer him a formal apology. Days later, Mike was no longer working for Maverick's. Looking back, Sam says that what was most intriguing was how the G.M. looked while reading the letter. Apparently, he was not familiar with some of the words Sam had used; this made Sam "seem smarter" than the G.M. had ever presumed. Also, the presence of the legal threat represented an exceptionally nice touch. A corporation *must* be legally bound in some way; otherwise, what is its motivation to effect change?

The Allegory of the Cave

Plato

• •

Plato (428–347 B.C.) was born into an aristocratic Athenian family and educated according to the best precepts available. He eventually became a student of Socrates and later involved himself closely with Socrates' work and teaching.

Plato was not only Socrates' finest student but was also the student who immortalized Socrates in his works. Most of Plato's works are philosophical essays, with Socrates as a character speaking in a dialogue with one or more students or listeners. Thus, Plato permits us the vision of Socrates written by one who knew him and listened carefully to what he said.

The times in which Plato lived were turbulent indeed. In 404 B.C. Athens was defeated by Sparta and was governed by tyrants. Political life in Athens was dangerous. Plato felt, however, that he could effect positive change in Athenian politics until, in 384 B.C., Socrates was tried unjustly for corrupting the youth of Athens and put to death. After that, Plato withdrew from public life and devoted himself to writing and to the Academy which he founded in an olive grove in Athens. The Academy endured for almost a thousand years, which tells us how greatly Plato's thought was valued.

Although it is not easy to condense Plato's views, he may be said to have held the world of sense perception as inferior to the world of ideal entities that exist only in a pure spiritual realm. These ideals, or forms, had been perceived directly by everyone before birth, and then dimly remembered here on earth. But the memory, even dim as it is, makes it possible for people to understand what is perceived by the senses despite the fact that the senses are so unreliable and perceptions are so imperfect.

This view of reality has long been important to philosophers because it gives a philosophical basis to antimaterialistic thought. It values the spirit first and frees people from the tyranny of sensory perception and sensory reward. In the case of love, Plato held that Eros leads us to a reverence for the body and its pleasures; but the thrust of his teaching is that the body is a metaphor for spiritual delights. Plato assures us that the body is only a starting point and that it can eventually lead both to spiritual fulfillment and to the appreciation of true beauty.

"The Allegory of the Cave" is, on the one hand, a discussion of politics—the Republic is a treatise on justice and the ideal government. On the other hand, it has long stood for a kind of demonstration of the fact that if our perceptions are what we must rely upon to know the truth about the world, then we actually know very little about it. We know what we perceive, but we have no way of knowing anything beyond that. This allegory has been persuasive for centuries and remains at the center of thought that attempts to counter the pleasures of the sensual. Most religions aim for spiritual refinement and praise the qualities of the soul, which lies beyond perception. Thus, it comes as no surprise that Christianity and other religions have not only praised Plato, but have developed systems of thought that bear a close resemblance to his. Late refinements of his thought, usually called Neo-Platonism, have been influential even into modern times.

• • • • • • • • •

Plato's Rhetoric

Two very important rhetorical techniques are at work in the following section. The first and more obvious—at least on one level—is his reliance on the allegory, a story in which the characters and situations are meant to resemble people and situations in another example. It is a difficult technique to use well, although we have the example of Aesop's fables in which hares and tortoises represent people and their foibles. The advantage of the technique is that a complex and sometimes unpopular argument can be fought and won before the audience realizes that an argument is being fought. The disadvantage of the technique is that the terms of the allegory may only approximate the situation which it reflects; thus, the argument may fail to be convincing.

Another rhetorical technique Plato uses is the dialogue. In fact, it is a hallmark of Plato's work, since most of his writings are called dialogues. The Symposium, Apology, Phaedo, Crito, Meno, and most of the famous works are all written in dialogue form. Usually Socrates is speaking to a student or a friend about highly abstract issues. Socrates asks questions which require simple answers. Slowly, the questioning proceeds to unravel the answers to the most complex of issues.

This use of the question-and-answer dialogue is basically the Socratic method. Socrates analyzes the answer to each question, examines the implications of those answers, then asserts the truth. The method is functional in part because Plato's theory is that people do not learn things; they remember *them. That is, since people came originally from heaven, where they knew the truth, they already possess that knowledge and must recover it by means of the dialogue. Socrates' method is ideally suited to that purpose.*

Beyond these techniques, however, we must look at Plato's style. It is true that he is working with very difficult ideas, but the style of the work is so clear, simple, and direct that few people would have trouble understanding what is said at any given moment. Considering the influence this work has had on world thought and the reputation Plato had earned by the time he came to write the Republic, it is remarkable that the style is so plain and so accessible. It is significant that such a great mind can express itself with such impressive clarity. Part of that capacity is due to Plato's respect for rhetoric and its proper uses.

• • • • • • • • •

And now, I said, let me show in a figure how far our nature is enlightened or unenlightened:—Behold! human beings living in an underground den, which has a mouth open towards the light and reaching all along the den; here they have been from their childhood, and have their legs and necks chained so that they cannot move, and can only see before them, being prevented by the chains from turning round their heads. Above and behind them a fire is blazing at a distance, and between the fire and the prisoners there is a raised way; and you will see, if you look, a low wall built along the way, like the screen which marionette players have in front of them, over which they show the puppets.

I see.

And do you see, I said, men passing along the wall carrying all sorts of vessels, and statues and figures of animals made of wood and stone and various materials, which appear over the wall? Some of them are talking, others silent.

You have shown me a strange image, and they are strange prisoners.

Like ourselves, I replied; and they see only their own shadows, or the shadows of one another, which the fire throws on the opposite wall of the cave?

True, he said; how could they see anything but the shadows if they were never allowed to move their heads?

And of the objects which are being carried in like manner they would only see the shadows?

Yes, he said.

And if they were able to converse with one another, would they not suppose that they were naming what was actually before them?

Very true.

And suppose further that the prison had an echo which came from the other side, would they not be sure to fancy, when one of the passers-by spoke that the voice which they heard came from the passing shadow?

No question, he replied.

To them, I said, the truth would be literally nothing but the shadows of the images.

That is certain.

And now look again, and see what will naturally follow if the prisoners are released and disabused of their error. At first, when any of them is liberated and compelled suddenly to stand up and turn his neck round and walk and look towards the light, he will suffer sharp pains; the glare will distress him, and he will be unable to see the realities of which in his former state he had seen the shadows; and then conceive some one saying to him, that what he saw before was an illusion, but that now, when he is approaching nearer to being and his eye is turned towards more real existence, he has a clearer vision—what will be his reply? And you may further imagine that his instructor is pointing to the objects as they pass and requiring him to name them,—will he not be perplexed? Will he not fancy that the shadows which he formerly saw are truer than the objects which are now shown to him?

Far truer.

And if he is compelled to look straight at the light, will he not have a pain in his eyes which will make him turn away to take refuge in the objects of vision which he can see, and which he will conceive to be in reality clearer than the things which are now being shown to him?

True, he said.

And suppose once more, that he is reluctantly dragged up a steep and rugged ascent, and held fast until he is forced into the presence of the sun himself, is he not likely to be pained and irritated? When he approaches the light his eyes will be dazzled, and he will not be able to see anything at all of what are now called realities.

Not all in a moment, he said.

He will require to grow accustomed to the sight of the upper world. And first he will see the shadows best, next the reflections of men and other objects in the water, and then the objects themselves; then he will gaze upon the light of the moon and the stars and the spangled heaven; and he will see the sky and the stars by night better than the sun or the light of the sun by day?

Certainly.

Last of all he will be able to see the sun, and not mere reflections of him in the water, but he will see him in his own proper place, and not in another; and he will contemplate him as he is.

Certainly.

He will then proceed to argue that this is he who gives the season and the years, and is the guardian of all that is in the visible world, and in a certain way the cause of all things which he and his fellows have been accustomed to behold?

Clearly, he said, he would first see the sun and then reason about him.

And when he remembered his old habitation, and the wisdom of the den and his fellow prisoners, do you not suppose that he would felicitate himself on the change, and pity them?

Certainly, he would.

And if they were in the habit of conferring honors among themselves on those who were quickest to observe the passing shadows and to remark which of them went before, and which followed after, and which were together; and who were therefore best able to draw conclusions as to the future, do you think that he would care for such honors and glories, or envy the possessors of them? Would he not say with Homer,

Better to be the poor servant of a poor master, and to endure anything, rather than think as they do and live after their manner?

Yes, he said, I think that he would rather suffer anything than entertain these false notions and live in this miserable manner.

Imagine once more, I said, such a one coming suddenly out of the sun to be replaced in his old situation; would he not be certain to have his eyes full of darkness?

To be sure, he said.

And if there were a contest, and he had to compete in measuring the shadows with the prisoners who had never moved out of the den, while his sight was still weak, and before his eyes had become steady (and the time which would be needed to acquire this new habit of sight might be very considerable), would he not be ridiculous? Men would say of him that up he went and down he came without his eyes; and that it was better not even to think of ascending; and if any one tried to loose another and lead him up to the light, let them only catch the offender, and they would put him to death.

No question, he said.

This entire allegory, I said, you may now append, dear Glaucon, to the previous argument; the prison house is the world of sight, the light of the fire is the sun, and you will not misapprehend me if you interpret the journey upwards to be the ascent of the soul into the intellectual world according to my poor belief, which, at your desire, I have expressed—whether rightly or wrongly God knows. But, whether true or false, my opinion is that in the world of knowledge the idea of good appears last of all, and is seen only with an effort; and, when seen, is also inferred to be the universal author of all things beautiful and right, parent of light and of the lord of light in this visible world, and the immediate source of reason and truth in the intellectual; and that this is the power upon which he who would act rationally either in public or private life must have his eye fixed.

I agree, he said, as far as I am able to understand you.

Moreover, I said, you must not wonder that those who attain to this beatific vision are unwilling to descend to human affairs; for their souls are ever hastening into the upper world where they desire to dwell; which desire of theirs is very natural, if our allegory may be trusted.

Yes, very natural.

And is there anything surprising in one who passes from divine contemplations to the evil state of man, misbehaving himself in a ridiculous manner; if, while his eyes are blinking and before he has become accustomed to the surrounding darkness, he is compelled to fight in courts of law, or in other places, about the images or the shadows of images of justice, and is endeavoring to meet the conceptions of those who have never yet seen absolute justice?

Anything but surprising, he replied.

Any one who has common sense will remember that the bewilderments of the eyes are of two kinds, and arise from two causes, either from coming out of the light or from going into the light, which is true of the mind's eye, quite as much as of the bodily eye; and he who remembers this when he sees any one whose vision is perplexed and weak, will not be too ready to laugh; he will first ask whether that soul of man has come out of the brighter life, and is unable to see because unaccustomed to the dark, or having turned from darkness to the day is dazzled by excess of light. And he will count the one happy in his condition and state of being, and he will pity the other; or, if he have a mind to laugh at the soul which comes from below into the light, there will be more reason in this than in the laugh which greets him who returns from above out of the light into the den.

That, he said, is a very just distinction.

But then, if I am right, certain professors of education must be wrong when they say that they can put a knowledge into the soul which was not there before, like sight into blind eyes.

They undoubtedly say this, he replied.

Whereas, our argument shows that the power and capacity of learning exists in the soul already; and that just as the eye was unable to turn from darkness to light without the whole body, so too the instrument of knowledge can only by the movement of the whole soul be turned from the world of becoming into that of being, and learn by degrees to endure the sight of being, and of the brightest and best of being, or in other words, of the good.

Very true.

And must there not be some art which will effect conversion in the easiest and quickest manner; not implanting the faculty of sight, for that exists already, but has been turned in the wrong direction, and is looking away from the truth?

Yes, he said, such an art may be presumed.

And whereas the other so-called virtues of the soul seem to be akin to bodily qualities, for even when they are not originally innate they can be implanted later by habit and exercise, the virtue of wisdom more than anything else contains a divine element which always remains, and by this conversion is rendered useful and profitable; or, on the other hand, hurtful and useless. Did you never observe the narrow intelligence flashing from the keen eye of a clever rogue—how eager he is, how clearly his paltry soul sees the way to his end; he is the reverse of blind, but his keen eye-sight is forced into the service of evil, and he is mischievous in proportion to his cleverness?

Very true, he said.

But what if there had been a circumcision of such natures in the days of their youth; and they had been severed from those sensual pleasures, such as eating and drinking, which, like leaden weights, were attached to them at their birth, and which drag them down and turn the vision of their souls upon the things that are below—if, I say, they had been released from these impediments and turned in the opposite direction, the very same faculty in them would have seen the truth as keenly as they see what their eyes are turned to now.

Very likely.

Yes, I said; and there is another thing which is likely, or rather a necessary inference from what has preceded, that neither the uneducated and uninformed of the truth, nor yet those who never make an end of their education, will be able ministers of State; not the former, because they have no single aim of duty which is the rule of all their actions, private as well as public; nor the latter, because they will not act at all except upon compulsion, fancying that they are already dwelling apart in the islands of the blessed.

Very true, he replied.

Then, I said, the business of us who are the founders of the State will be to compel the best minds to attain that knowledge which we have already shown to be the greatest of all—they must continue to ascend until they arrive at the good; but when they have ascended and seen enough we must not allow them to do as they do now.

What do you mean?

I mean that they remain in the upper world: but this must not be allowed; they must be made to descend again among the prisoners in the den, and partake of their labors and honors, whether they are worth having or not.

But is not this unjust? he said; ought we to give them a worse life, when they might have a better?

You have again forgotten, my friend, I said, the intention of the legislator, who did not aim at making any one class in the State happy above the rest; the happiness was to be in the whole State, and he held the citizens together by persuasion and necessity, making them benefactors of the State, and therefore benefactors of one another; to this end he created them, not to please themselves, but to be his instruments in binding up the State.

True, he said, I had forgotten.

Observe, Glaucon, that there will be no injustice in compelling our philosophers to have a care and providence of others; we shall explain to them that in other States, men of their class are not obliged to share in the toils of politics: and this is reasonable, for they grow up at their own sweet will, and the government would rather not have them. Being self-taught, they cannot be expected to show any gratitude for a culture which they have never received. But we have brought you into the world to be rulers of the hive, kings of yourselves and of the other citizens, and have educated you far better and more perfectly than they have been educated, and you are better able to share in the double duty. That is why each of you, when his turn comes, must go down to the general underground abode, and get the habit of seeing in the dark. When you have acquired the habit, you will see ten thousand times better than the inhabitants of the den, and you will know what the several images are, and what they represent, because you have seen the beautiful and just and good in their truth. And thus our State, which is also yours will be a reality, and not a dream only, and will be administered in a spirit unlike that of other States, in which men fight with one another about shadows only and are distracted in the struggle for power, which in their eyes is a great good. Whereas the truth is that the State in which the rulers are most reluctant to govern is always the best and most quietly governed, and the State in which they are most eager, the worst.

Quite true, he replied.

And will our pupils, when they hear this, refuse to take their turn at the toils of State, when they are allowed to spend the greater part of their time with one another in the heavenly light?

Impossible, he answered; for they are just men, and the commands which we impose upon them are just; there can be no doubt that every one of them will take office as a stern necessity, and not after the fashion of our present rulers of State.

Yes, my friend, I said; and there lies the point. You must contrive for your future rulers another and a better life than that of a ruler, and then you may have a well-ordered State; for only in the State which offers this, will they rule who are truly rich, not in silver and gold, but in virtue and wisdom, which are the true blessings of life. Whereas if they go to the administration of public affairs, poor and hungering after their own private advantage, thinking that hence they are to snatch the chief good, order there can never be; for they will be fighting about office, and the civil and domestic broils which thus arise will be the ruin of the rulers themselves and of the whole State.

Most true, he replied.

And the only life which looks down upon the life of political ambition is that of true philosophy. Do you know of any other?

Indeed, I do not, he said.

• •

Thoughts, Ideas, and Discussion Questions

1. Define *allegory, marionette,* and any other unfamiliar terms.
2. Articulate Plato's claim in one sentence.
3. How can "Allegory of the Cave" be considered a whistle blower's manifesto?
4. Using concrete language, create a modern day "Allegory of the Cave." What shadows represent reality in America today?

Application

1. In essay form, identify your cave(s). Use this exercise as a vehicle to promote awareness. Once you have become fully aware of your cave, and once you have become fully aware of what it will take to escape, eventually leaving your cave can become a reality. Of course, once you actually leave, it is your duty as a thinking being to return to the cave to rescue the others. (And how will they feel when you blow the whistle?)

For more information on whistle blowing, read Jack Anderson's "The Reward Is," and then respond to the following.

Thoughts, Ideas, and Discussion Questions

1. Define *graft, pariah,* and any other unfamiliar terms.
2. Based on the information in the article, what does one gain by blowing the whistle?
3. The author refers to her whistle-blowing experience as a rite of passage. Ostensibly, this "passage" comprises many steps. What do these steps involve?

Applications

1. Rent one of these films: *Serpico, Brubaker, Marie, Silkwood,* or *The Insider.* Based on the information provided by the film(s) and any other text(s), offer a response to this question: Is it worth it?
2. Compare two whistleblowers to Jeffrey Weigand or Lowell Bergman of *The Insider.* They show how "The Reward Is?", "Allegory of the Cave," "Self-reliance," and/or "Civil Disobedience" relate to whistleblowing. Finally, discuss whether you think whistleblowing is an act representative of critical thinkers.

Observations

Before you begin reading the next chapter, take some time to reflect on what you learned in Chapter 6. Specifically, note what you think about what you learned, for in the spirit of promoting consciousness, it is essential that you not only become aware of your observations but that you commit them to paper. Use these observations like one would use a journal: as a tool for measuring growth and insight.

Preliminary Observations

_____

_____

_____

_____

_____

_____

_____

_____

_____

_____

_____

_____

_____

_____

_____

_____

_____

_____

_____

Refined Observations

_____

_____

_____

_____

_____

_____

_____

_____

_____

_____

_____

_____

_____

_____

_____

_____

_____

New Observations

_____

_____

_____

_____

_____

Common Fallacies

Just as focusing on one claim can help you control an argument, having the ability to identify fallacies in written or spoken discourse can ameliorate your position in an argument by making you a more critical reader/listener and by making your opponent's argument more or less credible.

False Analogy

. . . .

The false analogy fallacy makes a comparison between two things, but often the comparison is without the required connection or required evidence necessary to advance the argument. False analogies sound good when delivered quickly, but they do not hold water when scrutinized. Here are some examples:

"The U.S. Government should have an open-door immigration policy. Currently, we have walls we call borders which keep potential immigrants in their respective countries. This can be likened to what we do to animals in zoos. We cage them, surround them by walls, and say, 'you can't get out.' Only, it seems like, at least in this scenario, we're the animals."

Guns do kill people, but so do knives. It would be absurd to ban knives, so why do you want to ban guns?"

"Alcohol is legal, and tobacco is legal; both are addictive substances. Why shouldn't we legalize cocaine as well?"

Ad Hominem

. . . .

"Against the man" is the literal translation of the Latin term *ad hominem*. The *ad hominem* fallacy represents an ethos argument: it is an attack on the character of a person rather than on the argument, issue, problem, or concept. Here are some examples:

"He's Japanese. How can he teach Mexican-American Literature?"

"What can he tell us about being a pacifist? He was in the Vietnam War."

Hasty Generalization
· · · · · · · · · ·

If you are driving on the freeway and you get cut off three times, each time by the driver of a Honda, and you state, "Honda owners are bad drivers," you are making a hasty generalization. If you have a negative encounter with three Asian men, and if you boldly state, "All Asian men are rude," you are making a hasty generalization.

As a critical thinker, you know that some Honda owners may be good drivers, and you know that some Asian men might not be rude; hence, the hasty generalization becomes one of the easier fallacies to detect.

Faulty Use of Authority
· · · · · · · · · ·

If you are writing an essay about the benefits of drinking alcoholic beverages, and if you cite an article which states, "Having one glass of wine before you go to bed each night will help reduce the risk of a heart attack," you are engaging in faulty use of authority if you do not let the reader know that the article was funded by a prominent wine distributor and written by a doctor whose credentials are suspect.

TV, radio, and billboard advertisements are replete with the faulty use of authority fallacy. Contrary to what Sprint would like you to believe, Michael Jordan is not an authority in the telecommunications industry, and neither is Candice Bergman.

It is difficult to argue without appealing to authorities; thus, simply make a conscious attempt to cite credible sources who will not waver under scrutiny.

Post Hoc or Doubtful Cause

• • • • • • • • • • •

The Latin phrase, *post hoc, ergo propter hoc,* means "After this, therefore because of this." An example often cited to illustrate this fallacy reads: "After the rooster crows, the sun comes up. Therefore, the sun comes up because the rooster crows." Though it's quite evident that the rooster doesn't have anything to do with the earth's rotation, it is important to become aware of the form in which the *post hoc* fallacy often appears. Here are some examples:

"Ever since we outlawed prayer in public schools, a lot of bad things have happened. For instance, those two lunatics went on a shooting spree at Columbine High School. This type of violence didn't occur when prayer was legal. Therefore, it's obvious that we must re-institute prayer in public schools."

"After Bob started dating Rachel, he forgot all about his friends. Dating Rachel made Bob forget about his friends."

Dicto Simpliciter

• • • • • • • • • •

The *dicto simpliciter* fallacy is committed when an argument is based on an unqualified generalization. For instance, if someone said "Drugs are bad," the person has made an unqualified generalization. Are all drugs bad? Are only illegal drugs bad? Is aspirin bad? Simply saying, "Drugs are bad," is irresponsible, for it presents an argument based on an unqualified generalization.

False Dilemma (Either-or Arguments)

• • • • • • • • • •

This fallacy presents only two alternatives when many may be available. It's not uncommon to hear salespeople using this fallacy. When buying a car, the salesperson might say, "In truth, Mr. Jones, there is only one question to ask: should you buy the sedan or the coupe?" Of course, there is more than one question; one is "Do I even wish to buy a car?" A financial planner might say, "Look, you can either invest in stocks or lose to inflation each year by putting your money in the bank." Unfortunately, the financial planner hamstrings her customer by limiting the options to two when, in reality, myriad options exist.

Two Wrongs Make a Right

• • • • • • • • • • •

If someone says, "Columbus Day should not be celebrated because Columbus took Arawak Indians as slaves," and you respond, "Well, we celebrate Washington's birthday, and he owned slaves," you are not addressing the issue; you are attempting to sidestep the issue by showing how two wrongs make a right. If somebody does this to you, restate your claim, and ask that your opponent pledge strict adherence to the claim.

Ad Ignorantiam (Appeal to Ignorance)

• • • • • • • • • • •

The appeal to ignorance argues that a claim must be true simply because it has never been proven false. Here are some examples:

"No one has ever proven that Bob is not a homosexual; therefore, we may assume that he is a homosexual."

"No one has ever proven that aliens don't exist; therefore, aliens exist."

Slippery Slope

• • • • • • • • • • •

The slippery slope fallacy refers to a "dangerous and irreversible course." If a person claims that doing one thing will lead to another thing (usually something undesirable), and if the person does not provide adequate evidence to support his claim, he is guilty of the slippery slope fallacy. Here are some examples:

"The legalization of physician-assisted suicide will lead to suicide-based requests by not only the terminally ill but those who suffer from depression, anxiety, or even the common cold."

"If a woman were elected president, male leaders of other nations would see it as a weakness, and the United States would eventually be forced to give up its place as the world's economic leader."

"Offering an open-door immigration policy will lead to gross overcrowding and the death of America."

In the following essay, note four fallacies which have not yet been addressed: contradictory premises, *ad misericordiam,* hypothesis contrary to fact, and poisoning the well.

Love Is a Fallacy

Max Shulman

• •

Max Shulman (1919–1988) began his career as a writer when he was a journalism student at the University of Minnesota. Later he wrote humorous novels, stories, and plays. One of his novels, Barefoot Boy with Cheek *(1943), was made into a musical and another,* Rally Round the Flag, Boys! *(1957), was made into a film starring Paul Newman and Joanne Woodward.* The Tender Trap *(1954), a play which he wrote with Robert Paul Smith, still retains its popularity with theater groups. "Love Is a Fallacy" was first published in 1951.*

• • • • • • • • • •

Cool was I and logical. Keen, calculating, perspicacious, acute, and astute—I was all of these. My brain was as powerful as a dynamo, as precise as a chemist's scales, as penetrating as a scalpel. And—think of it!—I was only eighteen.

It is not often that one so young has such a giant intellect. Take, for example, Petey Bellows, my roommate at the university. Same age, same background, but dumb as an ox. A nice enough fellow, you understand, but nothing upstairs. Emotional type. Unstable. Impressionable. Worst of all, a faddist. Fads, I submit, are the very negation of reason. To be swept up in every new craze that comes along, to surrender yourself to idiocy just because everybody else is doing it—this, to me, is the acme of mindlessness. Not, however, to Petey.

One afternoon I found Petey lying on his bed with an expression of such distress on his face that I immediately diagnosed appendicitis. "Don't move," I said. "Don't take a laxative. I'll get a doctor."

"Raccoon," he mumbled thickly.

"Raccoon?" I said, pausing in my flight.

"I want a raccoon coat," he wailed.

I perceived that his trouble was not physical, but mental. "Why do you want a raccoon coat?"

"I should have known it," he cried, pounding his temples. "I should have known they'd come back when the Charleston came back. Like a fool I spent all my money for textbooks, and now I can't get a raccoon coat."

"Can you mean," I said incredulously, "that people are actually wearing raccoon coats again?"

"All the Big Men on Campus are wearing them. Where've you been?"

"In the library," I said, naming a place not frequented by Big Men on Campus.

He leaped from the bed and paced the room. "I've got to have a raccoon coat," he said passionately. "I've got to!"

"Petey, why? Look at it rationally. Raccoon coats are unsanitary. They shed. They smell bad. They weigh too much. They're unsightly. They—"

"You don't understand," he interrupted impatiently. "It's the thing to do. Don't you want to be in the swim?"

"No," I said truthfully.

"Well, I do," he declared. "I'd give anything for a raccoon coat. Anything!"

My brain, that precision instrument, slipped into high gear. "Anything?" I asked, looking at him narrowly.

"Anything," he affirmed in ringing tones.

I stroked my chin thoughtfully. It so happened that I knew where to get my hands on a raccoon coat. My father had had one in his undergraduate days; it lay now in a trunk in the attic back home. It also happened that Petey had something I wanted. He didn't *have* it exactly, but at least he had first rights on it. I refer to his girl, Polly Espy.

I had long coveted Polly Espy. Let me emphasize that my desire for this young woman was not emotional in nature. She was, to be sure, a girl who excited the emotions, but I was not one to let my heart rule my head. I wanted Polly for a shrewdly calculated, entirely cerebral reason.

I was a freshman in law school. In a few years I would be out in practice. I was well aware of the importance of the right kind of wife in furthering a lawyer's career. The successful lawyers I had observed were, almost without exception, married to beautiful, gracious, intelligent women. With one omission, Polly fitted these specifications perfectly.

Beautiful she was. She was not yet of pin-up proportions, but I felt sure that time would supply the lack. She already had the makings.

Gracious she was. By gracious I mean full of graces. She had an erectness of carriage, an ease of bearing, a poise that clearly indicated the best of breeding. At table her manners were exquisite. I had seen her at the Kozy Kampus Korner eating the specialty of the house—a sandwich that contained scraps of pot roast, gravy, chopped nuts, and a dipper of sauerkraut—without even getting her fingers moist.

Intelligent she was not. In fact, she veered in the opposite direction. But I believed that under my guidance she would smarten up. At any rate, it was worth a try. It is, after all, easier to make a beautiful dumb girl smart than to make an ugly smart girl beautiful.

"Petey," I said, "are you in love with Polly Espy?"

"I think she's a keen kid," he replied, "but I don't know if you'd call it love. Why?"

"Do you," I asked, "have any kind of formal arrangement with her? I mean are you going steady or anything like that?"

"No. We see each other quite a bit, but we both have other dates. Why?"

"Is there," I asked, "any other man for whom she has a particular fondness?"

"Not that I know of. Why?"

I nodded with satisfaction. "In other words, if you were out of the picture, the field would be open. Is that right?"

"I guess so. What are you getting at?"

"Nothing, nothing," I said innocently, and took my suitcase out of the closet.

"Where you going?" asked Petey.

"Home for the weekend." I threw a few things into the bag.

"Listen," he said, clutching my arm eagerly, "while you're home, you couldn't get some money from your old man, could you, and lend it to me so I can buy a raccoon coat?"

"I may do better than that," I said with a mysterious wink and closed my bag and left.

"Look," I said to Petey when I got back Monday morning. I threw open the suitcase and revealed the huge, hairy, gamy object that my father had worn in his Stutz Bearcat in 1925.

"Holy Toledo!" said Petey reverently. He plunged his hands into the raccoon coat and then his face. "Holy Toledo!" he repeated fifteen or twenty times.

"Would you like it?" I asked.

"Oh yes!" he cried, clutching the greasy pelt to him. Then a canny look came into his eyes. "What do you want for it?"

"Your girl," I said, mincing no words.

"Polly?" he said in a horrified whisper. "You want Polly?"

"That's right."

He flung the coat from him. "Never," he said stoutly.

I shrugged. "Okay. If you don't want to be in the swim, I guess it's your business."

I sat down in a chair and pretended to read a book, but out of the corner of my eye I kept watching Petey. He was a torn man. First he looked at the coat with the expression of a waif at a bakery window. Then he turned away and set his jaw resolutely. Then he looked back at the coat, with even more longing in his face. Then he turned away, but with not so much resolution this time. Back and forth his head swiveled, desire waxing, resolution waning. Finally he didn't turn away at all; he just stood and stared with mad lust at the coat.

"It isn't as though I was in love with Polly," he said thickly. "Or going steady or anything like that."

"That's right," I murmured.

"What's Polly to me, or me to Polly?"

"Not a thing," said I.

"It's just been a casual kick—just a few laughs, that's all."

"Try on the coat," said I.

He complied. The coat bunched high over his ears and dropped all the way down to his shoe tops. He looked like a mound of dead raccoons. "Fits fine," he said happily.

I rose from my chair. "Is it a deal?" I asked, extending my hand.

He swallowed. "It's a deal," he said and shook my hand.

I had my first date with Polly the following evening. This was in the nature of a survey; I wanted to find out just how much work I had to do to get her mind up to the standard I required. I took her first to dinner. "Gee, that was a delish dinner," she said as we left the restaurant. Then I took her to a movie. "Gee, that was a marvy movie," she said as we left the theater. And then I took her home. "Gee, I had a sensaysh time," she said as she bade me good night.

I went back to my room with a heavy heart. I had gravely underestimated the size of my task. This girl's lack of information was terrifying. Nor would it be enough merely to supply her with information. First she had to be taught to *think*. This loomed as a project of no small dimensions, and at first I was tempted to give her back to Petey. But then I got to thinking about her abundant physical charms and about the way she entered a room and the way she handled a knife and fork, and I decided to make an effort.

I went about it, as in all things, systematically. I gave her a course in logic. It happened that I, as a law student, was taking a course in logic myself, so I had all the facts at my fingertips. "Polly," I said to her when I picked her up on our next date, "tonight we are going over to the Knoll and talk."

"Oo, terrif," she replied. One thing I will say for this girl. You would go far to find another so agreeable.

We went to the Knoll, the campus trysting place, and we sat down under an old oak, and she looked at me expectantly: "What are we going to talk about?" she asked.

"Logic."

She thought this over for a minute and decided she liked it. "Magnif," she said.

"Logic," I said, clearing my throat, "is the science of thinking. Before we can think correctly, we must first learn to recognize the common fallacies of logic. These we will take up tonight."

"Wow-dow!" she cried, clapping her hands delightedly.

I winced, but went bravely on. "First let us examine the fallacy called Dicto Simpliciter."

"By all means," she urged, batting her lashes eagerly.

"Dicto Simpliciter means an argument based on an unqualified generalization. For example: Exercise is good. Therefore everybody should exercise."

"I agree," said Polly earnestly. "I mean exercise is wonderful. I mean it builds the body and everything."

"Polly," I said gently, "the argument is a fallacy. *Exercise is good* is an unqualified generalization. For instance, if you have heart disease, exercise is bad, not good. Many people are ordered by their doctors not to exercise. You must *qualify* the generalization. You must say exercise is *usually* good, or exercise is good *for most people.* Otherwise you have committed a Dicto Simpliciter. Do you see?"

"No," she confessed. "But this is marvy. Do more! Do more!"

"It will be better if you stop tugging at my sleeve," I told her, and when she desisted, I continued. "Next we take up a fallacy called Hasty Generalization. Listen carefully: You can't speak French. I can't speak French. Petey Bellows can't speak French. I must therefore conclude that nobody at the University of Minnesota can speak French."

"Really?" said Polly, amazed. *"Nobody?"*

I hid my exasperation. "Polly, it's a fallacy. The generalization is reached too hastily. There are too few instances to support such a conclusion."

"Know any more fallacies?" she asked breathlessly. "This is more fun than dancing even."

I fought off a wave of despair. I was getting nowhere with this girl, absolutely nowhere. Still, I am nothing if not persistent. I continued. "Next comes Post Hoc. Listen to this: Let's not take Bill on our picnic. Every time we take him out with us, it rains."

"I know somebody just like that," she exclaimed. "A girl back home—Eula Becker, her name is. It never fails. Every single time we take her on a picnic—"

"Polly," I said sharply, "it's a fallacy. Eula Becker doesn't *cause* the rain. She has no connection with the rain. You are guilty of Post Hoc if you blame Eula Becker."

"I'll never do it again," she promised contritely. "Are you mad at me?"

I sighed. "No, Polly, I'm not mad."

"Then tell me some more fallacies."

"All right. Let's try Contradictory Premises."

"Yes, let's," she chirped, blinking her eyes happily.

I frowned, but plunged ahead. "Here's an example of Contradictory Premises: If God can do anything, can He make a stone so heavy that He won't be able to lift it?"

"Of course," she replied promptly.

"But if He can do anything, He can lift the stone," I pointed out.

"Yeah," she said thoughtfully. "Well, then I guess He can't make the stone."

"But He can do anything," I reminded her.

She scratched her pretty, empty head. "I'm all confused," she admitted.

"Of course you are. Because when the premises of an argument contradict each other, there can be no argument. If there is an irresistible force, there can be no immovable object. If there is an immovable object, there can be no irresistible force. Get it?"

"Tell me some more of this keen stuff," she said eagerly.

I consulted my watch. "I think we'd better call it a night. I'll take you home now, and you go over all the things you've learned. We'll have another session tomorrow night."

I deposited her at the girl's dormitory, where she assured me that she had had a perfectly terrif evening, and I went glumly home to my room. Petey lay snoring in his bed, the raccoon coat huddled like a great hairy beast at his feet. For a moment I considered waking him and telling him that he could have his girl back. It seemed clear that my project was doomed to failure. The girl simply had a logic-proof head.

But then I reconsidered. I had wasted one evening; I might as well waste another. Who knew? Maybe somewhere in the extinct crater of her mind a few embers still smoldered. Maybe somehow I could fan them into flame. Admittedly it was not a prospect fraught with hope, but I decided to give it one more try.

Seated under the oak the next evening I said, "Our first fallacy tonight is called Ad Misericordiam."

She quivered with delight.

"Listen closely," I said. "A man applies for a job. When the boss asks him what his qualifications are, he replies that he has a wife and six children at home, the wife is a helpless cripple, the children have nothing to eat, no clothes to wear, no shoes on their feet, there are no beds in the house, no coal in the cellar, and winter is coming."

A tear rolled down each of Polly's pink cheeks. "Oh, this is awful—awful," she sobbed.

"Yes, it's awful," I agreed, "but it's no argument. The man never answered the boss's question about his qualifications. Instead he appealed to the boss's sympathy. He committed the fallacy of Ad Misericordiam. Do you understand?"

"Have you got a handkerchief?" she blubbered.

I handed her a handkerchief and tried to keep from screaming while she wiped her eyes. "Next," I said in a carefully controlled tone, "we will discuss False Analogy. Here is an example: Students should be allowed to look at their textbooks during examinations. After all, surgeons have X rays to guide them during an operation, lawyers have briefs to guide them during a trial, carpenters have blueprints to guide them when they are building a house. Why, then, shouldn't students be allowed to look at their textbooks during an examination?"

"There now," she said enthusiastically, "is the most marvy idea I've heard in years."

"Polly," I said testily, "the argument is all wrong. Doctors, lawyers, and carpenters aren't taking a test to see how much they have learned, but students are. The situations are altogether different, and you can't make an analogy between them."

"I still think it's a good idea," said Polly.

"Nuts," I muttered. Doggedly I pressed on. "Next we'll try Hypothesis Contrary to Fact."

"Sounds yummy," was Polly's reaction.

"Listen: If Madame Curie had not happened to leave a photographic plate in a drawer with a chunk of pitchblende, the world today would not know about radium."

"True, true," said Polly, nodding her head. "Did you see the movie? Oh, it just knocked me out. That Walter Pidgeon is so dreamy. I mean he fractures me."

"If you can forget Mr. Pidgeon for a moment," I said coldly, "I would like to point out that the statement is a fallacy. Maybe Madame Curie would have discovered radium at some later date. Maybe somebody else would have discovered it. Maybe any number of things would have happened. You can't start with a hypothesis that is not true and then draw any supportable conclusions from it."

"They ought to put Walter Pidgeon in more pictures," said Polly. "I hardly ever see him any more."

One more chance, I decided. But just one more. There is a limit to what flesh and blood can bear. "The next fallacy is called Poisoning the Well."

"How cute!" she gurgled.

"Two men are having a debate. The first one gets up and says, 'My opponent is a notorious liar. You can't believe a word that he is going to say.' . . . Now, Polly, think. Think hard. What's wrong?"

I watched her closely as she knit her creamy brow in concentration. Suddenly a glimmer of intelligence—the first I had seen—came into her eyes. "It's not fair," she said with indignation. "It's not a bit fair. What chance has the second man got if the first man calls him a liar before he even begins talking?"

"Right!" I cried exultantly. "One hundred percent right. It's not fair. The first man has *poisoned the well* before anybody could drink from it. He has hamstrung his opponent before he could even start. . . . Polly, I'm proud of you."

"Pshaw," she murmured, blushing with pleasure.

"You see, my dear, these things aren't so hard. All you have to do is concentrate. Think—examine—evaluate. Come now, let's review everything we have learned."

"Fire away," she said with an airy wave of her hand.

Heartened by the knowledge that Polly was not altogether a cretin, I began a long, patient review of all I had told her. Over and over and over again I cited instances, pointed out flaws, kept hammering away without letup. It was like digging a tunnel. At first everything was work, sweat, and darkness. I had no idea when I would reach the light, or even *if* I would. But I persisted. I pounded and clawed and scraped, and finally I was rewarded. I saw a chink of light. And then the chink got bigger and the sun came pouring in and all was bright.

Five grueling nights this took, but it was worth it. I had made a logician out of Polly; I had taught her to think. My job was done.

She was worthy of me at last. She was a fit wife for me, a proper hostess for my many mansions, a suitable mother for my well-heeled children.

It must not be thought that I was without love for this girl. Quite the contrary. Just as Pygmalion loved the perfect woman he had fashioned, so I loved mine. I decided to acquaint her with my feelings at our very next meeting. The time had come to change our relationship from academic to romantic.

"Polly," I said when next we sat beneath our oak, "tonight we will not discuss fallacies."

"Aw, gee," she said, disappointed.

"My dear," I said, favoring her with a smile, "we have now spent five evenings together. We have gotten along splendidly. It is clear that we are well matched."

"Hasty Generalization," said Polly brightly.

"I beg your pardon," said I.

"Hasty Generalization," she repeated. "How can you say that we are well matched on the basis of only five dates?"

I chuckled with amusement. The dear child had learned her lessons well. "My dear," I said, patting her hand in a tolerant manner, "five dates is plenty. After all, you don't have to eat a whole cake to know that it's good."

"False Analogy," said Polly promptly. "I'm not a cake. I'm a girl."

I chuckled with somewhat less amusement. The dear child had learned her lesson perhaps too well. I decided to change tactics. Obviously the best approach was a simple, strong, direct declaration of love. I paused for a moment while my massive brain chose the proper words. Then I began:

"Polly, I love you. You are the whole world to me, and the moon and the stars and the constellations of outer space. Please, my darling, say that you will go steady with me, for if you will not, life will be meaningless. I will languish. I will refuse my meals. I will wander the face of the earth, a shambling, hollow-eyed hulk."

There, I thought, folding my arms, that ought to do it.

"Ad Misericordiam," said Polly.

I ground my teeth. I was not Pygmalion; I was Frankenstein, and my monster had me by the throat. Frantically I fought back the tide of panic surging through me. At all costs I had to keep cool.

"Well, Polly," I said, forcing a smile, "you certainly have learned your fallacies."

"You're darn right," she said with a vigorous nod.

"And who taught them to you, Polly?"

"You did."

"That's right. So you do owe me something, don't you, my dear? If I hadn't come along you never would have learned about fallacies."

"Hypothesis Contrary to Fact," she said instantly.

I dashed perspiration from my brow. "Polly," I croaked, "You mustn't take all these things so literally. I mean this is just classroom stuff. You know that the things you learn in school don't have anything to do with life."

"Dicto Simpliciter," she said, wagging her finger at me playfully.

That did it. I leaped to my feet, bellowing like a bull. "Will you or will you not go steady with me?"

"I will not," she replied.

"Why not?" I demanded.

"Because this afternoon I promised Petey Bellows that I would go steady with him."

I reeled back, overcome with the infamy of it. After he promised, after he made a deal, after he shook my hand! "That rat!" I shrieked, kicking up great chunks of turf. "You can't go with him, Polly. He's a liar. He's a cheat. He's a rat."

"Poisoning the Well," said Polly, "and stop shouting, I think shouting must be a fallacy too."

With an immense effort of will, I modulated my voice. "All right," I said. "You're a logician. Let's look at this thing logically, How could you choose Petey Bellows over me? Look at me—a brilliant student, a tremendous intellectual, a man with an assured future. Look at Petey—a knothead, a jitterbug, a guy who'll never know where his next meal is coming from. Can you give me one logical reason why you should go steady with Petey Bellows?"

"I certainly can," declared Polly. "He's got a raccoon coat."

• •

Thoughts, Ideas, and Discussion Questions

1. Define *perspicacious, acute, astute, dynamo, acme, incredulously, cerebral, carriage, reverently, mincing, waif, resolutely, bade, trysting, contritely, cretin, Pygmalion.*
2. Is there an underlying claim in "Love is a Fallacy?"
3. Did you identify any fallacies in addition to the ones pointed out by Polly and the narrator?
4. Do you find this story offensive to men, women, or certain "types" of people?

Applications

1. Watch a TV talk show for one hour. Identify any fallacies offered by hosts or guests of the show.
2. Watch *Dateline, 20/20,* or a thirty-minute news segment on TV, noting how many fallacies and, specifically, which fallacies are being consistently committed.
3. Identify fallacies in magazine articles, newspaper articles or headlines, or fallacies heard on live talk-radio stations.

Observations

Before you begin reading the next chapter, take some time to reflect on what you learned in Chapter 7. Specifically, note what you think about what you learned, for in the spirit of promoting consciousness, it is essential that you not only become aware of your observations but that you commit them to paper. Use these observations like one would use a journal: as a tool for measuring growth and insight.

Preliminary Observations

_____

_____

_____

_____

_____

_____

_____

_____

Refined Observations

_____

_____

_____

_____

_____

_____

_____

_____

_____

New Observations

CHAPTER

The Satire

Nothing soils the pallet like a good satire. Good satires can enthuse, infuriate, and edify diverse audiences. Maybe this is why the satire is a popular rhetorical mode.

The purpose for the satire is three tiered:

1. Satires break the monotony of traditionally written arguments. After reading ten arguments about why welfare should not be allowed, it is refreshing to encounter a good satirist's claim:

   "Because I enjoy getting paid to watch soap operas and talk shows, and because I especially enjoy getting a monetary promotion for every child I bear, I will continue embracing, with pride, my career title: Welfare Mom."

   Though you may disagree with the aforementioned claim, one thing is certain: out of anger or morbid curiosity, you *will* finish reading the essay. In fact, one blessing inherent in good satires is the ability to dangle glittering extremisms in front of readers, knowing they will bite the baited hook and join the argument. This, of course, is the goal. In order to persuade your readers, you must get them to engage in the argument. This is the only way they can sort through their own beliefs. This is the only way they can become conscious of their true feelings. This awareness promotes thinking. This thinking encourages the creation of a claim. And once your readers state a claim, you can begin sculpting your argument, adding to it and subtracting from it, realizing that the support for their claim is exactly what you'll use to refute it.

2. Satires can go to extremes without fearing the "fallacy trap." Eventually, the satire reveals a lightheartedness not usually apparent in the traditional argument. This lightheartedness, coupled with outrageous claims which are, no doubt, adorning readers with a ScoobyDoo look of confusion, often goads readers into accepting the occasional fallacy as an "occupational hazard," one necessary to bring the point home. However, despite this "Get Out of Jail Free" card which the satirist may use when committing fallacies, a good satire is poignant and effective. Not only are most satires read *in their entirety,* but they provoke readers by proffering new ways to look at an old issue.

3. Satires allow writers to retain sanity in insane situations. When little Johnny gets upset, he can get in a fistfight, or he can write in his journal. When an abortion clinic is bombed by people who consider themselves "ProLife," one can throw a handgrenade as a counterattack, or one can take an intelligent look at an insane situation. How can "ProLifers" kill people via abortion clinic bombings? You can attempt to write a structured, linear argument, or you may opt to try your hand at something which affords the writer more freedom.

Analyze the following four essays. Once you unearth the issues being addressed, note the different techniques employed by good satirists.

A Modest Proposal

Jonathan Swift

• •

This essay is acknowledged by almost all critics to be the most powerful example of irony in the English language. (Irony means saying one thing but meaning another.) In 1729 Jonathan Swift, prolific satirist and dean of St. Patrick's Cathedral in Dublin, was moved to write in protest against the terrible poverty in which the Irish were forced to live under British rule.

• • • • • • • • •

It is a melancholy object to those who walk through this great town* or travel in the country, when they see the streets, the roads, and cabin doors, crowded with beggars of the female sex, followed by three, four, or six children, all in rags and importuning every passenger for an alms. These mothers, instead of being able to work for their honest livelihood, are forced to employ all their time in strolling to beg sustenance for their helpless infants: who, as they grow up either turn thieves for want of work, or leave their dear native country to fight for the Pretender in Spain, or sell themselves to the Barbados.**

I think it is agreed by all parties that this prodigious number of children in the arms, or on the backs, or at the heels of their mothers, and frequently of their fathers, is in the present deplorable state of the kingdom a very great additional grievance; and, therefore, whoever could find out a fair, cheap, and easy method of making these children sound, useful members of the commonwealth, would deserve so well of the public as to have his statue set up for a preserver of the nation.

From *A Modest Proposal* by Jonathan Swift, 1729.
*Dublin.—Ed.
**The Pretender was James Stuart, who was exiled to Spain. Many Irishmen had joined an army attempting to return him to the English throne in 1715. Others had become indentured servants, agreeing to work for a set number of years in Barbados or other British colonies in exchange for their transportation out of Ireland.—Ed.

But my intention is very far from being confined to provide only for the children of professed beggars; it is of a much greater extent, and shall take in the whole number of infants at a certain age who are born of parents in effect as little able to support them as those who demand our charity in the streets.

As to my own part, having turned my thoughts for many years upon this important subject, and maturely weighed the several schemes of other projectors,* I have always found them grossly mistaken in the computation. It is true, a child just dropped from its dam may be supported by her milk for a solar year, with little other nourishment; at most not above the value of two shillings, which the mother may certainly get, or the value in scraps, by her lawful occupation of begging; and it is exactly at one year old that I propose to provide for them in such a manner as instead of being a charge upon their parents or the parish, or wanting food and raiment for the rest of their lives, they shall on the contrary contribute to the feeding, and partly to the clothing, of many thousands.

There is likewise another great advantage in my scheme, that it will prevent those voluntary abortions, and that horrid practice of women murdering their bastard children, alas, too frequent among us, sacrificing the poor innocent babes, I doubt, more to avoid the expense than the shame, which would move tears and pity in the most savage and inhuman breast.

The number of souls in this kingdom being usually reckoned one million and a half, of these I calculate there may be about two hundred thousand couples whose wives are breeders; from which number I subtract thirty thousand couples who are able to maintain their own children, although I apprehend there cannot be so many, under the present distresses of the kingdom; but this being granted, there will remain an hundred and seventy thousand breeders. I again subtract fifty thousand for those women who miscarry, or whose children die by accident or disease within the year. There only remains one hundred and twenty thousand children of poor parents annually born. The question therefore is, how this number shall be reared and provided for, which, as I have already said, under the present situation of affairs, is utterly impossible by all the methods hitherto proposed. For we can neither employ them in handicraft or agriculture; we neither build houses (I mean in the country) nor cultivate land. They can very seldom pick up a livelihood by stealing, till they arrive at six years

---

*Planners.—Ed.

old, except where they are of towardly parts;* although I confess they learn the rudiments much earlier, during which time they can however be properly looked upon only as probationers, as I have been informed by a principal gentleman in the county of Cavan, who protested to me that he never knew above one or two instances under the age of six, even in a part of the kingdom so renowned for the quickest proficiency in that art.

I am assured by our merchants that a boy or a girl before twelve years old is no salable commodity; and even when they come to this age they will not yield above three pounds, or three pounds and a half a crown at most on the Exchange; which cannot turn to account either to the parents or kingdom, the charge of nutriment and rags having been at least four times that value.

I shall now therefore humbly propose my own thoughts, which I hope will not be liable to the least objection.

I have been assured by a very knowing American of my acquaintance in London, that a young healthy child well nursed is at a year old a most delicious, nourishing, and wholesome food, whether stewed, roasted, baked, or boiled; and I make no doubt that it will equally serve in a fricassee or a ragout.**

I do therefore humbly offer it to public consideration that of the hundred and twenty thousand children already computed, twenty thousand may be reserved for breed, whereof only onefourth part to be males; which is more than we allow to sheep, black cattle or swine; and my reason is, that these children are seldom the fruits of marriage, a circumstance not much regarded by our savages, therefore one male will be sufficient to serve four females. That the remaining hundred thousand may, at a year old, be offered in the sale to the persons of quality and fortune through the kingdom, always advising the mother to let them suck plentifully in the last month, so as to render them plump and fat for a good table. A child will make two dishes at an entertainment for friends; and when the family dines alone, the fore or hind quarter will make a reasonable dish, and seasoned with a little pepper or salt will be very good boiled on the fourth day, especially in winter.

I have reckoned upon a medium that a child just born will weigh 12 pounds, and in a solar year, if tolerably nursed, increaseth to 28 pounds.

---

*Innate talents.—Ed.
**Stew.—Ed

I grant this food will be somewhat dear, and therefore very proper for landlords, who, as they have already devoured most of the parents, seem to have the best title to the children.

Infant's flesh will be in season throughout the year, but more plentiful in March, and a little before and after; for we are told by a grave author, an eminent French physician,* that fish being a prolific diet, there are more children born in Roman Catholic countries about nine months after Lent than at any other season; therefore, reckoning a year after Lent, the markets will be more glutted than usual, because the number of popish infants is at least three to one in this kingdom; and therefore it will have one other collateral advantage, by lessening the number of papists among us.

I have already computed the charge of nursing a beggar's child (in which list I reckon all cottagers, laborers, and fourfifths of the farmers) to be about two shillings per annum, rags included; and I believe no gentleman would repine to give ten shillings for the carcass of a good fat child, which, as I have said, will make four dishes of excellent nutritive meat, when he hath only some particular friend or his own family to dine with him. Thus the squire will learn to be a good landlord, and grow popular among his tenants; the mother will have eight shillings net profit, and be fit for work till she produces another child.

Those who are more thrifty (as I must confess the times require) may flay the carcass; the skin of which artificially** dressed will make admirable gloves for ladies, and summer boots for fine gentlemen.

As to our city of Dublin, shambles*** may be appointed for this purpose in the most convenient parts of it, and butchers we may be assured will not be wanting; although I rather recommend buying the children alive, and dressing them hot from the knife, as we do roasting pigs.

A very worthy person, a true lover of his country, and whose virtues I highly esteem, was lately pleased in discoursing on this matter to offer a refinement upon my scheme. He said that many gentlemen of this kingdom, having of late destroyed their deer, he conceived

---

*A reference to Swift's favorite French writer, Françalois Rabelais (1494?–1553), who was actually a broad satirist known for his coarse humor.—Ed.
**With art or craft.—Ed.
***Butcher shops or slaughterhouses.—Ed.

that the want of venison might be well supplied by the bodies of young lads and maidens, not exceeding fourteen years of age nor under twelve; so great a number of both sexes in every country being now ready to starve for want of work and service; and these to be disposed of by their parents, if alive, or otherwise by their nearest relations. But with due deference to so excellent a friend and so deserving a patriot, I cannot be altogether in his sentiments; for as to the males, my American acquaintance assured me, from frequent experience, that their flesh was generally tough and lean, like that of our schoolboys by continual exercise, and their taste disagreeable; and to fatten them would not answer the charge. Then as to the females, it would, I think, with humble submission be a loss to the public, because they soon would become breeders themselves; and besides, it is not improbable that some scrupulous people might be apt to censure such a practice (although indeed very unjustly), as a little bordering upon cruelty; which, I confess, hath always been with me the strongest objection against any project, however so well intended.

But in order to justify my friend, he confessed that this expedient was put into his head by the famous Psalmanazar,* a native of the island Formosa, who came from thence to London above twenty years ago, and in conversation told my friend, that in his country when any young person happened to be put to death, the executioner sold the carcass to persons of quality as a prime dainty; and that in his time the body of a plump girl of fifteen, who was crucified for an attempt to poison the emperor, was sold to his imperial majesty's prime minister of state, and other great mandarins of the court, in joints from the gibbet, at four hundred crowns. Neither indeed can I deny, that if the same use were made of several plump young girls in this town, who without one single groat to their fortunes cannot stir abroad without a chair, and appear at playhouse and assemblies in foreign fineries which they never will pay for, the kingdom would not be the worse.

Some persons of a desponding spirit are in great concern about that vast number of poor people, who are aged, diseased, or maimed, and I have been desired to employ my thoughts what course may be taken to ease the nation of so grievous an encumbrance. But I am not in the least pain upon that matter, because it is very well known that

---

*Georges Psalmanazar was a Frenchman who pretended to be Japanese and wrote an entirely imaginary *Description of the Isle Formosa.* He had become well known in gullible London society.—Ed.

they are every day dying and rotting by cold and famine, and filth and vermin, as fast as can be reasonably expected. And as to the young laborers, they are now in as hopeful a condition; they cannot get work, and consequently pine away for want of nourishment, to a degree that if at any time they are accidentally hired to common labor, they have not strength to perform it; and thus the country and themselves are happily delivered from the evils to come.

I have too long digressed, and therefore shall return to my subject. I think the advantages by the proposal which I have made are obvious and many, as well as of the highest importance.

For first, as I have already observed, it would greatly lessen the number of papists, with whom we are yearly overrun, being the principal breeders of the nation as well as our most dangerous enemies; and who stay at home on purpose with a design to deliver the kingdom to the Pretender, hoping to take their advantage by the absence of so many good protestants, who have chosen rather to leave their country than stay at home and pay tithes against their conscience to an episcopal curate.

Secondly, The poorer tenants will have something valuable of their own, which by law may be made liable to distress and help to pay their landlord's rent, their corn and cattle being already seized, and money a thing unknown.

Thirdly, Whereas the maintenance of an hundred thousand children, from two years old and upward, cannot be computed at less than ten shillings a piece per annum, the nation's stock will be thereby increased fifty thousand pounds per annum, beside the profit of a new dish introduced to the tables of all gentlemen of fortune in the kingdom who have any refinement in taste. And the money will circulate among ourselves, the goods being entirely of our own growth and manufacture.

Fourthly, The constant breeders, beside the gain of eight shillings sterling per annum by the sale of their children, will be rid of the charge of maintaining them after the first year.

Fifthly, This food would likewise bring great custom to taverns; where the vintners will certainly be so prudent as to procure the best receipts for dressing it to perfection, and consequently have their houses frequented by all the fine gentlemen, who justly value themselves upon their knowledge in good eating; and a skilful cook, who understands how to oblige his guests, will contrive to make it as expensive as they please.

Sixthly, This would be a great inducement to marriage, which all wise nations have either encouraged by rewards or enforced by laws and penalties. It would increase the care and tenderness of mothers toward their children, when they were sure of a settlement for life to the poor babes, provided in some sort by the public, to their annual profit instead of expense. We should see an honest emulation among the married women, which of them could bring the fattest child to the market. Men would become as fond of their wives during the time of their pregnancy as they are now of their mares in foal, their cows in calf, their sows when they are ready to farrow; nor offer to beat or kick them (as is too frequent a practice) for fear of a miscarriage.

Many other advantages might be enumerated. For instance, the addition of some thousand carcasses in our exportation of barreled beef, the propagation of swine's flesh, and improvement in the art of making good bacon, so much wanted among us by the great destruction of pigs, too frequent at our tables; which are no way comparable in taste or magnificence to a wellgrown, fat, yearling child, which roasted whole will make a considerable figure at a lord mayor's feast or any other public entertainment. But this and many others I omit, being studious of brevity.

Supposing that one thousand families in this city would be constant customers for infants' flesh, besides others who might have it at merry meetings, particularly weddings and christenings, I compute that Dublin would take off annually about twenty thousand carcasses, and the rest of the kingdom (where probably they will be sold somewhat cheaper) the remaining eighty thousand.

I can think of no one objection that will possibly be raised against this proposal, unless it should be urged that the number of people will be thereby much lessened in the kingdom. This I freely own, and it was indeed one principal design in offering it to the world. I desire the reader will observe, that I calculate my remedy for this one individual kingdom of Ireland and for no other that ever was, is, or I think ever can be upon earth. Therefore let no man talk to me of other expedients: of taxing our absentees at five shillings a pound: of using neither clothes nor household furniture except what is of our own growth and manufacture: of utterly rejecting the materials and instruments that promote foreign luxury: of curing the expensiveness of pride, vanity, idleness, and gaming in our women: of introducing a vein of parsimony, prudence, and temperance: of learning to love our country, in the want of which we differ even from laplanders and the inhabitants of Topinamboo:* of quitting our animosities and factions, nor acting any longer like the Jews, who were murdering one another at the very moment their city was taken:** of being a little cautious not to sell our country and conscience for nothing: of teaching landlords to have at least one degree of mercy toward their tenants: lastly, of putting a spirit of honesty, industry, and skill into our shopkeepers; who, if a resolution could now be taken to buy only our native goods, would immediately unite to cheat and exact upon us in the price, the measure, and the goodness, nor could ever yet be brought to make one fair proposal of just dealing, though often and earnestly invited to it.

Therefore I repeat, let no man talk to me of these and the like expedients, till he hath at least some glimpse of hope that there will ever be some hearty and sincere attempt to put them in practice.

But as to myself, having been wearied out for many years with offering vain, idle, visionary thoughts, and at length utterly despairing of success, I fortunately fell upon this proposal, which, as it is wholly new, so it hath something solid and real, of no expense and little trouble, full in our own power, and whereby we can incur no danger in disobliging England. For this kind of commodity will not bear exportation, the flesh being of too tender a consistence to admit a long continuance in salt, although perhaps I could name a country which would be glad to eat up our whole nation without it.

After all, I am not so violently bent upon my own opinion as to reject any offer proposed by wise men, which shall be found equally innocent, cheap, easy, and effectual. But before something of that kind shall be advanced in contradiction to my scheme, and offering a better, I desire the author or authors will be pleased maturely to consider two points. First, as things now stand, how they will be able to find food and raiment for an hundred thousand useless mouths and backs. And secondly, there being a round million of creatures in human figure throughout this kingdom, whose whole subsistence put into a common stock would leave them in debt two millions of pounds sterling, adding those who are beggars by profession to the bulk of farmers, cottagers, and laborers, with their wives and children who are beggars in effect; I desire those politicians who dislike my overture, and may perhaps be so bold as to attempt an answer, that they

*District of Brazil.—Ed.
**During the Roman siege of Jerusalem (A.D. 70), prominent Jews were charged with collaborating with the enemy and put to death.—Ed.

will first ask the parents of these mortals, whether they would not at this day think it a great happiness to have been sold for food, at a year old in the manner I prescribe, and thereby have avoided such a perpetual scene of misfortunes as they have since gone through by the oppression of landlords, the impossibility of paying rent without money or trade, the want of common sustenance, with neither house nor clothes to cover them from the inclemencies of the weather, and the most inevitable prospect of entailing the like or greater miseries upon their breed for ever.

I profess, in the sincerity of my heart, that I have not the least personal interest in endeavoring to promote this necessary work, having no other motive than the public good of my country, by advancing our trade, providing for infants, relieving the poor, and giving some pleasure to the rich. I have no children by which I can propose to get a single penny; the youngest being nine years old, and my wife past childbearing.

• •

Thoughts, Ideas, and Discussion Questions

1. Articulate Swift's stated claim in one sentence. Then, articulate his implied claim.
2. What issue is Jonathan Swift addressing?
3. How does his use of facts and statistics help bolster his credibility?
4. Swift seems to assume a persona, the persona of someone he, hopefully, is not. Describe the characteristics of his alterego.
5. What does Swift achieve by writing in such a serious manner?
6. What would you have thought if you were in Dublin and you read this in 1729?
7. How much of Swift's essay is spent refuting the opposition? Is this technique effective?

Dating Your Mom

Ian Frazier

• •

Ian Frazier lives on Canal Street in Manhattan. As an under-graduate at Harvard University, he wrote for the Lampoon.
"Dating Your Mom" is the title essay of Frazier's first col-lection. His second collection of essays, reportage rather than humor or satire, is called Nobody Better, Better than Nobody. *Published in 1987, it was followed by* Great Plains, *an account of the American great plains, which was pub-lished in 1989.*

• • • • • • • • •

In today's fastmoving, transient, rootless society, where people meet and make love and part without ever really touching, the rela-tionship every guy already has with his own mother is too valuable to ignore. Here is a grown, experienced, loving woman—one you do not have to go to a party or a singles bar to meet, one you do not have to go to great lengths to get to know. There are hundreds of times when you and your mother are thrown together naturally, without the ten-sion that usually accompanies courtship—just the two of you, alone. All you need is a little presence of mind to take advantage of these situations. Say your mom is driving you downtown in the car to buy you a new pair of slacks. First, find a nice station on the car radio, one that she likes. Get into the pleasant lull of freeway driving—tires humming along the pavement, airconditioner on max. Then turn to look at her across the front seat and say something like, "You know, you've really kept your shape, Mom, and don't think I haven't no-ticed." Or suppose she comes into your room to bring you some clean socks. Take her by the wrist, pull her close, and say, "Mom, you're the most fascinating woman I've ever met." Probably she'll tell you to cut out the foolishness, but I can guarantee you one thing: She will never tell your dad. Possibly she would find it hard to say, "Dear, Piper just made a pass at me," or possibly she is secretly flattered, but, whatever the reason, she will keep it to herself until the day comes when she is no longer ashamed to tell the world of your love.

Dating your mother seriously might seem difficult at first, but once you try it I'll bet you'll be surprised at how easy it is. Facing up to your intention is the main thing: You have to want it bad enough. One problem is that lots of people get hung up on feelings of guilt about their dad. They think, Oh, here's this kindly old guy who taught me how to hunt and whittle and dynamite fish—I can't let him go on into his twilight years alone. Well, there are two reasons you can dismiss those thoughts from your mind. First, every woman, I don't care who she is, prefers her son to her husband. That is a simple fact; ask any woman who has a son, and she'll admit it. And why shouldn't she prefer someone who is so much like herself, who represents nine months of special concern and love and intense physical closeness—someone whom she actually created? As more women begin to express the need to have something all their own in the world, more women are going to start being honest about this preference. When you and your mom begin going together, you will simply become part of a natural and inevitable historical trend.

Second, you must remember this about your dad: You have your mother, he has his! Let him go put the moves on his own mother and stop messing with yours. If his mother is dead or too old to be much fun anymore, that's not your fault, is it? It's not your fault that he didn't realize his mom for the woman she was, before it was too late. Probably he's going to try a lot of emotional blackmail on you just because you had a good idea and he never did. Don't buy it. Comfort yourself with the thought that your dad belongs to the last generation of guys who will let their moms slip away from them like that.

Once your dad is out of the picture—once he has taken up fly tying, joined the Single Again Club, moved to Russia, whatever—and your mom has been wooed and won, if you're anything like me you're going to start having so much fun that the good times you had with your mother when you were little will seem tame by comparison. For a while, Mom and I went along living a contented, quiet life, just happy to be with each other. But after several months we started getting into some different things, like the big motorized stroller. The thrill I felt the first time Mom steered me down the street! On the tray, in addition to my Big Jim doll and the wire with the colored wooden beads, I have my desk blotter, my typewriter, an inout basket, and my name plate. I get a lot of work done, plus I get a great chance to peoplewatch. Then there's my big, adultsized highchair, where I sit in the evening as Mom and I watch the news and discuss current events, while I paddle in my food and throw my dishes on the floor. When Mom reaches to wipe off my chin and I take her hand, and we fall to the floor in a heap—me, Mom, highchair, and all—well, those are the best times, those are the very best times.

It is true that occasionally I find myself longing for even more— for things I know I cannot have, like the feel of a firm, strong, gentle hand at the small of my back lifting me out of bed into the air, or someone who could walk me around and burp me after I've watched all the bowl games and had about nine beers. Ideally, I would like a mom about nineteen or twenty feet tall, and although I considered for a while asking my mom to start working out with weights and drinking Nutrament, I finally figured, Why put her through it? After all, she is not only my woman, she is my best friend. I have to take her as she is, and the way she is is plenty good enough for me.

• •

Thoughts, Ideas, and Discussion Questions

1. Articulate Frazier's stated claim in one sentence. Then, articulate his implied claim.
2. What is Frazier's purpose for writing "Dating Your Mom?" What would provoke a person to write an essay such as this?
3. How is Frazier's essay similar to Swift's "A Modest Proposal?"
4. Language devices, like sentence variety, parallel structures, and strong verbs, make one's writing much more enjoyable and poignant for the reader. Identify some of the language devices that Frazier uses effectively.

Why Doesn't GM Sell Crack?

Michael Moore

• •

Excerpted from Downsize This!, *which appeared in 1996,
"Why Doesn't GM Sell Crack?" is one of Michael Moore's
many satirical rants. Michael Moore is the awardwinning director of the groundbreaking documentary* Roger and Me,
*which became the largest grossing nonfiction film of all time.
He is the creator and host of "TV Nation," which won an
Emmy Award in 1995. His other films include* Canadian Bacon
*(an official selection of the 1995 Cannes International Film
Festival), the short film* Pets or Meat: The Return to Flint, *and
his most recent documentary feature* The Big One. *He was also
the editor of the* Flint Voice/Michigan Voice *and one of the
first eighteenyearolds elected to public office in this country.
Michael Moore can be reached at* MMFlint@aol.com *or at his
website,* www.michaelmoore.com.

• • • • • • • • •

People in the business world like to say, "Profit is supreme." They
like chanting that.

"Profit is king." That's another one they like to repeat. They don't
like to say, "I'll pick up the check." That means less profit. Profit is
what it's all about. When they say "the bottom line," they mean their
profit. They like that bottom line to contain a number followed by a
lot of zeros.

If I had a nickel for every time I heard some guy in a suit tell me
that "a company must do whatever is necessary to create the biggest
profit possible," I would have a very big bottom line right now. Here's
another popular mantra: "The responsibility of the CEO is to make
his shareholders as much money as he can."

Are you enjoying this lesson in capitalism? I get it every time I fly on a plane. The bottom line feeders have all seen *Roger & Me,* yet they often mistake the fuselage of a DC9 for the Oxford Debating Society. So I have to sit through lectures ad nauseam about the beauties of our free market system. Today the guy in the seat next to me is the owner of an American company that makes office supplies—in Taiwan. I ask the executive, "How much is 'enough?'"

"Enough what?" he replies.

"How much is 'enough' profit?"

He laughs and says, "There's no such thing as 'enough'!"

"So, General Motors made nearly $7 billion in profit last year but they could make $7.1 billion by closing a factory in Parma, Ohio, and moving it to Mexico—that would be okay?"

"Not only okay," he responds, "it is their duty to close that plant and make the extra $.1 billion."

"Even if it destroys Parma, Ohio? Why can't $7 billion be enough and spare the community? Why ruin thousands of families for the sake of $.1 billion? Do you think this is *moral?*"

"Moral?" he asks, as if this is the first time he's heard that word since First Communion class. "This is not an issue of morality. It is purely a matter of economics. A company must be able to do whatever it wants to make a profit." Then he leans over as if to make a revelation I've never heard before.

"Profit, you know, is supreme."

So here's what I don't understand: if profit is supreme, why doesn't a company like General Motors sell crack? Crack is a *very* profitable commodity. For every pound of cocaine that is transformed into crack, a dealer stands to make a profit of $45,000. The dealer profit on a two thousand-pound car is less than $2,000. Crack is also safer to use than automobiles. Each year 40,000 people die in car accidents. Crack, on the other hand, according to the government's own statistics, kills only a few hundred a year. And it doesn't pollute.

So why doesn't GM sell crack? If profit is supreme, why not sell crack?

GM doesn't sell crack because it is illegal. Why is it illegal? Because we, as a society, have determined that crack destroys people's lives. It ruins entire communities. It tears apart the very backbone of our country. That's why we wouldn't let a company like GM sell it, no matter what kind of profit they could make.

If we wouldn't let GM sell crack because it destroys our communities then why do we let them close factories? *That, too,* destroys our communities.

As my frequentflier friend would say, "We can't prevent them from closing factories because they have a right to do whatever they want to in order to make a profit."

No, they don't. They don't have a "right" to do a lot of things: sell child pornography, manufacture chemical weapons, or create hazardous products that could conceivably make them a profit. We can enact laws to prevent companies from doing anything to hurt us.

And downsizing is one of those things that is hurting us. I'm not talking legitimate layoffs, when a company is losing money and simply doesn't have the cash reserves to pay its workers. I'm talking about companies like GM, AT&T, and GE, which fire people at a time when the company is making record profits in the billions of dollars. Executives who do this are not scorned, picketed, or arrested—they are hailed as heroes! They make the covers of *Fortune* and *Forbes.* They lecture at the Harvard Business School about their success. They throw big campaign fundraisers and sit next to the President of the United States. They are the Masters of the Universe simply because they make huge profits regardless of the consequences to our society.

Are we insane or what? Why do we allow this to happen? It is *wrong* to make money off people's labor and then fire them after you've made it. It is *immoral* for a CEO to make millions of dollars when he has just destroyed the livelihood of 40,000 families. And it's just plain *nuts* to allow American companies to move factories overseas at the expense of our own people.

When a company fires thousands of people, what happens to the community? Crime goes up, suicide goes up, drug abuse, alcoholism, spousal abuse, divorce—everything bad spirals dangerously upward. The same thing happens with crack. Only crack is illegal, and downsizing is not. If there was a crack house in your neighborhood what would you do? You would try to get rid of it!

I think it's time we applied the same attitudes we have about crack to corporate downsizing. It's simple: if it hurts our citizens, it should be illegal. We live in a democracy. We enact laws based on what we believe is right and wrong. Murder? Wrong, so we pass a law making it illegal. Burglary? Wrong, and we attempt to prosecute those who commit it. Two really big hairy guys from Gingrich's office pummel me after they read this book? Five to ten in Sing Sing.

As a society, we have a right to protect ourselves from harm. As a democracy, we have a responsibility to legislate measures to protect us from harm.

Here's what I think we should do to protect ourselves:

1. Prohibit corporations from closing a profitable factory or business and moving it overseas. If they close a business and move it within the U.S., they must pay reparations to the community they are leaving behind. We've passed divorce laws that say that if a woman works hard to put her husband through school, and he later decides to leave her after he has become successful, he has a responsibility to compensate her for her sacrifices that allowed him to go on to acquire his wealth. The "marriage" between a company and a community should be no different. If a corporation packs up and leaves, it should have some serious alimony to pay.

2. Prohibit companies from pitting one state or city against another. We are all Americans. It is not victory for our society when one town wins at another's expense. Texas should not be able to raid Massachusetts for jobs. It is debilitating and, frankly, legal extortion.

3. Institute a 100 percent tax on any profits gained by shareholders when the company's stock goes up due to an announcement of firings. No one should be allowed to profit from such bad news.

4. Prohibit executives' salaries from being more than thirty times greater than an average employee's pay. When workers have to take a wage cut because of hard times, so, too, should the CEO. If a CEO fires a large number of employees, it should be illegal for him to collect a bonus that year.

5. Require boards of directors of publicly owned corporations to have representation from both workers and consumers. A company will run better if it has to listen to the people who have to build and/or use the products the company makes.

For those of you free-marketers who disagree with these modest suggestions and may end up on a plane sitting next to me, screaming, "You can't tell a business how it can operate!"—I have this to say: Oh, yes, we can! We legally require companies to build safe products, to ensure safe workplaces, to pay employees a minimum wage, to contribute to their Social Security, and to follow a host of other rules that we, as a society, have deemed necessary for our well-being. And we can legally require each of the steps I've outlined above.

GM can't sell crack. Soon, I predict, they and other companies will not be able to sell us out. Just keep firing more workers, my friends, and see what happens.

• •

Thoughts, Ideas, and Discussion Questions

1. Define *ad nauseam*.
2. Articulate Moore's stated claim in one sentence. Then, articulate his implied claim.
3. How is Moore's essay less satirical when compared to the essays written by Swift and Frazier?
4. What effect does Moore wish to impress upon his readers?

How to Raise a Pimp

Darryl L. Fortson, M.D.

• •

"How to Raise a Pimp" first appeared in Dr. Fortson's column in the Post Tribune *in Gary, Indiana. Dr. Fortson is currently a physician based in Gary, and he can be reached at Dlfortson@aol.com.*

• • • • • • • • •

"Pimpin'" is challenging work. It demands managerial skill, financial acumen, and an intimate knowledge of law enforcement policies and procedures. I've observed that a lot of women seem to be raising their sons (often unknowingly) to become pimps. Usually, when we think of a pimp, we think of a man driving around in a big car with a bunch of streetwalkers that he panders to other lusty men. But there are other types of pimps as well. You probably know one. He's the guy you know that is perpetually looking for a woman (usually his mother, wife, or girlfriend) to take total financial care of him. But contrary to popular belief, pimpin' is a learned behavior. You have to start training a boy to be a pimp in childhood. Here is how it's done.

First, raise him to think he's "cute." I'm not talking about a positive self-image. I'm talking about creating an impression in his mind at the earliest possible moment that his physical appearance is more important than how he treats his fellow man, more important than being knowledgeable and learning to think. Do this by piercing his ears and braiding his hair from day one, making him indistinguishable from a little girl. Of course, you would never think of making your baby daughter look like a boy, but that's okay. And don't worry, you won't make him gay, but by focusing on his physical appearance and fashion, you will teach him that a woman's role in his life is for her to cater to his every material desire just because he is so "cute" or "fine"—you know, like a pimp. Let him think that the world revolves around him by virtue of "cuteness." That way, when the steel mill, corporate America, or academia start hiring "cute" instead of "skilled," "strong," or "intelligent," he will finally be able to get a job—whatever that is.

To raise a pimp, you must act like a whore. How else will your son know how to handle them? You've got to swear and talk nasty at every available activity. Keep a steady stream of different men coming through your house. Let your son hear you moan in your bedroom as you consort with "the man of the week." Let him see how you manipulate men, this one to pay the rent, that one to pay the light bill. That way he learns that the only value men have in society is to use and be used by women. It won't make him a good man, but it will make him one helluva pimp.

Emphasize the importance of sexual rather than intellectual prowess. This is a favorite in black communities. For instance, they say black men have "big ones." If your son is black, make sure he keeps focused on this. That is essential to keeping him on the "pimp track." You see, if he starts valuing "heavy thinking" over being "heavy hung," he might stray from the pimpin' path that some in the black community—and for that matter, in some segments of white society as well—have chosen for some young black men. And you certainly wouldn't want that to happen, now would you? By the way, for what it's worth, since I'm a physician, I've seen a lot of "you-know-whats," some big, some not so big. I can't say whether black men's are bigger or not, but I am certain that I have never examined a black man with one that was bigger than his brain.

Make your son "your man." I'm not talking about sexually but emotionally. Let your young son talk to you like he's grown, even when he is a child. Get him involved in your personal affairs. Keep him away from his father, and put his father down to him; he will grow up with no respect for his father or himself. Since he is young and impressionable, your son may be the only "man" in your life you can "control." So don't love him; control him. Never let him accept responsibility for his actions. Remember, when he gets in trouble at school, it should always be some other child or the teacher's fault, never his. If he starts using drugs, blame his friends, not him. If he gets arrested, bail him out immediately and tell the judge that your son is "a good boy." Remember, sorry excuses make sorry men, and sorry men make excellent pimps. Look, if you follow my advice, your son will grow up to be a trifling, good-for-nothing, clothes-horsing, baby-making, no-job-having pimp, perpetually dependent on the women in his life (perhaps you) for his very sustenance. But you have to decide early if you want a pimp or a man for a son, because you certainly can't have both.

• •

Thoughts, Ideas, and Discussion Questions

1. Articulate Fortson's stated claim in one sentence. Then, articulate his implied claim.
2. What is Fortson's motivation for writing "How to Raise a Pimp?"

One of the simplest ways to write a satire is through inversion. Say, for instance, you are against ESL courses which prescribe English-only, full immersion tactics. (In these courses, non-native English speaking students enroll in classes where English is the only language spoken. You can imagine the confusion and obfuscation inherent in these classes.) If you are against these ESL courses, you might consider writing a satire which supports them. You'd use, however, support which would be better suited for an argument against ESL courses.

If you are against full-immersion ESL courses because they alienate the non-native English speakers, discourage assimilation, and encourage attrition, then you might write a satire like this:

Though many people are vehemently against full-immersion ESL courses which pit non-native English speakers against their "English-only" speaking teacher, this method for teaching English is, actually, a really good idea. Not only does it create a very uncomfortable environment for the students but it alienates non-native English speakers, discourages assimilation, and encourages attrition.

One of the greatest things about full-immersion ESL courses is how they alienate non-native English speakers. These students are new to America, willingly embracing novel customs and hackneyed traditions. They want to succeed. Unfortunately, when they enroll in a public school which preaches full immersion, they get confused, they panic, and they feel displaced. This is alienation. And it is a great idea, for it embodies the heart of Social Darwinism, and it lets these immigrants know that America will not cater to their needs; in fact, America will go out of its way to make these people feel uncomfortable. Of course, many are of the opinion that education provides people with understanding, and understanding keeps people from doing "stupid things," like committing crimes. If these non-native English speakers do not receive an education and the understanding expected to accompany it, then the crime rate can be expected to rise. Yes, alienating these students is just one of the many reasons why full-immersion ESL courses are a really good idea.

Note: This writer should complete the satire by supporting his claim's two additional tiers and by offering his readers a hearty conclusion. Though this writer chooses not to pull from sources (articles, essays, interviews) in order to bolster his credibility, he would be encouraged to do so in his following paragraphs.

Here are two examples of effective satires, both written by students of critical thinking:

Gail Rankin
Professor Jones
English 1C
10 October 2000

Yo! Like What's Wrong Wif Ma Rap?

Although many people are against teaching Ebonics in schools, it is actually a very good idea. Children who grow up in poverty-stricken areas such as Oakland, California are raised in households where their parents probably have only a third-or-fourth-grade education themselves, and because of this, their understanding of Standard English is very limited. Thus, their inability to speak Standard English, and only speak Ebonics, is passed down to the child. State government and educators need to understand that these children need to be coddled by teaching them a substandard style of English instead of teaching the proper style of English. According to an article written by Leon W. Todd in *Education Magazine*, "Unfortunately, some attempts to legitimize such poor language habits as being a culturally legitimate African or English language do more harm than good" (177). But this harm *is* good. It is good because it permanently disables the kids in the classroom by making them ignorant to Standard English. Then when they go to a bookstore or library, they will not be able to pick up a book and read it. But this is okay too, for the more ignorant children we have in society, the greater the chance of violence and unemployment. This unemployment would then probably lead to careers as drug dealers or gang members, pimps or prostitutes. Career choices such as these do not require a real grasp of the English language. According to Todd's article, "Alternate language forms become disorders when a child can not recognize proper speech . . . [and] It matters little if the inappropriate speech pattern derives from poverty, rap music, hip hop culture . . . the problem still needs to be diagnosed as a major language disorder and/or learning disability so the child can receive the help needed to correct the situation" (177). But proper speech recognition is not all that necessary. After all, there are other children who will speak Ebonics, and they can segregate themselves from the rest of society because they will not be able to understand what the majority of the population is saying. In fact, they will completely miss out in the area of career development and socializing outside of their small "ebonic group." But this is okay because children who grow up in an Ebonics-only class will probably have to take jobs like flipping hamburgers at restaurants or sweeping floors at some large corporate building. But someone has to take the dirty jobs, so why not one of these kids?

Another good thing about teaching Ebonics to children is that it teaches down to children. As Jesse Jackson stated in an online article "The Ebonics Debate Moves to the Senate—January 23, 1997," "Now I'm very much aware that teaching children in schools in the inner cities and in poor neighborhoods all over the country, rural or inner city, has never been easy, and it never will be" (1). But since teaching children is difficult, why should the educational system bend over backwards to teach kids Standard English like the rest of the country when they can simply teach them their own "English" and never make the children strive for any real achievement. According to another online article from CNN entitled Oakland schools adopt 'Black English' policy written by Don Knapp, ". . . black students make up only 53 percent of the 52,000-student district"(2). Even though black children just barely make up half the population of the Oakland school district, Ebonics should still be taught because one of the major fallacies is that only African-Americans speak Ebonics. The truth is that Ebonics is a multi-cutural, multi-ethnic plague, finding itself in the speech of Asians, Mexicans, Whites, and Native Americans (who, technically, speak Pow-wow-onics, according to Leon W. Todd, who will not simply lump various ethnicities under one "Ebonic" umbrella).

Another good thing about teaching Ebonics in school would be the expense of researching the subject to know how to teach the dialect. This is great because it is a good way to waste money. Instead of using the funds available to improve the schools and bring in better quality teachers to teach these kids in poorer areas, the states can simply throw the cash away into an area that is completely unnecessary and will help to cripple children in their speech. Also, funds must be spent to train and certify teachers and counselors. This is, then, a great opportunity for the teachers and counselors to demand higher pay because of their dual qualification in language; this puts an even bigger stress on educators in the school districts to distribute more money to their teaching staff. Thus, after all the money is spent on teaching the teachers and staff the language of Ebonics, one must ask this question: what use is Ebonics to the children once they are grown and out of school?

Society has now produced a population of children that speaks defective English. But there are many educators in the Oakland, California school district that believe this is okay. Many people believe that Ebonics is the language many African-Americans speak, which some linguists liken to a language spoken in West Africa. Ebonics is derived from a combination of the words "ebony" and "phonics" or "black sounds." But again, as stated earlier, though African- Americans have been fortunate enough to wear the Ebonics stigma, one need simply turn on the television and flip to an episode of "Jerry Springer" to see that people from all ethnic groups speak fluent Ebonics. Hence, instead of combating this equal-opportunity "language" by forcing these people to endure pure English-immersion classes, ones which force the children to speak proper English so they can adequately assimilate in school, school officials would rather teach these children street slang so they can be further hindered in life.

But handicapping children for life is why Ebonics should be taught in schools. It disables them in the classroom and hinders their learning process because they will not be able to read proper English. They will have faulty notions that everyone in this whole-wide world speaks the same as they, but once they grow up they will realize they were sadly mistaken, and their career paths will be limited. Their socialization will be limited to a small group of Ebonics-speaking friends, thus forcing them to be segregated from most of society. Then these children will be forced to move to other areas where other Ebonics-speaking people live. They can create their own town of Ebonics-literate people such as the communities created for Cubans called Little Havana in Miami, or Little Saigon in Garden Grove, California for the Vietnamese people. Now, in Oakland, the state of California could add another of these communities named Little Ebony.

Works Cited

Jackson, Jesse. "Online NewsHour: The Debate Moves to the Senate." http://www9.cnn.com/US/9612/30/ebonics/index.html (30 Dec. 1996).
Knapp, Don. "CNN—Oakland School Adopts 'Black English' Policy." http://www5.cnn.com/US/9612/19/black.english/index.html (19 Dec. 1996).
Todd, Leon W. "Ebonics." *Education Magazine*. Winter 1997: 177–181.

Note: Gail does a fine job of qualifying her argument so that she does not step on "ethnic toes." Also, she uses outside support to bolster her satire's credibility. And while she clearly makes many outlandish claims, they are made with a tone representative of a serious, sardonic individual.

Kriselle Gan
Professor Jones
English 1C
10 October 2000

Praising the SAT

"The SAT occupies a central place in the American psyche, lying at the terrifying intersection of ability, class and pride," writes John Cloud, a reporter for the education sector of Time.com. The SAT was first used experimentally in 1926 and continued to struggle to build its reputation shortly after World War II. The College Board, the gov-

erning authority of the controversial SAT, which stood for Standardized Aptitude Test, desperately wanted the University of California
to adopt the test as a requirement for admission to supposedly
raise the level of standard for incoming students. Nicholas Lemann,
a big SAT advocate and the author of "The Big Test," stated: "If they
drop the SAT, we will lose a great deal more than the revenue; we will
suffer a damaging blow to our prestige." Thus, while many argue that
the SAT is inconsequential, others firmly believe that it should be required, for it maintains standards of excellence in America's universities. Therefore, the SAT should be used as a measure of knowledge
and potential for college admission since it gives admissions officers
a consistent, nationally recognized standard.

First, the SAT is unfair. One argument that emerged in the 1970s
was that the test was inherently biased against African-Americans
and Latinos whose average scores were lower than those of Caucasian students. The SAT measures the skill and ability in the
preparation prior to taking the test-a skill that could be easily developed with expensive coaching and pampering SAT courses. Sta-
tistically, African-American and Latino families, on the average,
have shown a lower household income, and this provides a direct cor-
relation as to why their children score lower on the SAT. Princeton
Review, a pioneer in the SAT course industry, charges $799–$899

for six-week classes that teach students how to approach the SAT in order to raise their scores. However, because many families already struggle to make that payment on their monthly mortgage, they don't have an extra $899 to invest in their child's "potential" future. Of course, how else would the SAT school industry adroitly amass $400 million in revenue in 1999 if not for the overanxious, college-bound-soldier who needed to take the SAT because "kids [like him] live and die by what they score on that three-hour test . . . Or at least they think so," comments Ray Brown, dean of admissions at Texas Christian University. An SAT score accurately represents how well students do under pressure, how much use they've made of their parents' investments, and how well they regurgitate months of harvested knowledge into a productive ninety-minute block of time. This is precisely why this three-hour test should be the ultimate measure of intelligence and should play a crucial role in determining a student's academic fate.

Second, the SAT should be used, for it fails to measure anything meaningful. Few really argue that the SAT serves as an intelligence test anymore, and, therefore, it is commonly referred to as an "assessment test." Even President Kurt Landgraf of the Educational Testing Service, the company that designs the SAT under contract from the College Board, claimed the nature of the test: "It's a measure of a student's ability to answer questions at a given place and time." The test is not indicative of a person's intelligence, personality, nor diligence and, thus, offers colleges an excellent method to adequately assess an applicant's potential success. Both Tressa McAllister, a student at Muhlenberg College, and Laila Kouri of Westpot, Conn., both agree that the SAT isn't fair. McAllister told CNN that she didn't agree with the SAT because it only measures one's performance on a specific day on a specific test. Laila Kouri, on the contrary, had enrolled into an expensive coaching class and had seen the disparity that the SAT fostered. She had known people to blow off classes and fail in school and, yet, take the SAT and score surprisingly well. Such inconsistencies, however, simply endorse the notion that the SAT is clearly a measure of one's knowledge and, thus, reaffirms why it should be used as a gauge to measure a student's potential in his college and post-college success.

Another reason why the SAT should be used to determine a student's academic fate is because the test is culturally biased in favor of Anglo-Americans. For example, an "Americanized" story like The Wizard of Oz is a common bedtime story told to children in the United States; however, people from other ethnic groups are often not as familiar with Dorothy, Toto, and their journey along the Yellow-brick Road. Nevertheless, these cultural predilections could not possibly materialize, for "The SAT is probably the most thoroughly researched test in history," affirms College Board President Gatson

Caperton. It's supposedly designed to evaluate each student that takes the test in a fair and equal manner and, thus, allows for an adequate, indubitable indication of a student's knowledge and future success. Thus, with the SAT being as reputable as it is, the test could provide colleges with concrete, reliable information, reaffirming why a student's admission should heavily rely on his SAT score.

Society has produced a population of students eager to go only to the best universities our country has to offer, and, thus, it is rational to require these students to take the SAT. Regardless of the fact that the psychologist who runs the University of California believes that "the test hurls kids into months of practicing word games and math riddles at the expense of studying chemistry or poetry," the pressure continues to prime students' minds with "pedagogical phantoms instead of real learning." Despite the trauma and stress that the SAT causes many aspiring college-bound students, "that which does not kill them only serves to make them stronger." Even conservatives at the *Weekly Standard* have written about how the SAT has "shaped—and misshaped—modern American life." Students' childhoods are spent in classrooms learning Latin roots and coming in Saturday mornings to take their weekly practice test only to stay afterward to analyze what they've done wrong and how to improve on next week's test. Clearly, the SAT adds structure and requires immeasurable amounts of concentration and discipline, further substantiating the responsibly-noted assertion that a musician's time and devotion shouldn't be spend writing a concerto and a scientist's time shouldn't be spent playing in the physics lab; instead, both the aspiring Mozart and the next Einstein should confine themselves to the corner of the library, entertaining word games and solving math riddles.

The SAT assesses students' accumulated knowledge rather than their possibly advantageous genetics. This reaffirms the idea that the SAT is a measurement of knowledge, and its applications and should, therefore, be used as a significant factor when college admissions officers decide to admit or reject applicants. This is supported by Lemann when he states: "You want to measure people on something they've done, not on supposedly innate abilities." By "something they've done," he is referring to the amount of SAT classes the son of a wealthy doctor has attended or how much he has spent on that private tutor that came over to the house everyday after school rather than the natural talents possessed by the inner-city student who excels in tennis and whose love of Shakespeare and music demands hours of practice and refinement.

Students who do not do well on biased, unfair, and meaningless tests clearly do not have their priorities focused and, thus, need their limits set for them, for it would not be fair to take away one of the few tests that clearly defines one's "different educational opportunities . . . ," comments Donald Stewart, the first African-American to hold the job of College Board president. He continues: "Poor kids are getting a lousy education. It's as simple as that." For some students, the SAT has become a handicap in their opportunity to attend the country's finest universities and mingle with elite social circles. Therefore, the SAT should be used as a measurement of garnered knowledge for college admissions, for it not only provides a clear-cut disparity between families of differing income levels but also recognizes students who can perform exceptionally well at least three hours in their life. This is expected; otherwise, those countless hours of analogies, word problems, and reading comprehension sections devoted to the SAT would have been in vain.

Works Cited

Cloud, John. "Should SATs Matter?" http://www.time.com/time/education/article10,8599,1321-1,00.html (3 Oct. 2001).

"Standardized Tests Under Fire." http://www4.cnn.com/us/9906/15/standardized.tests/ (15 June 1999).

Note: Kriselle's satire is well-constructed for many reasons. First of all, it adheres to a formal, academic tone and is, hence, devoid of colloquialisms (contractions, street vernacular or "slang," inane questions) and replete with seemingly credible examples to advance each assertion. Also, she organizes her satire responsibly, clearly delegating the same task to each body paragraph. (Of course, each body paragraph's primal urge should be to directly advance the argument's claim.)

Kriselle also succeeds in delineating between a stated and implied claim. Clearly, the support she'd normally use to advance her implied claim is what she's using to advance her stated claim; this creates the desired satirical effect. Critical thinkers should note that the satire, because it's often an unfamiliar rhetorical mode to students, is extremely challenging. One challenge is simply avoiding the urge to try one's hand at comedy. Remember, satires (at least in this context) are not being assessed based on their comedic value. The goal is not to be funny but, rather, to articulate a stated claim, support it by using what would normally be used to support the implied claim, and use such an odd coupling to engage readers.

Applications

After choosing an issue, write a satire. Make sure to state your claim. Though you are free to choose your own, these claims have been provided for you:

1. Mentally defective men and women should be sterilized or otherwise prevented from producing children. See *eugenics.*
2. Bilingual instruction should not be permitted in the public schools.
3. Marijuana should be legalized.
4. Whale hunting should be banned by international law.
5. Capital punishment should be practiced in the United States.
6. Immigration to the United States should never be allowed.
7. Welfare is a just form of compensation.
8. Animal experimentation is terrific.
9. HMOs are excellent for patients and doctors.
10. We need the media. If we didn't have them, the rising bulimic/anorexic rate in America might actually experience its first decline in decades.
11. Ebonics should be taught in all schools.

Helpful Hints

- Write a traditional argument first. Then, make changes to it to fit the satirical format.

- Identify your implied claim. (It will, most likely, be the opposite of your stated claim.) Next, find much support to advance your implied claim. Finally, employ that support, using it to, technically, support your stated claim (this will seem illogical; however, simply note how Gail Rankin and Kriselle Gan, in the student examples, used support that would be much better suited for their implied claims as opposed to their stated claims).
- Do not deviate from formal academic discourse. The satire is not an opportunity for students to unveil their comedic prowess. Instead, it is an opportunity to compose a serious essay about a serious issue or problem; since the supporting elements, however, would more aptly advance a much different claim, readers should be fascinated by the argument's peculiar, satirical nature.

Observations

Before you begin reading the next chapter, take some time to reflect on what you learned in Chapter 8. Specifically, note what you think about what you learned, for in the spirit of promoting consciousness, it is essential that you not only become aware of your observations but that you commit them to paper. Use these observations like one would use a journal: as a tool for measuring growth and insight.

Preliminary Observations

_____

_____

_____

_____

_____

_____

_____

_____

Refined Observations

_____

_____

_____

_____

_____

_____

_____

_____

New Observations

The Debate

One could argue that any person taking a stand against immigration whose lineage does not stem from indigenous people should be diagnosed with cognitive dissonance. Others, however, could argue that it is the responsibility of the people who currently inhabit an area to protect it from anything which could lead to its destruction. In this case, Death is disguised as overpopulation. Specifically, in dense areas like Los Angeles, New York, Chicago, Portland, and Seattle, overpopulation has reared its ugly head in public school classrooms. And since parents, arguably, want the best for their children, they may be justified in their beliefs that first-generation immigrants and the children of first-generation immigrants are lowering the learning curves of the students for which the schools were originally built. But is this a reasonable argument?

Others are not as concerned with overpopulation as they are with a "let's take care of our own first, and then we will open our doors" mentality. People cite ghettos, malnourished children, overcrowded emergency rooms, and rising crime. Some even argue that immigrants revoke Americans of their rightful "Dream," the promise that it is possible to work hard and become a millionaire and live "the good life." (According to one statistic, first-generation immigrants are four times more

likely to become millionaires than those born in America.) Others argue, however, that there are plenty of American Dreams for people with the right work ethic.

Others are not as concerned with having their American Dream stolen as they are with the possibility of facing unemployment because their prospective jobs were filled by recent immigrants. The opposition, however, argues that many immigrants fill the jobs most Americans wouldn't consider anyway: working in fields, washing cars, mowing lawns, selling fruit.

Though many people have opinions on immigration, how many have *informed* opinions? Have you ever ruminated on this issue? Have you sufficiently investigated and interpreted before rendering a judgment? Read the following essays with the goal of formulating a reasonable claim addressing a complex issue.

The New Colossus

Emma Lazarus

• •

Emma Lazarus (1849–1887) was a Russian-born poet who settled in New York. Her works include Admetus and Other Poems *(1871),* Alide *(1874),* Songs of the Semite *(1882), and* By the Waters of Babylon *(1887). But of all her works, none is so famous as her sonnet to the Statue of Liberty. Now carved on the statue's pedestal, the poem was first published in 1883.*

• • • • • • • • •

Not like the brazen giant of Greek fame,
With conquering limbs astride from land to land;
Here at our sea-washed, sunset gates shall stand
A mighty woman with a torch, whose flame
Is the imprisoned lightning, and her name
Mother of Exiles. From her beacon-hand
Glows world-wide welcome; her mild eyes command
The air-bridged harbor that twin cities frame.
"Keep, ancient lands, your storied pomp!" cries she
With silent lips. "Give me your tired, your poor,
Your huddled masses yearning to breathe free,
The wretched refuse of your teeming shore.
Send these, the homeless, tempest-tost to me,
I lift my lamp beside the golden door!"

• •

From *The New Colossus* by Emma Lazarus, 1883.

Gatecrashers

Michael Kinsley

● ●

Responding to growing concerns about immigration, Michael Kinsley published the following editorial on December 28, 1992. A Harvard-educated attorney who was cohost of CNN's Crossfire, *Kinsley is senior editor of* The New Republic, *a magazine that usually reflects liberal political opinions.*

● ● ● ● ● ● ● ● ● ●

A new Census Bureau report predicts that there will be 383 million Americans in the year 2050. That's 128 million more than there are now, and 83 million more than the bureau was predicting just four years ago, when it appeared that the U.S. population would peak and stabilize at around 300 million.

Part of the startling upward revision reflects an unexpected increase in the birthrate. But most of it is due to an increase in immigration. The Census Bureau expects an average of 880,000 new arrivals a year, legal and illegal. By 2050 a fifth of the American population will be folks who arrived here after 1991 and their children. Almost half the population (47 percent) will be "minority"—black, Asian, Hispanic, Native American—compared with just a quarter today.

Immigration has not been much of a political issue lately. In fact a 1990 law increasing the annual legal quota by 40 percent passed almost unnoticed. And there's been little fuss over the total failure of the hotly contested 1986 immigration reform—which for the first time made it a crime to employ illegal aliens—to achieve its purpose of reducing illegal immigration.

But the politics of immigration may be heating up. And the political coloration of anti-immigrant sentiment may be changing too.

Despite the traditional association of the Democratic Party with immigrant groups, what little opposition there has been to immigration in recent years has come vaguely from the left. Some environmentalists believe that immigrants contribute to overpopulation and strain the nation's natural resources. And some blacks (and white sympathizers) worry that immigrants are stealing opportunities from America's oldest and still most down-trodden minority.

What's new, though, is the re-emergence of anti-immigrant sentiment on the right. Here it takes the traditional form of concern about the nation's ethnic character. This fits in with other social concerns about matters like multiculturalism and even gay rights: a sense that some classic and comfortable image of America is being changed before our eyes.

Presidential candidate Pat Buchanan sometimes included immigration in his riffs on this general theme. And the *National Review* (edited by an immigrant—although only from Britain) ran a long cover story (by another immigrant from Britain) condemning immigration as a liberal elitist plot and predicting an America of "ethnic strife . . . dual loyalties . . . collapsing like the Tower of Babel" if the foreign hordes aren't kept out. ("Tired? Poor? Huddled? Tempest-Tossed?" asked the witty cover. "Try Australia.") Free market capitalism itself, the author suggests at one point, may depend on the continued predominance of Anglo-Saxon stock.

There have been Americans who feared that our country is "running out of room" since the frontier closed off more than a century ago. Although 128 million extra people in the next six decades sounds like an awful lot, that is no greater than the population increase over the past six decades. (And it's a much smaller proportional increase.) Only environmentalist zealots could believe that America would be better off if our population were still only 125 million—even accepting the complacent assumption that everyone reading this column would be one of the lucky 125 million.

There is no answer to the argument that "at some point" the country becomes too crowded, but there's no particular reason to believe we're at that point yet. Germany, with less than a third of America's population in a far smaller area, is currently accepting new arrivals in almost the same volume.

Germany may not seem the happiest example for my side of the immigration argument. There, immigration is straining the social fabric and producing riots and violence by neo-Nazi punks. Not to defend such xenophobic outrages, but Germany is different from the

United States. Like most countries in the world (Israel, to pick a sensitive example), its sense of nationhood has a large ethnic component. This is neither good nor evil; it's just a fact. Although any civilized nation should be prepared to take in refugees from oppression, the "otherness" of foreigners will always be more vivid elsewhere than in America. In other countries, concern about diluting the nation's ethnic stock even has a certain validity.

Such concerns have no validity in America. In fact, they are un-American. If applied in earlier times, when they were raised with equal passion, they would have excluded the ancestors of many who make the ethnic/cultural preservation argument today. The anti-immigration literature seems to regard this point as some kind of cheap shot. But I cannot see why.

On the economic effects of immigration, there are studies to suit every taste. Immigrants take jobs from poor Americans; or they go on welfare and bloat the tax bill; or both; or neither. Basic economic logic suggests that even when a new arrival "takes" a job, the money he earns and spends will in turn create a job or so. The more the merrier is a tenet of capitalism dating back to Adam Smith, and nothing I've seen disproves it.

The propaganda from FAIR (Federation for American Immigration Reform, the liberal anti-immigration lobby) on these issues is unpersuasive because it tends to "prove too much" as the lawyers say. With a straight face, FAIR compares immigration to slavery and child labor, as if the trouble with these practices were the burden they placed on rival sources of labor. In one recent broadside FAIR's executive director, Dan Stein, suggests that America should have curtailed immigration after the Civil War in order to increase economic opportunities for ex-slaves. Whether this would actually have benefited blacks or not, it might have spared us Dan Stein.

The emerging case for curtailing immigration has many byways. There's the argument that we need "time to digest" the immigrant wave of the past couple of decades, just as previous waves were followed by periods of low immigration. There's the argument that today's ethnic assertiveness and social welfare apparatus mean that the machinery of assimilation no longer works to turn immigrants into middle-class Americans. There's the undeniable fact that instant communication and cheap transportation have eroded the natural restraints of distance and ignorance on the demand for places in America.

There are counterarguments to all these points, and others. And counter-counterarguments. No one can know the effect of future large-scale immigration on our country. It has always been beneficial in the past, but that's no guarantee it will be so in the future. The previous tenant of this column, the late Richard Strout believed passionately that America's achievement of a liberal welfare state depended on levels of both affluence and social cohesion that were threatened by large-scale immigration.

Immigration is a subject, I suspect, of which very few opinions are changed because of arguments or statistics. It's almost a matter of faith. Your views of immigration depend on your sense of what makes America America. For some it's endless open spaces. For some it's a demographic image frozen in time. For some that stuff on the Statue of Liberty still plucks a chord. All these visions of America have a large component of fantasy. But I know which fantasy I prefer.

• •

We Should Always Lift Our Lamp to the World

Susan Roosevelt Weld and William F. Weld

• •

Susan Roosevelt Weld is a research fellow in East Asian Legal Studies at Harvard University Law School. William F. Weld is governor of Massachusetts. This essay appeared in the Boston Globe *on January 11, 1996.*

• • • • • • • • •

From the building of the railroads to the building of space age technology, immigrants have left their imprint on our nation and our commonwealth. They have contributed to our art, religion, science, education, medicine, business, theater, and every aspect of the culture that is known throughout the world as American. There can be no question that the story of the United States is the story of immigration.

Lately, we have been amazed at the amount of confusion that surrounds immigration. Almost all Americans recognize the value of past immigration; however, many are uncertain of the value of immigration today. They point with pride to ancestors who came here with full hearts and empty pockets, who prospered and contributed mightily to the quality of life that all Americans enjoy today.

At the same time, many of them wonder if changing times have modified America's needs. Several bills before Congress reflect the idea that immigrants are no longer a tremendous national advantage but instead are a liability [that] must be controlled.

Is the United States now so self-sufficient, so rich, and so powerful that we no longer need immigrants?

We do not think so. We look at an economy that is rapidly becoming global, and we recognize the value of speaking more than one language. We look at the information highway, and we recognize that the world is getting smaller and the distances among continents are shrinking. More than ever, we see the need for new ideas, new problem-solving skills, new Americans.

But, we are asked, do immigrants impose an intolerable burden on our economy? Are we looking at an increase in immigration that is unprecedented in the history of our nation? Studies say otherwise. Census data show that immigrants were nearly 15 percent of our population in 1910; today they are 8 percent. Although the U.S. population has tripled during that time, the immigrant population has not doubled.

Other generally accepted "facts" about immigration are not supported by the figures. For example:

- A 1993 poll indicates that 70 percent of Americans think that "most of the people who have moved to the United States in the last few years are here illegally." The Urban Institute, however, estimates that in 1993 there were about 11 million aliens, of whom 2.5 million were undocumented.
- Many people believe that today's immigrants are not as well educated as native-born Americans. According to census figures, however, while more immigrants have not completed high school than natives, they are twice as likely to hold a Ph.D.
- Although it is widely believed that immigrants put people out of work, the Manhattan Institute tells us that of the ten states with the highest immigrant populations, only one—Illinois—is among the ten highest unemployment states. Immigrants start businesses, pay taxes, purchase goods and services, and create jobs.
- Nor are immigrants overloading our state prisons. A 1991 survey by the National Institute of Corrections showed that 4 percent of state prison populations are aliens. Federal prisons do have a higher percentage (25 percent) of aliens, but most are international drug smugglers and other border-hopping felons, not immigrants.
- There is a persistent belief that immigrants use far more welfare than the native-born. Actually, according to the Urban Institute, 2.3 percent of immigrants use these services, as opposed to 3.3 percent of natives. Only if you factor in refugees escaping intol-

erable conditions in their home countries does the percentage go higher, and refugees and asylum-seekers are allowed public benefits for eight months only. Immigrants generate $285 billion in income and pay more than $70 billion in taxes—far greater sums than the $5.7 billion they use in public assistance.

Any way you look at it, the economic evidence is overwhelming: Newcomers support themselves through work, not welfare.

We therefore question the wisdom of provisions in Congress's welfare compromise that would make legal immigrants ineligible for most federal social services for five years after their arrival. Legal immigrants should enjoy rights and protections that are not available to those who break the law to come here. We believe that denying ordinary citizen benefits to future American citizens is not only ungenerous and unwelcoming, but also unnecessary.

Those who sponsor immigrants pledge to take financial responsibility for them through a process called "deeming." If deeming were enforced, there would be little need to yank away the social safety net from legal arrivals. And, except in cases when it would tie immigrants to sponsors who batter them or when the sponsor is in financial distress, deeming should be enforced.

Another proposal before Congress would eliminate the "national interest waiver" that eases immigration for those with special skills and would make it much more difficult and expensive for employers to hire recent graduates of American universities. Right now, the best of these students are often hired by the best of our high-tech firms. If we start telling MIT Ph.D's that their employment future in the United States is uncertain, we're not improving the economy for the native-born, we're sending badly needed talent straight to our global competitors; we're depriving our businesses of the whizzes that can help them grow; and we're shrinking opportunities for everyone. We believe this proposal should be dumped into the "cutting off your nose to spite your face" file and promptly forgotten.

Many people believe that unlike the hard-working, eager-to-learn, grateful immigrants of the past, today's newcomers do not want to speak English, that they cling to their old cultures and tend to reject American society and culture. Our experience has been the opposite. We find that despite differences in culture and language, today's immigrants quickly recognize that they must learn English if they want to get ahead.

We also find that to an amazing degree, they share the most traditional of American values: a disciplined work ethic, strong family ties, religious values, an inclination toward entrepreneurship, respect for education, personal independence, appreciation of democracy and a determination that—whatever it takes, whatever sacrifices may be called for, whatever deprivations must be endured—their children will have a better life.

They share with other Americans a conviction that they and their children are smart enough, tough enough, and brave enough to answer questions, solve problems, avert disasters, and ultimately not only flourish and thrive themselves, but help bring prosperity and honor to their new country.

And they are right. Immigrants are not helpless victims relying on our charity and good will—far from it! They are survivors. It takes courage, creativity, determination, and commitment to abandon cherished possessions and people, leave the known for the unknown, cross unfamiliar territory, and set up a new life in a new land. It is a tribute to the indomitable human spirit that so many people continue to do this so well.

To those who say that the time has come to extinguish Lady Liberty's lamp and to slam shut the golden door, we say nonsense. Did you ever notice how, in the Olympic Games, the Norwegians look like Norwegians, the Chinese look like Chinese, the Ethiopians look like Ethiopians, the Spaniards look like Spaniards, and the Americans look like everybody?

There is a reason for this: Americans are everybody. America is still a young country, somewhat brash perhaps, occasionally prone to stumble and recover, and then stumble and recover again. But the United States possesses a vigor and a record for accomplishment that has prompted many an Old World aristocrat to drop his monocle and say, "Wow!"

Diversity has played a significant role in our success. We believe, as surely as we believe anything, that immigration is good for the United States and Massachusetts. We welcome new Americans and the legacy they bring with them. We firmly believe that with the help of our new Americans, the United States will do far more than survive: We will grow and mature, and we will witness the unfolding of a nation that is stronger, wiser, fairer, braver, kinder, and more prosperous than anything heretofore seen. We will be honored to be part of it.

• •

Immigration Straight-Talk

William Raspberry

• •

This column by William Raspberry, a syndicated columnist, appeared in the Boston Globe *on December 13, 1995.*

• • • • • • • • •

America, as Jim Sleeper of the New York Daily News once noted, is one of the few places where a charge of racial or ethnic bigotry is a serious indictment.

Even when Americans are being unfair to one group or another, they are at pains to protest that their objective is inclusion, not exclusion—that they believe in America as a welcoming place for all who share her ideals.

This desire not to be seen as bigoted has helped to change perceptions, laws, and attitudes. It has also kept at least one issue virtually off the table: immigration.

We have been worried about the deleterious effects of uncontrolled immigration for a long time, yet we've been fearful of speaking plainly about it lest we be viewed as bigots. We have seen the social costs of immigration (overcrowding and depressed wages, to name two). At least one poll found that some two-thirds of Hispanics—the category usually evoked by the phrase "immigration problem"—believe we're admitting too many immigrants.

Why is straight talk on the subject so difficult? One explanation may lie in the reaction to California's recent passage of Proposition 187—a decision by the voters there that they will no longer pay for the health, education, and welfare of *illegal* aliens.

A fair number of liberals have attacked the vote as "immigrant bashing," and at least two conservatives—Jack Kemp and Bill Bennett—called it "an ugly antipathy toward all immigrants."

As William B. Dickinson of the Biocentric Institute put it: "Those who favor open borders have long tried—with considerable success—to blur the distinction between legal and illegal immigrants. America's tradition as an immigrant nation, its congenital sympathy for underdogs, and its less-principled desire for an endless supply of cheap labor make it easy to excuse poor people who slip across our borders in the dead of night. Those of us who support an orderly immigration policy based on law find ourselves demonized as bigots, racists or nativists."

Even that quintessential liberal Barbara Jordan came in for her share of knocks when the commission she headed called for an end to public aid for illegal immigrants aside from immunizations and emergency food and health care.

It's easy enough to see what drove the Californians. The presence of the illegals in California (and in dozens of other cities) is the result of the failure of the federal government to keep them out. This same government, through the federal courts, has ruled that the state has the duty to provide services (including health, education, and welfare) for people whose very presence here is a violation of the law. But the states get little help from Washington in paying for these services, and the feds, though recently better at enforcing the borders, seem unable to deport the illegals they arrest here.

But passing Proposition 187 isn't the end of the matter. In the first place, unless the Supreme Court overturns its earlier ruling, California state law will not relieve Californians of the burden of educating the children of illegals (or undocumented workers, as the gentler, less accurate phrase has it). More importantly, it's not clear, upon sober reflection, that California has an interest in keeping large numbers of its residents poor and hungry and ignorant.

A counter argument is used by antiwelfare advocates: Harsh treatment of present illegals will seem inhumane, but generosity will only increase their numbers.

Dickinson, like Mortimer Zuckerman of *U.S. News,* argues that it's time to revamp American immigration law across the board—including those bedeviling questions of which country's immigrants should be favored, what skills should be required of those admitted, and how many immigrants are too many.

Certainly it seems reasonable to rethink the 1990 liberalization of the rules that allow immigrants to send home for members of their families, very broadly defined—and to reconsider as well the notion (unique to the United States?) that anyone born here is automatically a U.S. citizen.

But for now, I'd be happy to hear serious and candid discussion of the one problem that everybody acknowledges is a problem: illegal immigration.

As Zuckerman noted, these are the people who "have, by definition, broken the law, and they are guilty of an ethical breach as well: They have jumped the line of people patiently waiting for years for their visas."

Does it really make sense for the federal government to reward these violaters of law and civility with mandated services for themselves and their children, paid for by money-short states with no choice in the matter?

Can't we put aside our charges of bigotry and at least talk about it?

• •

Unchecked Immigration

Peter Brimelow

• •

Peter Brimelow is a senior editor of National Review *and* Forbes *magazine. This excerpt is from the November 1995 edition of* Commentary.

• • • • • • • • • •

I am not at all relaxed . . . about problems posed to the American national project by what the editors call, quite accurately, "unchecked immigration." The facts here are compelling. But they are not widely understood because of the romantic haze, intellectual inertia, and downright dishonesty that surrounds the subject.

The 1965 Immigration Act triggered an influx of historically high proportions, particularly compared to current U.S. birth rates. Thus the Census Bureau projects that Americans, left to themselves, are sta-bilizing their population around 250 to 260 million. But the govern-ment is in effect second-guessing them through immigration policy. If present trends continue, the U.S. population will reach 390 million by 2050. More than 130 million will be post-1970 immigrants and their descendants. Because the 1965 Act arbitrarily choked off immigration from Europe, this influx has been almost all from the Third World. So by 2050, whites, who were 90 percent of the population as recently as 1960, will be on the verge of becoming a minority.

This is a demographic transformation without precedent in the history of the world. It is incumbent on those who favor it to explain what makes them think it is going to work—and why they want to transform the American nation as it had evolved by 1965.

Because the new arrangements are clearly not working at the mo-ment. The 1990 Census revealed that native-born Americans, both black and white, were fleeing the immigrant-favored areas, where they were being replaced on an almost one-for-one basis by immigrants, and going to entirely separate sections of the country—whites to the white heartland of the Midwest, the Pacific Northwest, and so on; blacks to the black areas of the South, Atlanta, Washington, D.C., and so on.

The country is coming apart ethnically under the impact of the enormous influx. This must ultimately raise what might be called the National Question: Is America still that interlacing of ethnicity and culture that we call a nation—and can the American nation-state, the political expression of that nation, survive?

All of the unraveling that the editors instance—multiculturalism, dissolution of shared values, increased stratification—is exacerbated, at the very least, by immigration. This is not to say that immigration necessarily caused these policies, a point immigration enthusiasts invariably miss. "The fault, dear Peter, lies not in our immigrants but in ourselves," *New York Post* columnist Maggie Gallagher wrote in what was one of the nicer reactions to my arguments. But here's the rub: If there is a rainstorm when you have a cold, you stay indoors.

Unless there is another pause for assimilation, as there have been many times in the past, immigration will add to America's latent sectionalism and ultimately break the country up like the late Roman empire—a crisis as utterly unexpected as World War I by the American political elite, both Left and Right.

Illegal immigration should be ended with a second Operation Wetback, as the Eisenhower administration ended the similar illegal-immigration crisis of the 1950s: Seal the borders, deport the illegals already here. Legal immigration should be halted with a five- or ten-year moratorium: no net immigration, with admissions for hardship cases or needed skills balancing the 200,000 legal residents who leave each year. During that moratorium, there should be a debate in which Americans would be asked what they want—as they have not yet been. Immigration might then be resumed, at moderate levels, with an emphasis on skills, and on evidence of cultural compatibility such as speaking English.

• •

Geniuses from Abroad

George Gilder

• •

George Gilder is a fellow at Seattle's Discovery Institute. This column appeared in the Wall Street Journal *on December 18, 1995.*

• • • • • • • •

The current immigration debate founders on ignorance of one huge fact: Without immigration, the U.S. would not exist as a world power. Without immigration, the U.S. could not have produced the computerized weapons that induced the Soviet Union to surrender in the arms race. Without immigration, the U.S. could not have built the atomic bomb during World War II, or the hydrogen bomb in the early 1950s, or the MIRVs in the 1970s or the cruise missiles for the Gulf War in the 1990s.

Today, immigrants are vital not only for targeted military projects but also for the wide range of leading-edge ventures in an information age economy. No less than military superiority in previous eras, U.S. industrial dominance and high standards of living today depend on outsiders.

Every high-technology company, big or small is like a Manhattan Project. All must mobilize the personnel best trained and most able to perform a specific function, and deliver a product within a window of opportunity as fateful and remorseless as a war deadline. This requires access to the small elite of human beings in the world capable of pioneering these new scientific and engineering frontiers. For many specialized high-technology tasks, the pool of potential talent around the world numbers about 10 people, or even fewer.

The Right People

If you are running such a technology company, you will quickly discover that the majority of this cognitive elite are not citizens of your country. Unless you can find the right people wherever they may be, you will not be able to launch the exotic innovation that changes the world. Unless you can fill the key technology jobs, you will not create any other jobs at all, and your country will forgo the cycle of new products, skills, and businesses that sustain a world-leading standard of living.

Discussing the impact of immigration, economists and their followers are beady-eyed gnatcatchers, experts on the movement of cabbage pickers and au pair girls and the possible impact of Cubans on Miami wage levels. But like hunters in a cartoon, they ignore the tyrannosaurus rex crouching behind them. Thus sophisticated analysts, such as George Borjas of the University of California, San Diego, and artful writers, such as Peter Brimelow, conclude that the impact of immigration on the U.S. economy is slight or negligible.

In fact, the evidence is overwhelming and undeniable; it is all around us, in a spate of inventions and technical advances, from microwaves and air bags to digital cable and satellite television, from home computers and air conditioners to cellular phones and life saving pharmaceuticals and medical devices. Without immigration over the last 50 years, I would estimate that the U.S. real living standards would be at least 40% lower.

The underplaying of immigration as an economic force stems from a basic flaw in macroeconomic analysis. Economists fail to account for the indispensable qualitative effects of genius. Almost by definition, genius is the ability to generate unique products and concepts and bring them to fruition. Geniuses are literally thousands of times more productive than the rest of us. We all depend on them for our livelihoods and opportunities.

The feats of genius are necessarily difficult to identify or predict, except in retrospect. But judging from the very rough metric of awards of mathematical doctorates and other rigorous scientific and engineering degrees, prizes, patents, and publications, about a third of the geniuses in the U.S. are foreign born, and another 20% are the offspring of immigrants. A third of all American Nobel Prize winners, for example, were born overseas.

A stellar example of these elites in action is Silicon Valley in California. Silicon Valley companies have reduced the price of computer

MIPs and memory bits by a factor of some 10,000 in 2 1/2 decades. Although mainstream economists neglect to measure the qualitative impact of these innovations, most of the new value in the world economy over the last decade has stemmed, directly or indirectly, from the semiconductor and computer industries, both hardware and software.

Consider Intel Corp. Together with its parent, Fairchild Semiconductor, Intel developed the basic processes of microchip manufacture and created dynamic and static random access memory. In other words, Intel laid the foundations for the personal computer revolution and scores of other chip-based industries that employ the vast bulk of U.S. engineers today.

Two American born geniuses, Robert Noyce and Gordon Moore, were key founders of Fairchild and Intel. But their achievements would have been impossible without the help of Jean Hourni, inventor of planar processing; Dov Frohmann-Benchkowski, inventor of electrically erasable programmable ROMs; Federico Faggin, inventor of silicon gate technology and builder of the first microprocessor; Mayatoshi Shima, layout designer of key 8086 family devices; and of course Andrew Grove, the company's now revered CEO who solved several intractable problems of the metal oxide silicon technology at the heart of Intel's growth. All these Intel engineers—and hundreds of other key contributors—were immigrants.

The pattern at Intel was repeated throughout Silicon Valley, from National Semiconductor and Advanced Micro Devices to Applied Materials, LSI Logic, Actel, Atmel, Integrated Device Technologies, Xicor, Cypress, Sun Microsystems and Hewlett-Packard, all of which from the outset heavily depended on immigrants in the laboratories and on engineering work benches. LSI, IDT, Actel, Atmel, Xicor, and Sun were all founded or led by immigrants. Today, fully one-third of all the engineers in Silicon Valley are foreign born.

Now, with Silicon Valleys proliferating throughout the U.S. economy, with Silicon Deserts, Prairies, Mountains, and even Alleys being hopefully launched from Manhattan to Oregon, immigration becomes ever more vital to the future of the U.S. economy. And microchips are just the beginning. On the foundation of silicon have arisen world-leading software and medical equipment industries almost equally dependent on immigrants. As spearhead of the fastest growing U.S. industry, software, Microsoft offers some of the most coveted jobs in the U.S. economy. But for vital functions, it still must turn to immigrants for 5% of its domestic work force, despite the difficult and expensive legal procedures required to import an alien.

Freedom of Enterprise

In recent congressional testimony, Ira Rubenstein, a Microsoft attorney, declared that immigration bars could jeopardize the 58 percent of its revenue generated overseas, threaten American dominance of advance "client-server" business applications, and render "stillborn" the information superhighway. In particular, Corning and other producers of fiber-optic technology have faced a severe shortage of native engineers equipped to pursue this specialty crucial to both telecommunications and medical instruments.

With U.S. high school students increasingly shunning mathematics and the hard sciences, America is the global technology and economic leader in spite of, not because of, any properties of the American gene pool or dominant culture. America prevails only because it offers the freedom of enterprise and innovation to people from around the world.

A decision to cut back legal immigration today, as Congress is contemplating, is a decision to wreck the key element of the American technological miracle. After botching the issues of telecom deregulation and tax rate reduction, and wasting a year on Hooverian myths about the magic of a balanced budget, the Republican Congress now proposes to issue a deadly body blow to the intellectual heart of U.S. growth. Congress must not cripple the new Manhattan Projects of the U.S. economy in order to pursue some xenophobic and archaic dream of ethnic purity and autarky.

• •

How about Home-Grown Geniuses?

Mark Krikorian

• •

This letter in response to George Gilder's "Geniuses from Abroad" appeared in the December 27, 1995, issue of the Wall Street Journal.

• • • • • • • • •

The move in Congress to rationalize our nation's Rube-Goldberg immigration policy, which Mr. Gilder tars as "some xenophobic and archaic dream of ethnic purity and autarky," would not, as he appears to think, cut the number of skills-tested immigrants. The bill approved by the Senate immigration subcommittee more than covers current demand for such visas, while the bill soon to be debated on the House floor actually increases the number of available visas.

Like other amateur opponents of a sustainable immigration policy, Mr. Gilder offers no solutions to the real problems we face in this area: millions of people on waiting lists, a large and growing education gap between natives and immigrants, a politicized and racialized visa lottery, a refugee system which admits few genuine refugees, and a political asylum policy which is metastasizing to cover virtually everyone on the planet. Perhaps instead of waxing poetic about the role of genius in economic growth, Mr. Gilder could have made some useful suggestions for managing these real problems.

Mark Krikorian
Executive Director
Center for Immigration Studies

• •

Get Out of Dodge!

Wanda Coleman

• •

Wanda Coleman is a poet who writes regularly for the Los Angeles Times. *This selection originally appeared in the February 15, 1993, issue of* The Nation, *and was then excerpted in this form in the May–June 1994 issue of* Utne Reader.

• • • • • • • • •

I am terrorized by the murder of a child. Intermittently, dramatic images of her death unreel. Two years after it happened, I'm still enraged, upset, unable to sleep. I'm haunted by her murder and by the thousands of murders of black youths since 1955, when a brutally bludgeoned Emmett Till rose from the autumn waters of Mississippi's Tallahatchie River. Each afternoon, as I wait for my fourteen-year-old son to return from school, I pray. I'm not a religious woman. But when I hear him coming through that door, I'm overjoyed. How long, I wonder, will America allow him to live?

It allowed Latasha Harlins barely fifteen years. In March and April 1991, a year before South Central Los Angeles erupted, local residents repeatedly witnessed news broadcasts of the videotaped Empire Liquor Market killing of fifteen-year-old Latasha Harlins by fifty-one-year-old Soon Ja Du. Central to the black-Korean tensions that fueled the riots, this incident was scarcely a footnote in national media coverage of the riots.

The video, filmed by an in-store camera, is painfully graphic: Latasha approaches Du, alone behind the counter, with money in her hand. Du accuses her of stealing a $1.79 bottle of orange juice. Latasha turns to show Du the juice in her knapsack, then waves the $2. After a heated verbal exchange, Latasha throws the orange juice down on the counter. The angry Du grabs for Latasha's pack, then catches the flap of her jacket. Latasha slaps Du, who immediately lets go. Latasha turns and walks away. Du fumbles for the .38 caliber, fires once. Latasha pitches forward and drops to the floor as the bullet strikes the back of her head.

Initial newspaper accounts of the incident were careful to describe Latasha as "studious and self-assured." But the slant of so-called objective coverage betrayed tacit sympathy for Du. She had lived every bigot's fantasy. She had shot *one of them.*

The fear that motivated Soon Ja Du was couched in statistics designed to justify her killing of Latasha: "In the surrounding 32 blocks, 936 felonies reported last year . . . 5 murders . . . 9 rapes . . . 184 robberies and 254 assaults." The fact that Du's son was the victim in one of those assaults was subtly emphasized. The nasties of ghetto life were responsible, not the "feeble and overwhelmed" grocer forced to work fourteen-hour days, at the mercy of shoplifters, street hoodlums, and chronic migraines, and certainly not white society.

Local protests over the Harlins shooting were swift and raucous, the culmination of complaints by black community leaders about "the Korean invasion" and lack of dialogue between the two groups. For nearly a decade the local media, alternative and mainstream, had refused to investigate the problem initially brought to their attention by a handful of concerned black writers, including me.

During that period, I had had three especially infuriating run-ins with Korean merchants. One was a fight at a hamburger stand, when the Koreans across the counter refused to accept my newly minted $20 bill. They'd been burned before, and they thought the bill was bogus. I was guilty of the crime someone else, also black, had committed. Using my own stubby fuse and lofty blood pressure as a gauge seemed unfair. But when even my demure sixty-year-old mother complained of abuse by "some Koreans because I'm black," I saw that violence was inevitable in my community.

Black protest over the Harlins-Du incident increased, but was unexpectedly dissipated when attorney Charles Lloyd was hired for Du's defense. Lloyd is black. As in the Hill versus Thomas fiasco, many were reluctant to go against one of our own. A "wait and see" attitude was adopted toward the previously hotly disputed case. When Soon Ja Du's bail was set at $250,000 and her release made imminent, the courtroom, crowded with Korean Americans, broke into applause. The black community was virtually silent. It would remain so until after the verdict in the Rodney King beating trial.

The socioeconomic reversals and unchecked discrimination of the Nixon/Ford/Reagan/Bush years stymied progress for most African Americans. And the high expectations many had for President Carter were gradually deflated. One year into the Carter administration, NAACP executive director Benjamin Hooks told 3,000 Urban League delegates, "Nearly 80 percent of the white people in America feel that enough has been done for black people." Since then, study after study has documented his gloomy insight: Blacks still disproportionately live in substandard and segregated housing; attend inferior public schools staffed by underpaid, underencouraged teachers; confront corporate America's glass ceiling; make do with lower wages as skilled labor devolves into low-paid service jobs; populate worsening neighborhoods plagued by unfettered drug traffic, increased violent crimes, overflowing prisons; battle homelessness. Factor in the unacceptably high rate of premature death due to hypertension and stroke, murder, and AIDS. While the richest 20 percent of America got richer, the largely disenfranchised fifteenth-generation African Americans struggled to "keep hope alive."

Blacks squeezed out of the L.A. economy were likewise being squeezed out nationally. Economic statistics repeatedly illuminated the concurrence of events that have conspired to marginalize struggling blacks. The increasing influx of immigrants exacerbated our crisis. While blacks were being pushed out of the marketplace by recession and widespread apathy, that same American marketplace was accommodating a groundswell of immigrants, privileged and underprivileged, from as far away as the former Soviet Union, the Middle East, Vietnam, and Korea. Their presence pushed blacks out of the marketplace altogether. Only lucky exceptions remained.

In his October 1992 *Atlantic* article "Blacks vs. Browns," Jack Miles sidesteps black-Korean conflicts to trace black-Latino clashes underscoring "Watts II." (A June 1983 issue of *Time* estimated that 90 percent of illegal immigrants come from Mexico. The Census Bureau reported a 16 percent increase in America's Latino population between 1981 and 1986, making one out of fourteen Americans Latino.) Miles observes that Latinos, even when they're foreign, seem native and safe while blacks, who are native, seem foreign and dangerous. Miles implies that blacks are so "nihilistic, so utterly alienated" that white Americans cannot "make a connection" with us. It's "just easier with the Mexicans." But the point is that the prejudice of white America has promoted the very attitude among blacks that whites like

Miles find so discomforting. No matter how many immigrants white America puts between itself and blacks, this national dilemma will persist.

Furthermore, as a price of entry, the majority of immigrants buy into the lie of American apartheid: Black people are inferior. To fail to accept this tenet of American life is to jeopardize what is already a tenuous existence for the newly arrived. When merchants like Soon Ja Du mimic whites' fear of blacks, their behavior is condoned, if not rewarded, by our society. Alliances between blacks and immigrants are troubled because the two groups profoundly misunderstand each other: While the immigrant populations (Koreans, Latinos, et al.) expect rational behavior from blacks driven mad by poverty and racism, blacks expect immigrants to empathize with our plight the minute they set foot on our turf—when too many of us don't grasp it ourselves. Newly arrived immigrants often do not understand that what may be interpreted as a mere inconvenience or slight by whites may be interpreted as disrespectful, even life-threatening, by blacks. "Objectivity" is impossible because racism prevents it.

Cooked under the pressures of the penal system, Latino-black conflicts have steadily worsened and are emphasized by the media. Violence on local campuses makes the front pages. Two black families in the Boyle Heights barrio of Ramona Gardens were firebombed. I got my taste of these tensions when I parked my car across the street from a liquor store and dashed in to play the lottery. Pulling up, I noticed about a dozen Latino men in a nearby alley and on the stoop next door, drinking and hanging out. My car is dilapidated and rusty, so I trusted no one would bother it. I left it open, windows down. When I returned the entire interior was wet. Not a Latino in sight. I wiped it down, sniffing to see if it was urine. It was water. And the message was clear: *Get out of Dodge.*

• •

Thoughts, Ideas, and Discussion Questions

1. If Lazarus' "New Colossus" does not adequately reflect your stance on immigration, compose a poem (adhering to similar line structure) which does.
2. Kinsley makes this assertion: "Your views of immigration depend on your sense of what makes America America." Do you agree? What does America comprise? Does your response have anything to do with the World View you articulated in Chapter One?
3. When Kinsley refers to "that stuff on the Statue of Liberty," what is he referring to? When he follows with "All these visions of America have a large component of fantasy," what is it that makes these visions so fantastic?
4. Note the presence of heterogeneity and homogeneity in different countries. Do Susan Roosevelt Weld and William F. Weld make a responsible assertion when they write, ". . . the Norwegians look like Norwegians, the Chinese look like Chinese, the Ethiopians look like Ethiopians, the Spaniards look like Spaniards, and the Americans look like everybody?"
5. What is Raspberry's claim?
6. Is Brimelow's argument based on a series of slippery slopes?
7. Coleman writes a compelling article, but what is her claim?
8. In "Unchecked Immigration," what is Brimelow's claim, and what solution does he propose? Using secondary sources to advance your argument, state whether you agree or disagree with Brimelow's claim and solutions.

Application

You are responsible for presenting a formal argument (10–15 minutes) on a problem or issue. The oral presentation affords you an awesome opportunity to showcase your talents, specifically the skills you have developed and sharpened as the semester has progressed. Think of the oral presentation as an extension of your written arguments, one which becomes transcendental, finding itself atop a soapbox, upon a stage, or behind a lectern or podium. Here are the requirements:

- Choose an issue or problem, one which is of interest to you and others. Make sure it is controversial, having at least two contending sides.

- Articulate a claim, and make sure your argument strictly adheres to the claim.
- Your support should comprise three types of appeals: logical, emotional, and ethical. (Logical appeals are factual, including dates, statistics, and the results of research by credible researchers. Emotional appeals include news coverage of children suffering, forced to work in sweatshops in third-world countries, descriptions of the emotional trauma a rabbit undergoes as it is skinned alive by poachers or fur enthusiasts, or gripping tales about a grandmother who is forced to endure agonizing pain because passive euthanasia was her doctor's prescription. Ethical appeals are used to identify with an audience's moral code: Is it right to take a human life? No matter how horrible the crime, can capital punishment be justified? Would you want death on your conscience?)
- Know that different "learners" exist. You may wish to not only use auditory stimuli (your voice, something excerpted from an audio tape or compact disc) but use visual stimuli (overheads, posters, pictures, slides, film or TV excerpts) and tactile stimuli (handouts, specimens).
- Identify your sources. Do not simply unleash your quotations, allowing them to run amuck in your audience. Use your support responsibly. This means identifying each source, giving your audience a moment to scrutinize your source's credibility. Hence, introduce your quotations in this manner: "According to Mark Jodstone of *Sports Illustrated* magazine's March 12, 1999 issue, 'Steroid use is very common among many professional football players.'"
- Refute the opposition. When you prepare this argument, do a "My Side/Their Side" exercise. Figure out who would support "your side" (and why), and figure out who would support "their side" (and why). Remember, the people who already agree with you need not be persuaded. You are delivering this argument for one purpose: to convince the people who do not agree with you that your claim is reasonable; moreover, you want these people to see that your claim is worth considering for adoption, for as critical thinkers, those who did not agree with you may want to make a new decision based on the new information with which you provided them.
- Focus on your diction. Is it a used car or a pre-owned car? Does the collection agent ask, "How are you going to *pay* for this?" or "How are you going to *take care* of this?" Note how the dentist does not say, "Please *spit*. Here comes the *needle*. Are you feeling any *pain?*" The dentist says, "Please *empty your mouth*. Here comes the *injection*. Are you feeling any *discomfort?*" Does the receptionist call you at home to *remind* you of the appointment or to *confirm* the appointment? (Of course, if the receptionist is *reminding* you, she is subtly implying that you forgot.) In your oral presentation, word choice affects how others hear and understand your argument. Choose your words with care and great tact.

- Do not read. If you read your argument to your audience, you'll accomplish one thing: you'll lose your audience. Many agree that note cards are helpful. However, most master orators memorize their speeches. Mark Twain, for instance, memorized his speeches but delivered them as if they were extemporaneous.
- Your typed, written proposal (due one week before your actual presentation) should include a clearly identified claim, a list of the sources you have employed, and a summary of either your viewpoint or the implications you perceive. Do not do your presentation on a topic for which you have already written an argument paper.
- Your oral presentation should last 10–15 minutes. Upon its completion, a 5–10 minute Question/Answer session will follow.

When searching for a topic, flip through the newspaper. Keep an eye out for "hot" topics. Affirmative action, euthanasia, immigration, animal experimentation, violence in the media, capital punishment, pornography on the Internet, and the legalization of marijuana are all "hot" topics. However, whether or not Homer Simpson is the greatest cartoon character of all time is not appropriate for this assignment. Also, arguing that lawyers and politicians are corrupt is equally futile. These arguments are based on preference (prejudice) rather than evidence.

When you deliver your argument, restate your claim often. Remember, the reason for your oral presentation is to persuade audience members to embrace your point of view. Hence, you should be regularly connecting your support to your claim. Also, it is a good idea to move around. Just as attention shifts are used by TV advertisers to break viewer monotony, hand gestures and mobility ought to be considered when giving an oral presentation. And because you do not want to invite fallacies, avoid using *all* and its relatives: *always, every, none, never.*

Finally, here are some words from Mark Twain:

1. *Say* what you are proposing to say, not merely come near it.
2. Use the right word, not its second cousin.
3. Eschew surplusage.
4. Not omit necessary details.
5. Avoid slovenliness of form.
6. Use good grammar.
7. Employ a simple and straightforward style.

Note: While each oral presentation is being delivered, students should be critically taking notes, identifying the speaker's claim, identifying appeals (logical, emotional, ethical), noting organization and faulty reasoning. A Question/Answer session should immediately follow the presentation. Afterwards, students should produce a written evaluation.

Observations

Before you begin reading the next chapter, take some time to reflect on what you learned in Chapter 9. Specifically, note what you think about what you learned, for in the spirit of promoting consciousness, it is essential that you not only become aware of your observations but that you commit them to paper. Use these observations like one would use a journal: as a tool for measuring growth and insight.

Preliminary Observations

_____

_____

_____

_____

_____

_____

_____

Refined Observations

_____

_____

_____

_____

_____

_____

_____

_____

_____

_____

_____

_____

_____

_____

_____

_____

_____

_____

_____

New Observations

_____

_____

_____

_____

_____

_____

Self-Reliance

Ralph Waldo Emerson

• •

Ralph Waldo Emerson (1803–1882) was born in Boston and descended from nine successive generations of prominent New England ministers. He grew up in a home and a community extremely proud of traditional theology and social ritual. An intellectual radical, Emerson entered Harvard at age fourteen, graduating thirtieth in a class of fifty-nine. Emerson, however, became the subject of much controversy. His focus on individualism in "Self-reliance" (1842) is the result of his first prolonged exposure to public censure.

• • • • • • • •

"Ne te quaesiveris extra."

Man is his own star; and the soul that can
Render an honest and a perfect man,
Commands all light, all influence, all fate;
Nothing to him falls early or too late.
Our acts our angels are, or good or ill,
Our fatal shadows that walk by us still.

    Epilogue to Beaumont and Fletcher's Honest Man's Fortune

Cast the bantling on the rocks,
    Suckle him with the she-wolf's teat,
    Wintered with the hawk and fox,
    Power and speed be hands and feet.

From *Selected Writings of Emerson* by Ralph Waldo Emerson, Modern Libaray College Education.

I read the other day some verses written by an eminent painter which were original and not conventional. The soul always hears an admonition in such lines, let the subject be what it may. The sentiment they instill is of more value than any thought they may contain. To believe your own thought, to believe that what is true for you in your private heart is true for all men—that is genius. Speak your latent conviction, and it shall be the universal sense; for the inmost in due time becomes the outmost, and our first thought is rendered back to us by the trumpets of the Last Judgment. Familiar as the voice of the mind is to each, the highest merit we ascribe to Moses, Plato, and Milton is, that they set at naught books and traditions, and spoke not what men, but what *they* thought. A man should learn to detect and watch that gleam of light which flashes across his mind from within, more than the luster of the firmament of bards and sages. Yet he dismisses without notice his thought, because it is his. In every work of genius we recognize our own rejected thoughts; they come back to us with a certain alienated majesty. Great works of art have no more affecting lesson for us than this. They teach us to abide by our spontaneous impression with good-humored inflexibility than most when the whole cry of voices is on the other side. Else, tomorrow a stranger will say with masterly good sense precisely what we have thought and felt all the time, and we shall be forced to take with shame our own opinion from another.

There is a time in every man's education when he arrives at the conviction that envy is ignorance; that imitation is suicide; that he must take himself for better, for worse, as his portion; that though the wide universe is full of good, no kernel of nourishing corn can come to him but through his toil bestowed on that plot of ground which is given to him to till. The power which resides in him is new in nature, and none but he knows what that is which he can do, nor does he know until he has tried. Not for nothing one face, one character, one fact, makes much impression on him, and another none. This sculpture in the memory is not without preestablished harmony. The eye was placed where one ray should fall, that it might testify of that particular ray. We but half express ourselves, and are ashamed of that divine idea which each of us represents. It may be safely trusted as proportionate and of good issues, so it be faithfully imparted, but God will not have his work made manifest by cowards. A man is relieved and gay when he has put his heart into his work and done his best; but what he has said or done otherwise, shall give him no peace. It is a deliverance which does not deliver. In the attempt his genius deserts him; no muse befriends; no invention, no hope.

Trust thyself: every heart vibrates to that iron string. Accept the place the divine providence has found for you, the society of your contemporaries, the connection of events. Great men have always done so, and confided themselves childlike to the genius of their age, betraying their perception that the absolutely trustworthy was seated at their heart, working through their hands, predominating in all their being. And we are now men, and must accept in the highest mind the same transcendent destiny; and not minors and invalids in a protected corner, not cowards fleeing before a revolution, but guides, redeemers, and benefactors, obeying the Almighty effort, and advancing on Chaos and the Dark.

What pretty oracles nature yields us on this text, in the face and behaviour of children, babes, and even brutes! That divided and rebel mind, that distrust of a sentiment because our arithmetic has computed the strength and means opposed to our purpose, these have not. Their mind being whole, their eye is as yet unconquered, and when we look in their faces, we are disconcerted. Infancy conforms to nobody: all conform to it, so that one babe commonly makes four or five out of the adults who prattle and play to it. So God has armed youth and puberty and manhood no less with its own piquancy and charm, and made it enviable and gracious and its claims not to be put by, if it will stand by itself. Do not think the youth has no force, because he cannot speak to you and me. Hark! in the next room his voice is sufficiently clear and emphatic. It seems he knows how to speak to his contemporaries. Bashful or bold, then, he will know how to make us seniors very unnecessary.

The nonchalance of boys who are sure of a dinner, and would disdain as much as a lord to do or say aught to conciliate one, is the healthy attitude of human nature. A boy is in the parlour what the pit is in the playhouse; independent, irresponsible, looking out from his corner on such people and facts as pass by, he tries and sentences them on their merits, in the swift, summary way of boys, as good, bad, interesting, silly, eloquent, troublesome. He cumbers himself never about consequences, about interests: he gives an independent, genuine verdict. You must court him: he does not court you. But the man is, as it were, clapped into jail by his consciousness. As soon as he has once acted or spoken with *éclat* he is a committed person, watched by the sympathy or the hatred of hundreds, whose affections must now enter into his account. There is no Lethe for this. Ah, that he could pass again into his neutrality! Who can thus avoid all pledges, and having observed, observe again from the same unaffected, unbiased, unbribable, unaffrighted innocence, must always be formidable. He would utter opinions on all passing affairs, which being seen to be not private, but necessary, would sink like darts into the ear of men, and put them in fear.

These are the voices which we hear in solitude, but they grow faint and inaudible as we enter into the world. Society everywhere is in conspiracy against the manhood of every one of its members. Society is a joint-stock company, in which the members agree, for the better securing of his bread to each shareholder, to surrender the liberty and culture of the eater. The virtue in most request is conformity. Self-reliance is its aversion. It loves not realities and creators, but names and customs.

Whoso would be a man must be a nonconformist. He who would gather immortal palms must not be hindered by the name of goodness, but must explore if it be goodness. Nothing is at last sacred but the integrity of your own mind. Absolve you to yourself, and you shall have the suffrage of the world. I remember an answer which when quite young I was prompted to make to a valued adviser, who was wont to importune me with the dear old doctrines of the church. On my saying, What have I to do with the sacredness of traditions, if I live wholly from within? my friend suggested—"But these impulses may be from below, not from above." I replied, "They do not seem to me to be such; but if I am the Devil's child, I will live then from the Devil." No law can be sacred to me but that of my nature. Good and bad are but names very readily transferable to that or this; the only right is what is after my constitution, the only wrong what is against it. A man is to carry himself in the presence of all opposition, as if every thing were titular and ephemeral but he. I am ashamed to think how easily we capitulate to badges and names, to large societies and dead institutions. Every decent and well-spoken individual affects and sways me more than is right. I ought to go upright and vital, and speak the rude truth in all ways. If malice and vanity wear the coat of philanthropy, shall that pass? If an angry bigot assumes this bountiful cause of Abolition, and comes to me with his last news from Barbadoes, why should I not say to him, 'Go love thy infant; love thy wood-chopper; be good-natured and modest; have that grace; and never varnish your hard, uncharitable ambition with this incredible tenderness for black folk a thousand miles off. Thy love afar is spite at home.' Rough and graceless would be such greeting, but truth is handsomer than the affectation of love. Your goodness must have some edge to it—else it is none. The doctrine of hatred must be preached as the counteraction of the doctrine of love when that pules and whines. I shun father and mother and wife and brother, when my genius calls me. I would write on the lintels of the door-post, *Whim.* I hope it is somewhat better than whim at last, but we cannot spend the day in explanation. Expect me not to show cause why I seek or why I exclude company. Then, again, do not tell me, as a good man did today, of my obligation to put all poor men in good situations. Are they *my* poor? I tell thee, thou foolish philanthropist, that I grudge the dollar, the dime, the cent, I give to such men as do not belong to me and to whom I do not belong. There is a class of persons to whom by all spiritual affinity I am bought and sold; for them I will go to prison, if need be; but your miscellaneous popular charities; the education at college of fools; the building of meeting-houses to the vain end to which many now stand; alms to sots; and the thousandfold Relief Societies; though I confess with shame I sometimes succumb and give the dollar, it is a wicked dollar which by and by I shall have the manhood to withhold.

Virtues are, in the popular estimate, rather the exception than the rule. There is the man *and* his virtues. Men do what is called a good action, as some piece of courage or charity, much as they would pay a fine in expiation of daily non-appearance on parade. Their works are done as an apology or extenuation of their living in the world—as invalids and the insane pay a high board. Their virtues are penances. I do not wish to expiate, but to live. My life is for itself and not for a spectacle. I much prefer that it should be of a lower strain, so it be genuine and equal, than that it should be glittering and unsteady. I wish it to be sound and sweet, and not to need diet and bleeding. I ask primary evidence that you are a man, and refuse this appeal from the man to his actions. I know that for myself it makes no difference whether I do or forbear those actions which are reckoned excellent. I cannot consent to pay for a privilege where I have intrinsic right. Few and mean as my gifts may be, I actually am, and do not need for my own assurance or the assurance of my fellows any secondary testimony.

What I must do is all that concerns me, not what the people think. This rule, equally arduous in actual and in intellectual life, may serve for the whole distinction between greatness and meanness. It is the harder, because you will always find those who think they know what is your duty better than you know it. It is easy in the world to live after the world's opinion; it is easy in solitude to live after our own; but the great man is he who in the midst of the crowd keeps with perfect sweetness the independence of solitude.

The objection to conforming to usages that have become dead to you is, that it scatters your force. It loses your time and blurs the impression of your character. If you maintain a dead church, contribute to a dead Bible-society, vote with a great party either for the government or against it, spread your table like base housekeepers—under all these screens I have difficulty to detect the precise man you are. And, of course, so much force is withdrawn from your proper life. But do your work, and I shall know you. Do your work, and you shall reinforce yourself. A man must consider what a blindman's bluff is this game of conformity. If I know your sect, I anticipate your argument. I hear a preacher announce for his text and topic the expediency of one of the institutions of his church. Do I not know beforehand that not possibly can he say a new and spontaneous word? Do I not know that, with all this ostentation of examining the grounds of the institution, he will do no such thing? Do I not know that he is pledged to himself not to look but at one side, the permitted side, not as a man, but as a parish minister? He is a retained attorney, and these airs of the bench are the emptiest affectation. Well, most men have bound their eyes with one or another handkerchief, and attached themselves to some one of these communities of opinion. This conformity makes them not false in a few particulars, authors of a few lies, but false in all particulars. Their every truth is not quite true. Their two is not the real two, their four not the real four; so that every word they say chagrins us, and we know not where to begin to set them right. Meantime nature is not slow to equip us in the prison-uniform of the party to which we adhere. We come to wear one cut of face and figure, and acquire by degrees the gentlest asinine expression. There is a mortifying experience in particular, which does not fail to wreak itself also in the general history; I mean "the foolish face of praise," the forced smile which we put on in company where we do not feel at ease in answer to conversation which does not interest us. The muscles, not spontaneously moved, but moved by a low usurping wilfulness, grow tight about the outline of the face with the most disagreeable sensation.

For nonconformity the world whips you with its displeasure. And therefore a man must know how to estimate a sour face. The bystanders look askance on him in the public street or in the friend's parlour. If this aversation had its origin in contempt and resistance like his own, he might well go home with a sad countenance; but the sour faces of the multitude, like their sweet faces, have no deep cause, but are put on and off as the wind blows and a newspaper directs. Yet is the discontent of the multitude more formidable than that of the senate and the college. It is easy enough for a firm man who knows the world to brook the rage of the cultivated classes. Their rage is decorous and prudent, for they are timid as being very vulnerable themselves. But when to their feminine rage the indignation of the people is added, when the ignorant and the poor are aroused, when the unintelligent brute force that lies at the bottom of society is made to growl and mow, it needs the habit of magnanimity and religion to treat it godlike as a trifle of no concernment.

The other terror that scares us from self-trust is our consistency; a reverence for our past act or word, because the eyes of others have no other data for computing our orbit than our past acts, and we are loath to disappoint them.

But why should you keep your head over your shoulder? Why drag about this corpse of your memory, lest you contradict what you have stated in this or that public place? Suppose you should contradict yourself; what then? It seems to be a rule of wisdom never to rely on your memory alone, scarcely even in acts of pure memory, but to bring the past for judgment into the thousand-eyed present, and live ever in a new day. In your metaphysics you have denied personality to the Deity, yet when the devout motions of the soul come, yield to them heart and life, though they should clothe God with shape and color. Leave your theory, as Joseph his coat in the hand of the harlot, and flee.

A foolish consistency is the hobgoblin of little minds, adored by little statesmen and philosophers and divines. With consistency a great soul has simply nothing to do. He may as well concern himself with his shadow on the wall. Speak what you think now in hard words, and to-morrow speak what to-morrow thinks in hard words again, though it contradict every thing you said to-day.—'Ah, so you shall be sure to be misunderstood.'—Is it so bad, then, to be misunderstood? Pythagoras was misunderstood, and Socrates, and Jesus, and Luther, and Copernicus, and Galileo, and Newton, and every pure and wise spirit that ever took flesh. To be great is to be misunderstood.

I suppose no man can violate his nature. All the sallies of his will are rounded in by the law of his being, as the inequalities of Andes and Himmaleh are insignificant in the curve of the sphere. Nor does it matter how you gauge and try him. A character is like an acrostic or Alexandrian stanza; read it forward, backward, or across, it still spells the same thing. In this pleasing, contrite wood-life which God allows me, let me record day by day my honest thought without prospect or retrospect, and, I cannot doubt, it will be found symmetrical, though I mean it not, and see it not. My book should smell of pines and resound with the hum of insects. The swallow over my window should interweave that thread or straw he carries in his bill into my web also. We pass for what we are. Character teaches above our wills. Men imagine that they communicate their virtue or vice only by overt actions, and do not see that virtue or vice emit a breath every moment.

There will be an agreement in whatever variety of actions, so they be each honest and natural in their hour. For of one will, the actions will be harmonious, however unlike they seem. These varieties are lost sight of at a little distance, at a little height of thought. One tendency unites them all. The voyage of the best ship is a zigzag line of a hundred tacks. See the line from a sufficient distance, and it straightens itself to the average tendency. Your genuine action will explain itself, and will explain your other genuine actions. Your conformity explains nothing. Act singly, and what you have already done singly will justify you now. Greatness appeals to the future. If I can be firm enough to-day to do right, and scorn eyes, I must have done so much right before as to defend me now. Be it how it will, do right now. Always scorn appearances, and you always may. The force of character is cumulative. All the foregone days of virtue work their health into this. What makes the majesty of the heroes of the senate and the field, which so fills the imagination? The consciousness of a train of great days and victories behind. They shed a united light on the advancing actor. He is attended as by a visible escort of angels. That is it which throws thunder into Chatham's voice, and dignity into Washington's port, and America into Adams's eye. Honor is venerable to us because it is no ephemeris. It is always ancient virtue. We worship it to-day because it is not of to-day. We love it and pay it homage, because it is not a trap for our love and homage, but is self-dependent, self-derived, and therefore of an old immaculate pedigree, even if shown in a young person.

I hope in these days we have heard the last of conformity and consistency. Let the words be gazetted and ridiculous henceforward. Instead of the gong for dinner, let us hear a whistle from the Spartan fife. Let us never bow and apologize more. A great man is coming to eat at my house. I do not wish to please him; I wish that he should wish to please me. I will stand here for humanity, and though I would make it kind, I would make it true. Let us affront and reprimand the smooth mediocrity and squalid contentment of the times, and hurl in the face of custom, and trade, and office, the fact which is the upshot of all history, that there is a great responsible Thinker and Actor working wherever a man works; that a true man belongs to no other time or place, but is the center of things. Where he is, there is nature. He measures you, and all men, and all events. Ordinarily, every body in society reminds us of someone else, or of some other person. Character, reality, reminds you of nothing else; it takes place of the whole creation. The man must be so much, that he must make all circumstances indifferent. Every true man is a cause, a country, and an age; requires infinite spaces and numbers and time fully to accomplish his design; and posterity seem to follow his steps as a train of clients. A man Caesar is born, and for ages after we have a Roman Empire. Christ is born, and millions of minds so grow and cleave to his genius, that he is confounded with virtue and the possible of man. An institution is the lengthened shadow of one man; as, Monachism, of the Hermit Antony; the Reformation, of Luther; Quakerism, of Fox; Methodism, of Wesley; Abolition, of Clarkson. Scipio, Milton called "the height of Rome"; and all history resolves itself very easily into the biography of a few stout and earnest persons.

Let a man then know his worth, and keep things under his feet. Let him not peep or steal, or skulk up and down with the air of a charity boy, a bastard, or an interloper, in the world which exists for him. But the man in the street, finding no worth in himself which corresponds to the force which built a tower or sculptured a marble god, feels poor when he looks on these. To him a palace, a statue, or a costly book have an alien and forbidding air, much like a gay equipage, and seem to say like that, "Who are you, Sir?" Yet they all are his, suitors for his notice, petitioners to his faculties that they will come out and take possession. The picture waits for my verdict; it is not to command me, but I am to settle its claims to praise. That popular fable of the sot who was picked up dead drunk in the street, carried to the duke's house, washed and dressed and laid in the duke's bed, and, on his waking, treated with all obsequious ceremony like the duke, and assured that he had been insane, owes its popularity to the fact that it symbolizes so well the state of man, who is in the world a sort of sot, but now and then wakes up, exercises his reason, and finds himself a true prince.

Our reading is mendicant and sycophantic. In history, our imagination plays us false. Kingdom and lordship, power and estate, are a gaudier vocabulary than private John and Edward in a small house and common day's work; but the things of life are the same to both; the sum total of both is the same. Why all this deference to Alfred, and Scanderbeg, and Gustavus? Suppose they were virtuous; did they wear out virtue? As great a stake depends on your private act to-day, as followed their public and renowned steps. When private men shall act with original views, the luster will be transferred from the actions of kings to those of gentlemen.

The world has been instructed by its kings, who have so magnetized the eyes of nations. It has been taught by this colossal symbol the mutual reverence that is due from man to man. The joyful loyalty with which men have everywhere suffered the king, the noble, or the great proprietor to walk among them by a law of his own, make his own scale of men and things, and reverse theirs, pay for benefits not with money but with honor, and represent the law in his person, was the hieroglyphic by which they obscurely signified their consciousness of their own right and comeliness, the right of every man.

The magnetism which all original action exerts is explained when we inquire the reason of self-trust. Who is the Trustee? What is the aboriginal Self, on which a universal reliance may be grounded? What is the nature and power of that science-baffling star, without parallax, without calculable elements, which shoots a ray of beauty even into trivial and impure actions, if the least mark of independence appear? The inquiry leads us to that source, at once the essence of genius, of virtue, and of life, which we call Spontaneity or Instinct. We denote this primary wisdom as Intuition, whilst all later teachings are tuitions. In that deep force, the last fact behind which analysis cannot go, all things find their common origin. For, the sense of being which in calm hours rises, we know not how, in the soul, is not diverse from things, from space, from light, from time, from man, but one with them, and proceeds obviously from the same source whence their life and being also proceed. We first share the life by which things exist, and afterwards see them as appearances in nature, and forget that we have shared their cause. Here is the fountain of action and of thought. Here are the lungs of that inspiration which giveth man wisdom, and which cannot be denied without impiety and atheism. We lie in the lap of immense intelligence, which makes us receivers of its truth and organs of its activity. When we discern justice, when we discern truth, we do nothing of ourselves, but allow a passage to its beams. If we ask whence this comes, if we seek to pry into the soul that causes, all philosophy is at fault. Its presence or its absence is all we can affirm. Every man discriminates between the voluntary acts of his mind, and his involuntary perceptions, and knows that to his involuntary perceptions a perfect faith is due. He may err in the expression of them, but he knows that these things are so, like day and night, not to be disputed. My willful actions and acquisitions are but roving; the idlest reverie, the faintest native emotion, command my curiosity and respect. Thoughtless people contradict as readily the statement of perceptions as of opinions, or rather much more readily; for, they do not distinguish between perception and notion. They fancy that I choose to see this or that thing. But perception is not whimsical, but fatal. If I see a trait, my children will see it after me, and in course of time, all mankind—although it may chance that no one has seen it before me. For my perception of it is as much a fact as the sun.

The relations of the soul to the divine spirit are so pure, that it is profane to seek to interpose helps. It must be that when God speaketh he should communicate, not one thing, but all things; should fill the world with his voice; should scatter forth light, nature, time, souls, from the center of the present thought; and new date and new create the whole. Whenever a mind is simple, and receives a divine wisdom, old things pass away—means, teachers, texts, temples fall; it lives now, and absorbs past and future into the present hour. All things are made sacred by relation to it—one as much as another. All things are dissolved to their centre by their cause, and, in the universal miracle, petty and particular miracles disappear. If, therefore, a man claims to know and speak of God, and carries you backward to the phraseology of some old mouldered nation in another country, in another world, believe him not. Is the acorn better than the oak which is its fullness and completion? Is the parent better than the child into whom he has cast his ripened being? Whence, then, this worship of the past? The centuries are conspirators against the sanity and authority of the soul. Time and space are but physiological colors which the eye makes, but the soul is light; where it is, is day; where it was, is night; and history is an impertinence and an injury, if it be any thing more than a cheerful apologue or parable of my being and becoming.

Man is timid and apologetic; he is no longer upright; he dares not say 'I think,' 'I am,' but quotes some saint or sage. He is ashamed before the blade of grass or the blowing rose. These roses under my window make no reference to former roses or to better ones; they are for what they are; they exist with God to-day. There is no time to them. There is simply the rose; it is perfect in every moment of its existence. Before a leaf-bud has burst, its whole life acts; in the full-blown flower there is no more; in the leafless root there is no less. Its nature is satisfied, and it satisfies nature, in all moments alike. But man postpones or remembers; he does not live in the present, but with reverted eye laments the past, or, heedless of the riches that surround him, stands on tiptoe to foresee the future. He cannot be happy and strong until he too lives with nature in the present, above time.

This should be plain enough. Yet see what strong intellects dare not yet hear God himself, unless he speak the phraseology of I know not what David, or Jeremiah, or Paul. We shall not always set so great a price on a few texts, on a few lives. We are like children who repeat by rote the sentences of grandames and tutors, and, as they grow older, of the men of talents and character they chance to see— painfully recollecting the exact words they spoke; afterwards, when they come into the point of view which those had who uttered these sayings, they understand them, and are willing to let the words go; for, at any time, they can use words as good when occasion comes. If we live truly, we shall see truly. It is as easy for the strong man to be strong, as it is for the weak to be weak. When we have new perception, we shall gladly disburden the memory of its hoarded treasures as old rubbish. When a man lives with God, his voice shall be as sweet as the murmur of the brook and the rustle of the corn.

And now at last the highest truth on this subject remains unsaid; probably cannot be said; for all that we say is the far-off remembering of the intuition. That thought, by what I can now nearest approach to say it, is this. When good is near you, when you have life in yourself, it is not by any known or accustomed way; you shall not discern the footprints of any other; you shall not see the face of man; you shall not hear any name; the way, the thought, the good, shall be wholly strange and new. It shall exclude example and experience. You take the way from man, not to man. All persons that ever existed are its forgotten ministers. Fear and hope are alike beneath it. There is somewhat low even in hope. In the hour of vision, there is nothing that can be called gratitude, nor properly joy. The soul raised over passion beholds identity and eternal causation, perceives the self-existence of Truth and Right, and calms itself with knowing that all things go well. Vast spaces of nature, the Atlantic Ocean, the South Sea; long intervals of time, years, centuries, are of no account. This which I think and feel underlay every former state of life and circumstances, as it does underlie my present, and what is called life, and what is called death.

Life only avails, not the having lived. Power ceases in the instant of repose; it resides in the moment of transition from a past to a new state, in the shooting of the gulf, in the darting to an aim. This one fact the world hates, that the soul *becomes*; for that forever degrades the past, turns all riches to poverty, all reputation to a shame, confounds the saint with the rogue, shoves Jesus and Judas equally aside. Why, then, do we prate of self-reliance? Inasmuch as the soul is present, there will be power not confident but agent. To talk of reliance is a poor external way of speaking. Speak rather of that which relies, because it works and is. Who has more obedience than I masters me, though he should not raise his finger. Round him I must revolve by the gravitation of spirits. We fancy it rhetoric, when we speak of eminent virtue. We do not yet see that virtue is Height, and that a man or a company of men, plastic and permeable to principles, by the law of nature must overpower and ride all cities, nations, kings, rich men, poets, who are not.

This is the ultimate fact which we so quickly reach on this, as on every topic, the resolution of all into the ever-blessed ONE. Self-existence is the attribute of the Supreme Cause, and it constitutes the measure of good by the degree in which it enters into all lower forms. All things real are so by so much virtue as they contain. Commerce, husbandry, hunting, whaling, war, eloquence, personal weight, are somewhat, and engage my respect as examples of its presence and impure action. I see the same law working in nature for conservation and growth. Power is in nature the essential measure of right. Nature suffers nothing to remain in her kingdoms which cannot help itself. The genesis and maturation of a planet, its poise and orbit, the bended tree recovering itself from the strong wind, the vital resources of every animal and vegetable, are demonstrations of the self-sufficing, and therefore self-relying soul.

Thus all concentrates: let us not rove; let us sit at home with the cause. Let us stun and astonish the intruding rabble of men and books and institutions, by a simple declaration of the divine fact. Bid the invaders take the shoes from off their feet, for God is here within. Let our simplicity judge them, and our docility to our own law demonstrate the poverty of nature and fortune beside our native riches.

But now we are a mob. Man does not stand in awe of man, nor is his genius admonished to stay at home, to put itself in communication with the internal ocean, but it goes abroad to beg a cup of water of the urns of other men. We must go alone. I like the silent church before the service begins, better than any preaching. How far off, how cool, how chaste the persons look, begirt each one with a precinct or sanctuary! So let us always sit. Why should we assume the faults of our friend, or wife, or father, or child, because they sit around our hearth, or are said to have the same blood? All men have my blood, and I have all men's. Not for that will I adopt their petulance or folly, even to the extent of being ashamed of it. But your isolation must not be mechanical, but spiritual, that is, must be elevation. At times the whole world seems to be in conspiracy to importune you with emphatic trifles. Friend, client, child, sickness, fear, want, charity, all knock at once at thy closet door, and say—'Come out unto us.' But keep thy state; come not into their confusion. The power men possess to annoy me, I give them by a weak curiosity. No man can come near me but through my act. "What we love that we have, but by desire we bereave ourselves of the love."

If we cannot at once rise to the sanctities of obedience and faith, let us at least resist our temptations; let us enter into the state of war, and wake Thor and Woden, courage and constancy, in our Saxon breasts. This is to be done in our smooth times by speaking the truth. Check this lying hospitality and lying affection. Live no longer to the expectation of these deceived and deceiving people with whom we converse. Say to them, 'O father, O mother, O wife, O brother, O friend, I have lived with you after appearances hitherto. Henceforward I am the truth's. Be it known unto you that henceforward I obey no law less than the eternal law. I will have no covenants but proximities. I shall endeavour to nourish my parents, to support my family, to be the chaste husband of one wife—but these relations I must fill after a new and unprecedented way. I appeal from your customs. I must be myself. I cannot break myself any longer for you, or you. If you can love me for what I am, we shall be the happier. If you cannot, I will still seek to deserve that you should. I will not hide my tastes or aversions. I will so trust that what is deep is holy, that I will do strongly before the sun and moon whatever inly rejoices me, and the heart appoints. If you are noble, I will love you; if you are not, I will not hurt you and myself by hypocritical attentions. If you are true, but not in the same truth with me, cleave to your companions; I will seek my own. I do this not selfishly, but humbly and truly. It is alike your interest, and mine, and all men's, however long we have dwelt in lies, to live in truth. Does this sound harsh to-day? You will soon love what is dictated by your nature as well as mine, and, if we follow the truth, it will bring us out safe at last.'—But so you may give these friends pain. Yes, but I cannot sell my liberty and my power, to save their sensibility. Besides, all persons have their moments of reason, when they look out into the region of absolute truth; then will they justify me, and do the same thing.

The populace think that your rejection of popular standards is a rejection of all standard, and mere antinomianism; and the bold sensualist will use the name of philosophy to gild his crimes. But the law of consciousness abides. There are two confessionals, in one or the other of which we must be shriven. You may fulfil your round of duties by clearing yourself in the *direct,* or in the *reflex* way. Consider whether you have satisfied your relations to father, mother, cousin, neighbour, town, cat, and dog; whether any of these can upbraid you. But I may also neglect this reflex standard, and absolve me to myself. I have my own stern claims and perfect circle. It denies the name of duty to many offices that are called duties. But if I can discharge its debts, it enables me to dispense with the popular code. If any one imagines that this law is lax, let him keep its commandment one day.

And truly it demands something godlike in him who has cast off the common motives of humanity, and has ventured to trust himself for a taskmaster. High be his heart, faithful his will, clear his sight, that he may in good earnest be doctrine, society, law, to himself, that a simple purpose may be to him as strong as iron necessity is to others!

If any man consider the present aspects of what is called by distinction *society,* he will see the need of these ethics. The sinew and heart of man seem to be drawn out, and we have become timorous, desponding whimperers. We are afraid of truth, afraid of fortune, afraid of death, and afraid of each other. Our age yields no great and perfect persons. We want men and women who shall renovate life and our social state, but we see that most natures are insolvent, cannot satisfy their own wants, have an ambition out of all proportion to their practical force, and do lean and beg day and night continually. Our housekeeping is mendicant, our arts, our occupations, our marriages, our religion, we have not chosen, but society has chosen for us. We are parlour soldiers. We shun the rugged battle of fate, where strength is born.

If our young men miscarry in their first enterprises, they lose all heart. If the young merchant fails, men say he is *ruined.* If the finest genius studies at one of our colleges, and is not installed in an office within one year afterwards in the cities or suburbs of Boston or New York, it seems to his friends and to himself that he is right in being disheartened, and in complaining the rest of his life. A sturdy lad from New Hampshire or Vermont, who in turn tries all the professions, who *teams it, farms it, peddles,* keeps a school, preaches, edits a newspaper, goes to Congress, buys a township, and so forth, in successive years, and always, like a cat, falls on his feet, is worth a hundred of these city dolls. He walks abreast with his days, and feels no shame in not 'studying a profession,' for he does not postpone his life, but lives already. He has not one chance, but a hundred chances. Let a Stoic open the resources of man, and tell men they are not leaning willows, but can and must detach themselves; that with the exercise of self-trust, new powers shall appear; that a man is the word made flesh, born to shed healing to the nations, that he should be ashamed of our compassion, and that the moment he acts from himself, tossing the laws, the books, idolatries, and customs out of the window, we pity him no more, but thank and revere him; and that teacher shall restore the life of man to splendor, and make his name dear to all history.

It is easy to see that a greater self-reliance must work a revolution in all the offices and relations of men; in their religion; in their education; in their pursuits; their modes of living; their association; in their property; in their speculative views.

1. In what prayers do men allow themselves! That which they call a holy office is not so much as brave and manly. Prayer looks abroad and asks for some foreign addition to come through some foreign virtue, and loses itself in endless mazes of natural and supernatural, and mediatorial and miraculous. Prayer that craves a particular commodity, anything less than all good, is vicious. Prayer is the contemplation of the facts of life from the highest point of view. It is the soliloquy of a beholding and jubilant soul. It is the spirit of God pronouncing his works good. But prayer as a means to effect a private end is meanness and theft. It supposes dualism and not unity in nature and consciousness. As soon as the man is at one with God, he will not beg. He will then see prayer in all action. The prayer of the farmer kneeling in his field to weed it, the prayer of the rower kneeling with the stroke of his oar, are true prayers heard throughout nature, though for cheap ends. Caratach, in Fletcher's "Bonduca," when admonished to inquire the mind of the god Audate, replies—

His hidden meaning lies in our endeavours;
Our valors are our best gods.

Another sort of false prayers are our regrets. Discontent is the want of self-reliance: it is infirmity of will. Regret calamities, if you can thereby help the sufferer; if not, attend your own work, and already the evil begins to be repaired. Our sympathy is just as base. We come to them who weep foolishly, and sit down and cry for company, instead of imparting to them truth and health in rough electric shocks, putting them once more in communication with their own reason. The secret of fortune is joy in our hands. Welcome evermore to gods and men is the self-helping man. For him all doors are flung wide; him all tongues greet, all honors crown, all eyes follow with desire. Our love goes out to him and embraces him, because he did not need it. We solicitously and apologetically caress and celebrate him, because he held on his way and scorned our disapprobation. The gods love him because men hated him. "To the persevering mortal," said Zoroaster, "the blessed Immortals are swift."

As men's prayers are a disease of the will, so are their creeds a disease of the intellect. They say with those foolish Israelites, 'Let not God speak to us, lest we die. Speak thou, speak any man with us, and we will obey.' Everywhere I am hindered of meeting God in my brother, because he has shut his own temple doors, and recites fables merely of his brother's, or his brother's brother's God. Every new mind is a new classification. If it prove a mind of uncommon activity and power, a Locke, a Lavoisier, a Hutton, a Bentham, a Fourier, it imposes its classification on other men, and lo! a new system. In proportion to the depth of the thought, and so to the number of the objects it touches and brings within reach of the pupil, is his complacency. But chiefly is this apparent in creeds and churches, which are also classifications of some powerful mind acting on the elemental thought of duty, and man's relation to the Highest. Such is Calvinism, Quakerism, Swedenborgism. The pupil takes the same delight in subordinating every thing to the new terminology, as a girl who has just learned botany in seeing a new earth and new seasons thereby. It will happen for a time, that the pupil will find his intellectual power has grown by the study of his master's mind. But in all unbalanced minds, the classification is idolized, passes for the end, and not for a speedily exhaustible means, so that the walls of the system blend to their eye in the remote horizon with the walls of the universe; the luminaries of heaven seem to them hung on the arch their master built. They cannot imagine how you aliens have any right to see—how you can see; 'It must be somehow that you stole the light from us.' They do not yet perceive, that light, unsystematic, indomitable, will break into any cabin, even into theirs. Let them chirp awhile and call it their own. If they are honest and do well, presently their neat new pinfold will be too strait and low, will crack, will lean, will rot and vanish, and the immortal light, all young and joyful, million-orbed, million-colored, will beam over the universe as on the first morning.

2. It is for want of self-culture that the superstition of Travelling, whose idols are Italy, England, Egypt, retains its fascination for all educated Americans. They who made England, Italy, or Greece venerable in the imagination did so by sticking fast where they were, like an axis of the earth. In manly hours, we feel that duty is our place. The soul is no traveller; the wise man stays at home, and when his necessities, his duties, on any occasion call him from his house, or into foreign lands, he is at home still, and shall make men sensible by the expression of his countenance, that he goes the missionary of wisdom and virtue, and visits cities and men like a sovereign, and not like an interloper or a valet.

I have no churlish objection to the circumnavigation of the globe, for the purposes of art, of study, and benevolence, so that the man is first domesticated, or does not go abroad with the hope of finding somewhat greater than he knows. He who travels to be amused, or to get somewhat which he does not carry, travels away from himself, and grows old even in youth among old things. In Thebes, in Palmyra, his will and mind have become old and dilapidated as they. He carries ruins to ruins. Travelling is a fool's paradise. Our first journeys discover to us the indifference of places. At home I dream that at Naples, at Rome, I can be intoxicated with beauty, and lose my sadness. I pack my trunk, embrace my friends, embark on the sea, and at last wake up in Naples, and there beside me is the stern fact, the sad self, unrelenting, identical, that I fled from. I seek the Vatican, and the palaces. I affect to be intoxicated with sights and suggestions, but I am not intoxicated. My giant goes with me wherever I go.

3. But the rage of travelling is a symptom of a deeper unsoundness affecting the whole intellectual action. The intellect is vagabond, and our system of education fosters restlessness. Our minds travel when our bodies are forced to stay at home. We imitate; and what is imitation but the travelling of the mind? Our houses are built with foreign taste; our shelves are garnished with foreign ornaments; our opinions, our tastes, our faculties, lean, and follow the Past and the Distant. The soul created the arts wherever they have flourished. It was in his own mind that the artist sought his model. It was an application of his own thought to the thing to be done and the conditions to be observed. And why need we copy the Doric or the Gothic model? Beauty, convenience, grandeur of thought, and quaint expression are as near to us as to any, and if the American artist will study with hope and love the precise thing to be done by him, considering the climate, the soil, the length of the day, the wants of the people, the habit and

form of the government, he will create a house in which all these will find themselves fitted, and taste and sentiment will be satisfied also.

Insist on yourself; never imitate. Your own gift you can present every moment with the cumulative force of a whole life's cultivation; but of the adopted talent of another, you have only an extemporaneous, half possession. That which each can do best, none but his Maker can teach him. No man yet knows what it is, nor can, till that person has exhibited it. Where is the master who could have taught Shakspeare? Where is the master who could have instructed Franklin, or Washington, or Bacon, or Newton? Every great man is a unique. The Scipionism of Scipio is precisely that part he could not borrow. Shakspeare will never be made by the study of Shakspeare. Do that which is assigned you, and you cannot hope too much or dare too much. There is at this moment for you an utterance brave and grand as that of the colossal chisel of Phidias, or trowel of the Egyptians, or the pen of Moses, or Dante, but different from all these. Not possibly will the soul all rich, all eloquent, with thousand-cloven tongue, deign to repeat itself; but if you can hear what these patriarchs say, surely you can reply to them in the same pitch of voice; for the ear and the tongue are two organs of one nature. Abide in the simple and noble regions of thy life, obey thy heart, and thou shalt reproduce the Foreworld again.

4. As our Religion, our Education, our Art look abroad, so does our spirit of society. All men plume themselves on the improvement of society, and no man improves.

Society never advances. It recedes as fast on one side as it gains on the other. It undergoes continual changes; it is barbarous, it is civilized, it is christianized, it is rich, it is scientific; but this change is not amelioration. For every thing that is given, something is taken. Society acquires new arts, and loses old instincts. What a contrast between the well-clad, reading, writing, thinking American, with a watch, a pencil, and a bill of exchange in his pocket, and the naked New Zealander, whose property is a club, a spear, a mat, and an undivided twentieth of a shed to sleep under! But compare the health of the two men, and you shall see that the white man has lost his aboriginal strength. If the traveller tell us truly, strike the savage with a broad axe, and in a day or two the flesh shall unite and heal as if you struck the blow into soft pitch, and the same blow shall send the white to his grave.

The civilized man has built a coach, but has lost the use of his feet. He is supported on crutches, but lacks so much support of muscle. He has a fine Geneva watch, but he fails of the skill to tell the hour by the sun. A Greenwich nautical almanac he has, and so being sure of the information when he wants it, the man in the street does not know a star in the sky. The solstice he does not observe; the equinox he knows as little; and the whole bright calendar of the year is without a dial in his mind. His note-books impair his memory; his libraries overload his wit; the insurance-office increases the number of accidents; and it may be a question whether machinery does not encumber; whether we have not lost by refinement some energy, by a Christianity entrenched in establishments and forms, some vigor of wild virtue. For every Stoic was a Stoic; but in Christendom where is the Christian?

There is no more deviation in the moral standard than in the standard of height or bulk. No greater men are now than ever were. A singular equality may be observed between the great men of the first and of the last ages; nor can all the science, art, religion, and philosophy of the nineteenth century avail to educate greater men than Plutarch's heroes, three or four and twenty centuries ago. Not in time is the race progressive. Phocion, Socrates, Anaxagoras, Diogenes, are great men, but they leave no class. He who is really of their class will not be called by their name, but will be his own man, and, in his turn, the founder of a sect. The arts and inventions of each period are only its costume, and do not invigorate men. The harm of the improved machinery may compensate its good. Hudson and Behring accomplished so much in their fishing-boats, as to astonish Parry and Franklin, whose equipment exhausted the resources of science and art. Galileo, with an opera-glass, discovered a more splendid series of celestial phenomena than any one since. Columbus found the New World in an undecked boat. It is curious to see the periodical disuse and perishing of means and machinery, which were introduced with loud laudation a few years or centuries before. The great genius returns to essential man. We reckoned the improvements of the art of war among the triumphs of science, and yet Napoleon conquered Europe by the bivouac, which consisted of falling back on naked valor, and disencumbering it of all aids. The Emperor held it impossible to make a perfect army, says Las Casas, "without abolishing our arms, magazines, commissaries, and carriages, until, in imitation of the Roman custom, the soldier should receive his supply of corn, grind it in his hand-mill, and bake his bread himself."

Society is a wave. The wave moves onward, but the water of which it is composed does not. The same particle does not rise from the valley to the ridge. Its unity is only phenomenal. The persons who make up a nation to-day, next year die, and their experience with them.

And so the reliance on Property, including the reliance on governments which protect it, is the want of self-reliance. Men have looked away from themselves and at things so long, that they have come to esteem the religious, learned, and civil institutions as guards of property, and they deprecate assaults on these, because they feel them to be assaults on property. They measure their esteem of each other by what each has, and not by what each is. But a cultivated man becomes ashamed of his property, out of new respect for his nature. Especially he hates what he has, if he sees that it is accidental—came to him by inheritance, or gift, or crime; then he feels that it is not having; it does not belong to him, has no root in him, and merely lies there, because no revolution or no robber takes it away. But that which a man is, does always by necessity acquire, and what the man acquires is living property, which does not wait the beck of rulers, or mobs, or revolutions, or fire, or storm, or bankruptcies, but perpetually renews itself wherever the man breathes. "Thy lot or portion of life," said the Caliph Ali, "is seeking after thee; therefore be at rest from seeking after it." Our dependence on these foreign goods leads us to our slavish respect for numbers. The political parties meet in numerous conventions; the greater the concourse, and with each new uproar of announcement, The delegation from Essex! The Democrats from New Hampshire! The Whigs of Maine! the young patriot feels himself stronger than before by a new thousand of eyes and arms. In like manner the reformers summon conventions, and vote and resolve in multitude. Not so, O friends! will the God deign to enter and inhabit you, but by a method precisely the reverse. It is only as a man puts off all foreign support, and stands alone, that I see him to be strong and to prevail. He is weaker by every recruit to his banner. Is not a man better than a town? Ask nothing of men, and in the endless mutation, thou only firm column must presently appear the upholder of all that surrounds thee. He who knows that power is inborn, that he is weak because he has looked for good out of him and elsewhere, and so perceiving, throws himself unhesitatingly on his thought, instantly rights himself, stands in the erect position, commands his limbs, works miracles; just as a man who stands on his feet is stronger than a man who stands on his head.

So use all that is called Fortune. Most men gamble with her, and gain all, and lose all, as her wheel rolls. But do thou leave as unlawful these winnings, and deal with Cause and Effect, the chancellors of God. In the Will work and acquire, and thou hast chained the wheel of Chance, and shalt sit hereafter out of fear from her rotations. A political victory, a rise of rents, the recovery of your sick, or the return of your absent friend, or some other favorable event, raises your spirits, and you think good days are preparing for you. Do not believe it. Nothing can bring you peace but yourself. Nothing can bring you peace but the triumph of principles.

• •

Civil Disobedience

Henry David Thoreau

• •

Henry David Thoreau (1817–1862), philosphoer and writer, is best known for Walden, *an account of his solitary retreat to Walden Pond, near Concord, Massachusetts. Here he remained for more than two years in an effort to "live deliberately, to front only the essential facts of life." "Civil Disobedience" was first given as a lecture in 1848 and published in 1849. It was widely read and influenced both Mahatma Gandhi in the passive-resistance campaign he led against the British in India and Martin Luther King, Jr., in the civil rights movement.*

• • • • • • • •

I heartily accept the motto, "That government is best which governs least"; and I should like to see it acted up to more rapidly and systematically. Carried out, it finally amounts to this, which also I believe—"That government is best which governs not at all"; and when men are prepared for it, that will be the kind of government which they will have. Government is at best but an expedient; but most governments are usually, and all governments are sometimes, inexpedient. The objections which have been brought against a standing army, and they are many and weighty, and deserve to prevail, may also at last be brought against a standing government. The standing army is only an arm of the standing government. The government itself, which is only the mode which the people have chosen to execute their will, is equally liable to be abused and perverted before the people can act through it. Witness the present Mexican war, the work of comparatively a few individuals using the standing government as their tool; for in the outset, the people would not have consented to this measure.

Civil Disobedience by Henry David Thoreau, 1849.

This American government,—what is it but a tradition, though a recent one, endeavoring to transmit itself unimpaired to posterity, but each instant losing some of its integrity? It has not the vitality and force of a single living man; for a single man can bend it to his will. It is a sort of wooden gun to the people themselves. But it is not the less necessary for this; for the people must have some complicated machinery or other, and hear its din, to satisfy that idea of government which they have. Governments show thus how successfully men can be imposed upon, even impose on themselves, for their own advantage. It is excellent, we must all allow. Yet this government never of itself furthered any enterprise, but by the alacrity with which it got out of its way. *It* does not keep the country free. *It* does not settle the West. *It* does not educate. The character inherent in the American people has done all that has been accomplished; and it would have done somewhat more, if the government had not sometimes got in its way. For government is an expedient, by which men would fain succeed in letting one another alone; and, as has been said, when it is most expedient, the governed are most let alone by it. Trade and commerce, if they were not made of india-rubber, would never manage to bounce over obstacles which legislators are continually putting in their way; and if one were to judge these men wholly by the effects of their actions and not partly by their intentions, they would deserve to be classed and punished with those mischievous persons who put obstructions on the railroads.

But, to speak practically and as a citizen, unlike those who call themselves no-government men, I ask for, not at once no government, but *at once* a better government. Let every man make known what kind of government would command his respect, and that will be one step toward obtaining it.

After all, the practical reason why, when the power is once in the hands of the people, a majority are permitted, and for a long period continue, to rule is not because they are most likely to be in the right, nor because this seems fairest to the minority, but because they are physically the strongest. But a government in which the majority rule in all cases cannot be based on justice, even as far as men understand it. Can there not be a government in which the majorities do not virtually decide right and wrong, but conscience?—in which majorities decide only those questions to which the rule of expediency is applicable? Must the citizen ever for a moment, or in the least degree, resign his conscience to the legislator? Why has every man a conscience then? I think that we should be men first, and subjects afterward. It is not desirable to cultivate a respect for the law, so much as for the right. The only obligation which I have a right to assume is to do at any time what I think right. It is truly enough said that a corporation has no conscience; but a corporation of conscientious men is a corporation *with* a conscience. Law never made men a whit more just; and, by means of their respect for it, even the well-disposed are daily made the agents of injustice. A common and natural result of an undue respect for the law is, that you may see a file of soldiers, colonel, captain, corporal, privates, powder-monkeys, and all, marching in admirable order over hill and dale to the wars, against their wills, ay, against their common sense and consciences, which makes it very steep marching indeed, and produces a palpitation of the heart. They have no doubt that it is a damnable business in which they are concerned; they are all peaceably inclined. Now, what are they? Men at all? or small movable forts and magazines, at the service of some unscrupulous man in power? Visit the Navy Yard, and behold a marine, such a man as an American government can make, or such as it can make a man with its black arts— a mere shadow and reminiscence of humanity, a man laid out alive and standing, and already, as one may say, buried under arms with funeral accompaniment, though it may be,—

> Not a drum was heard, not a funeral note,
> As his corse to the rampart we hurried;
> Not a soldier discharged his farewell shot
> O'er the grave where our hero we buried.

The mass of men serve the state thus, not as men mainly, but as machines, with their bodies. They are the standing army, and the militia, jailers, constables, posse comitatus. In most cases there is no free exercise whatever of the judgment or of the moral sense; but they put themselves on a level with wood and earth and stones; and wooden men can perhaps be manufactured that will serve the purpose as well. Such command no more respect than men of straw or a lump of dirt. They have the same sort of worth only as horses and dogs. Yet such as these even are commonly esteemed good citizens. Others,—as most legislators, politicians, lawyers, ministers, and office-holders,—serve the state chiefly with their heads; and, as they rarely make any moral distinctions, they are as likely to serve the devil, without *intending* it, as God. A very few, as heroes, patriots, martyrs, reformers in the great sense, and *men,* serve the state with their consciences also, and so necessarily resist it for the most part; and they are commonly treated as enemies by it. A wise man will only be useful as a man, and will not submit to be "clay," and "stop a hole to keep the wind away," but leave that office to his dust at least:—

I am too high born to be propertied,
To be a second at control,
Or useful serving-man and instrument
To any sovereign state throughout the world.

He who gives himself entirely to his fellow men appears to them useless and selfish; but he who gives himself partially to them is pronounced a benefactor and philanthropist.

How does it become a man to behave toward the American government today? I answer, that he cannot without disgrace be associated with it. I cannot for an instant recognize that political organization as *my* government which is the *slave's* government also.

All men recognize the right of revolution; that is, the right to refuse allegiance to, and to resist, the government, when its tyranny or its inefficiency are great and unendurable. But almost all say that such is not the case now. But such was the case, they think, in the Revolution of '75. If one were to tell me that this was a bad government because it taxed certain foreign commodities brought to its ports, it is most probable that I should not make an ado about it, for I can do without them. All machines have their friction; and possibly this does enough good to counter-balance the evil. At any rate, it is a great evil to make a stir about it. But when the friction comes to have its machine, and oppression and robbery are organized, I say, let us not have such a machine any longer. In other words, when a sixth of the population of a nation which has undertaken to be the refuge of liberty are slaves, and a whole country is unjustly overrun and conquered by a foreign army, and subjected to military law, I think that it is not too soon for honest men to rebel and revolutionize. What makes this duty the more urgent is that fact that the country so overrun is not our own, but ours is the invading army.

Paley, a common authority with many on moral questions, in his chapter on the "Duty of Submission to Civil Government," resolves all civil obligation into expediency; and he proceeds to say that "so long as the interest of the whole society requires it, that is, so long as the established government cannot be resisted or changed without public inconveniency, it is the will of God . . . that the established government be obeyed—and no longer. This principle being admitted, the justice of every particular case of resistance is reduced to a computation of the quantity of the danger and grievance on the one side, and of the probability and expense of redressing it on the other." Of this, he says, every man shall judge for himself. But Paley appears never to have contemplated those cases to which the rule of expediency does not apply, in which a people, as well as an individual, must do justice, cost what it may. If I have unjustly wrested a plank from a drowning man, I must restore it to him though I drown myself. This, according to Paley, would be inconvenient. But he that would save his life, in such a case, shall lose it. This people must cease to hold slaves, and to make war on Mexico, though it cost them their existence as a people.

In their practice, nations agree with Paley; but does anyone think that Massachusetts does exactly what is right at the present crisis?

> *A drab of state, a cloth-o'-silver slut,*
> *To have her train borne up, and her soul trail in the dirt.*

Practically speaking, the opponents to a reform in Massachusetts are not a hundred thousand politicians at the South, but a hundred thousand merchants and farmers here, who are more interested in commerce and agriculture than they are in humanity, and are not prepared to do justice to the slave and to Mexico, *cost what it may.* I quarrel not with far-off foes, but with those who, near at home, co-operate with, and do the bidding of, those far away, and without whom the latter would be harmless. We are accustomed to say, that the mass of men are unprepared; but improvement is slow, because the few are not as materially wiser or better than the many. It is not so important that many should be good as you, as that there be some absolute goodness somewhere; for that will leaven the whole lump. There are thousands who are *in opinion* opposed to slavery and to the war, who yet in effect do nothing to put an end to them; who, esteeming themselves children of Washington and Franklin, sit down with their hands in their pockets, and say that they know not what to do, and do nothing; who even postpone the question of freedom to the question of free-trade, and quietly read the prices-current along with the latest advices from Mexico, after dinner, and, it may be, fall asleep over them both. What is the price-current of an honest man and patriot today? They hesitate, and they regret, and sometimes they petition; but they do nothing in earnest and with effect. They will wait, well disposed, for others to remedy the evil, that they may no longer have it to regret. At most, they give up only a cheap vote, and a feeble countenance and Godspeed, to the right, as it goes by them. There are nine hundred and ninety-nine patrons of virtue to one virtuous man. But it is easier to deal with the real possessor of a thing than with the temporary guardian of it.

All voting is a sort of gaming, like checkers or backgammon, with a slight moral tinge to it, a playing with right and wrong, with moral questions; and betting naturally accompanies it. The character of the voters is not staked. I cast my vote, perchance, as I think right; but I am not vitally concerned that that right should prevail. I am willing to leave it to the majority. Its obligation, therefore, never exceeds that of expediency. Even voting *for the right is doing* nothing for it. It is only expressing to men feebly your desire that it should prevail. A wise man will not leave the right to the mercy of chance, nor wish it to prevail through the power of the majority. There is but little virtue in the action of masses of men. When the majority shall at length vote for the abolition of slavery, it will be because they are indifferent to slavery, or because there is but little slavery left to be abolished by their vote. *They* will then be the only slaves. Only *his* vote can hasten the abolition of slavery who asserts his own freedom by his vote.

I hear of a convention to be held at Baltimore, or elsewhere, for the selection of a candidate for the Presidency, made up chiefly of editors, and men who are politicians by profession; but I think, what is it to any independent, intelligent, and respectable man what decision they may come to? Shall we not have the advantage of this wisdom and honesty, nevertheless? Can we not count upon some independent votes? Are there not many individuals in the country who do not attend conventions? But no: I find that the respectable man, so called, has immediately drifted from his position, and despairs of his country, when his country has more reasons to despair of him. He forthwith adopts one of the candidates thus selected as the only *available* one, thus proving that he is himself *available* for any purposes of the demagogue. His vote is of no more worth than that of any unprincipled foreigner or hireling native, who may have been bought. O for a man who is a *man,* and, and my neighbor says, has a bone in his back which you cannot pass your hand through! Our statistics are at fault: the population has been returned too large. How many *men* are there to a square thousand miles in the country? Hardly one. Does not America offer any inducement for men to settle here? The American has dwindled into an Odd Fellow,—one who may be known by the development of his organ of gregariousness, and a manifest lack of intellect and cheerful self-reliance; whose first and chief concern, on coming into the world, is to see that the Almshouses are in good repair; and, before yet he has lawfully donned the virile garb, to collect a fund to the support of the widows and orphans that may be; who, in short, ventures to live only by the aid of the Mutual Insurance company, which has promised to bury him decently.

It is not a man's duty, as a matter of course, to devote himself to the eradication of any, even to most enormous, wrong; he may still properly have other concerns to engage him; but it is his duty, at least, to wash his hands of it, and, if he gives it no thought longer, not to give it practically his support. If I devote myself to other pursuits and contemplations, I must first see, at least, that I do not pursue them sitting upon another man's shoulders. I must get off him first, that he may pursue his contemplations too. See what gross inconsistency is tolerated. I have heard some of my townsmen say, "I should like to have them order me out to help put down an insurrection of the slaves, or to march to Mexico;—see if I would go"; and yet these very men have each, directly by their allegiance, and so indirectly, at least, by their money, furnished a substitute. The soldier is applauded who refuses to serve in an unjust war by those who do not refuse to sustain the unjust government which makes the war; is applauded by those whose own act and authority he disregards and sets at naught; as if the state were penitent to that degree that it hired one to scourge it while it sinned, but not to that degree that it left off sinning for a moment. Thus, under the name of Order and Civil Government, we are all made at last to pay homage to and support our own meanness. After the first blush of sin comes its indifference; and from immoral it becomes, as it were, *un*moral, and not quite unnecessary to that life which we have made.

The broadest and most prevalent error requires the most disinterested virtue to sustain it. The slight reproach to which the virtue of patriotism is commonly liable, the noble are most likely to incur. Those who, while they disapprove of the character and measures of a government, yield to it their allegiance and support are undoubtedly its most conscientious supporters, and so frequently the most serious obstacles to reform. Some are petitioning the State to dissolve the Union, to disregard the requisitions of the President. Why do they not dissolve it themselves,—the union between themselves and the State,— and refuse to pay their quota into its treasury? Do not they stand in the same relation to the State that the State does to the Union? And have not the same reasons prevented the State from resisting the Union which have prevented them from resisting the State?

How can a man be satisfied to entertain an opinion merely, and enjoy *it?* Is there any enjoyment in it, if his opinion is that he is aggrieved? If you are cheated out of a single dollar by your neighbor, you do not rest satisfied with knowing you are cheated, or with saying that you are cheated, or even with petitioning him to pay you your due; but you take effectual steps at once to obtain the full amount, and see to it that you are never cheated again. Action from principle, the perception and the performance of right, changes things and relations; it is essentially revolutionary, and does not consist wholly with anything which was. It not only divides States and churches, it divides families; ay, it divides the *individual,* separating the diabolical in him from the divine.

Unjust laws exist: shall we be content to obey them, or shall we endeavor to amend them, and obey them until we have succeeded, or shall we transgress them at once? Men, generally, under such a government as this, think that they ought to wait until they have persuaded the majority to alter them. They think that, if they should resist, the remedy would be worse than the evil. But it is the fault of the government itself that the remedy *is* worse than the evil. *It* makes it worse. Why is it not more apt to anticipate and provide for reform? Why does it not cherish its wise minority? Why does it cry and resist before it is hurt? Why does it not encourage its citizens to put out its faults, and *do* better than it would have them? Why does it always crucify Christ, and excommunicate Copernicus and Luther, and pronounce Washington and Franklin rebels?

One would think, that a deliberate and practical denial of its authority was the only offense never contemplated by its government; else, why has it not assigned its definite, its suitable and proportionate, penalty? If a man who has no property refuses but once to earn nine shillings for the State, he is put in prison for a period unlimited by any law that I know, and determined only by the discretion of those who put him there; but if he should steal ninety times nine shillings from the State, he is soon permitted to go at large again.

If the injustice is part of the necessary friction of the machine of government, let it go, let it go: Perchance it will wear smooth,—certainly the machine will wear out. If the injustice has a spring, or a pulley, or a rope, or a crank, exclusively for itself, then perhaps you may consider whether the remedy will not be worse than the evil; but if it is of such a nature that it requires you to be the agent of injustice to another, then I say, break the law. Let your life be a counter-friction to stop the machine. What I have to do is to see, at any rate, that I do not lend myself to the wrong which I condemn.

As for adopting the ways of the State has provided for remedying the evil, I know not of such ways. They take too much time, and a man's life will be gone. I have other affairs to attend to. I came into this world, not chiefly to make this a good place to live in, but to live in it, be it good or bad. A man has not everything to do, but something; and because he cannot do *everything,* it is not necessary that he should do *something* wrong. It is not my business to be petitioning the Governor or the Legislature any more than it is theirs to petition me; and if they should not hear my petition, what should I do then? But in this case the State has provided no way: Its very Constitution is the evil. This may seem to be harsh and stubborn and unconcilliatory; but it is to treat with the utmost kindness and consideration the only spirit that can appreciate or deserves it. So is all change for the better, like birth and death, which convulse the body.

I do not hesitate to say, that those who call themselves Abolitionists should at once effectually withdraw their support, both in person and property, from the government of Massachusetts, and not wait till they constitute a majority of one, before they suffer the right to prevail through them. I think that it is enough if they have God on their side, without waiting for that other one. Moreover, any man more right than his neighbors constitutes a majority of one already.

I meet this American government, or its representative, the State government, directly, and face to face, once a year—no more—in the person of its tax-gatherer; this is the only mode in which a man situated as I am necessarily meets it; and it then says distinctly, Recognize me; and the simplest, the most effectual, and, in the present posture of affairs, the indispensablest mode of treating with it on this head, of expressing your little satisfaction with and love for it, is to deny it then. My civil neighbor, the tax-gatherer, is the very man I have to deal with,—for it is, after all, with men and not with parchment that I quarrel,—and he has voluntarily chosen to be an agent of the government. How shall he ever know well what he is and does as an officer of the government, or as a man, until he is obliged to consider whether he will treat me, his neighbor, for whom he has respect, as a neighbor and well-disposed man, or as a maniac and disturber of the peace, and see if he can get over this obstruction to his neighborliness without a ruder and more impetuous thought or speech corresponding with his action. I know this well, that if one thousand, if one hundred, if ten men whom I could name—if ten *honest* men only—

ay, if *one* HONEST man, in this State of Massachusetts, *ceasing to hold slaves,* were actually to withdraw from this co-partnership, and be locked up in the county jail therefor, it would be the abolition of slavery in America. For it matters not how small the beginning may seem to be: what is once well done is done forever. But we love better to talk about it: that we say is our mission. Reform keeps many scores of newspapers in its service, but not one man. If my esteemed neighbor, the State's ambassador, who will devote his days to the settlement of the question of human rights in the Council Chamber, instead of being threatened with the prisons of Carolina, were to sit down the prisoner of Massachusetts, that State which is so anxious to foist the sin of slavery upon her sister,—though at present she can discover only an act of inhospitality to be the ground of a quarrel with her,—the Legislature would not wholly waive the subject of the following winter.

Under a government which imprisons unjustly, the true place for a just man is also a prison. The proper place today, the only place which Massachusetts has provided for her freer and less despondent spirits, is in her prisons, to be put out and locked out of the State by her own act, as they have already put themselves out by their principles. It is there that the fugitive slave, and the Mexican prisoner on parole, and the Indian come to plead the wrongs of his race should find them; on that separate but more free and honorable ground, where the State places those who are not *with* her, but *against* her,— the only house in a slave State in which a free man can abide with honor. If any think that their influence would be lost there, and their voices no longer afflict the ear of the State, that they would not be as an enemy within its walls, they do not know by how much truth is stronger than error, nor how much more eloquently and effectively he can combat injustice who has experienced a little in his own person. Cast your whole vote, not a strip of paper merely, but your whole influence. A minority is powerless while it conforms to the majority; it is not even a minority then; but it is irresistible when it clogs by its whole weight. If the alternative is to keep all just men in prison, or give up war and slavery, the State will not hesitate which to choose. If a thousand men were not to pay their tax bills this year, that would not be a violent and bloody measure, as it would be to pay them, and enable the State to commit violence and shed innocent blood. This is, in fact, the definition of a peaceable revolution, if any such is possible. If the tax-gatherer, or any other public officer, asks me, as one has done, "But what shall I do?" my answer is, "If you really wish to do anything, resign your office." When the subject has refused allegiance, and the officer has resigned from office, then the revolution is accomplished. But even suppose blood should flow. Is there not a sort of blood shed when the conscience is wounded? Through this wound a man's real manhood and immortality flow out, and he bleeds to an everlasting death. I see this blood flowing now.

I have contemplated the imprisonment of the offender, rather than the seizure of his goods—though both will serve the same purpose—because they who assert the purest right, and consequently are most dangerous to a corrupt State, commonly have not spent much time in accumulating property. To such the State renders comparatively small service, and a slight tax is wont to appear exorbitant, particularly if they are obliged to earn it by special labor with their hands. If there were one who lived wholly without the use of money, the State itself would hesitate to demand it of him. But the rich man,—not to make any invidious comparison,—is always sold to the institution which makes him rich. Absolutely speaking, the more money, the less virtue; for money comes between a man and his objects, and obtains them for him; it was certainly no great virtue to obtain it. It puts to rest many questions which he would otherwise be taxed to answer; while the only new question which it puts is the hard but superfluous one, how to spend it. Thus his moral ground is taken from under his feet. The opportunities of living are diminished in proportion as that are called the "means" are increased. The best thing a man can do for his culture when he is rich is to endeavor to carry out those schemes which he entertained when he was poor. Christ answered the Herodians according to their condition. "Show me the tribute-money," said he;—and one took a penny out of his pocket;—if you use money which has the image of Caesar on it, and which he has made current and valuable, that is, *if you are men of the State,* and gladly enjoy the advantages of Caesar's government, then pay him back some of his own when he demands it. "Render therefore to Caesar that which is Caesar's and to God those things which are God's",—leaving them no wiser than before as to which was which; for they did not wish to know.

When I converse with the freest of my neighbors, I perceive that, whatever they may say about the magnitude and seriousness of the question, and their regard for the public tranquility, the long and the short of the matter is, that they cannot spare the protection of the existing government, and they dread the consequences to their property and families of disobedience to it. For my own part, I should not like to think that I ever rely on the protection of the State. But, if I deny the authority of the State when it presents its tax bill, it will soon take and waste all my property, and so harass me and my children without end. This is hard. This makes it impossible for a man to live honestly, and at the same time comfortably, in outward respects. It will not be worth the while to accumulate property; that would be sure to go again. You must hire or squat somewhere, and raise but a small crop, and eat that soon. You must live within yourself, and depend upon yourself always tucked up and ready for a start, and not have many affairs. A man may grow rich in Turkey even, if he will be in all respects a good subject of the Turkish government. Confucius said: "If a state is governed by the principles of reason, poverty and misery are subjects of shame; if a state is not governed by the principles of reason, riches and honors are subjects of shame." No: Until I want the protection of Massachusetts to be extended to me in some distant Southern port, where my liberty is endangered, or until I am bent solely on building up an estate at home by peaceful enterprise, I can afford to refuse allegiance to Massachusetts, and her right to my property and life. It costs me less in every sense to incur the penalty of disobedience to the State than it would to obey. I should feel as if I were worth less in that case.

Some years ago, the State met me in behalf of the Church, and commanded me to pay a certain sum toward the support of a clergyman whose preaching my father attended, but never I myself. "Pay," it said, "or be locked up in the jail." I declined to pay. But, unfortunately, another man saw fit to pay it. I did not see why the schoolmaster should be taxed to support the priest, and not the priest the schoolmaster; for I was not the State's schoolmaster, but I supported myself by voluntary subscription. I did not see why the lyceum should not present its tax bill, and have the State to back its demand, as well as the Church. However, at the request of the selectmen, I condescended to make some such statement as this in writing:— "Know all men by these presents, that I, Henry Thoreau, do not wish to be regarded as a member of any society which I have not joined." This I gave to the town clerk; and he has it. The State, having thus learned that I did not wish to be regarded as a member of that church, has never made a like demand on me since; though it said that it must adhere to its original presumption that time. If I had known how to name them, I should then have signed off in detail from all the societies which I never signed on to; but I did not know where to find such a complete list.

I have paid no poll tax for six years. I was put into a jail once on this account, for one night; and, as I stood considering the walls of solid stone, two or three feet thick, the door of wood and iron, a foot thick, and the iron grating which strained the light, I could not help being struck with the foolishness of that institution which treated me as if I were mere flesh and blood and bones, to be locked up. I wondered that it should have concluded at length that this was the best use it could put me to, and had never thought to avail itself of my services in some way. I saw that, if there was a wall of stone between me and my townsmen, there was a still more difficult one to climb or break through before they could get to be as free as I was. I did nor for a moment feel confined, and the walls seemed a great waste of stone and mortar. I felt as if I alone of all my townsmen had paid my tax. They plainly did not know how to treat me, but behaved like persons who are underbred. In every threat and in every compliment there was a blunder; for they thought that my chief desire was to stand the other side of that stone wall. I could not but smile to see how industriously they locked the door on my meditations, which followed them out again without let or hindrance, and *they* were really all that was dangerous. As they could not reach me, they had resolved to punish my body; just as boys, if they cannot come at some person against whom they have a spite, will abuse his dog. I saw that the State was half-witted, that it was timid as a lone woman with her silver spoons, and that it did not know its friends from its foes, and I lost all my remaining respect for it, and pitied it.

Thus the state never intentionally confronts a man's sense, intellectual or moral, but only his body, his senses. It is not armed with superior wit or honesty, but with superior physical strength. I was not born to be forced. I will breathe after my own fashion. Let us see who is the strongest. What force has a multitude? They only can force me who obey a higher law than I. They force me to become like themselves. I do not hear of *men* being *forced* to live this way or that by masses of men. What sort of life were that to live? When I meet a government which says to me, "Your money or your life," why should I be in haste to give it my money? It may be in a great strait, and not know what to do: I cannot help that. It must help itself; do as I do. It is not worth the while to snivel about it. I am not responsible for the successful working of the machinery of society. I am not the son of the engineer. I perceive that, when an acorn and a chestnut fall side by side, the one does not remain inert to make way for the other, but both obey their own laws, and spring and grow and flourish as best they can, till one, perchance, overshadows and destroys the other. If a plant cannot live according to nature, it dies; and so a man.

The night in prison was novel and interesting enough. The prisoners in their shirtsleeves were enjoying a chat and the evening air in the doorway, when I entered. But the jailer said, "Come, boys, it is time to lock up"; and so they dispersed, and I heard the sound of their steps returning into the hollow apartments. My roommate was introduced to me by the jailer as "a first-rate fellow and clever man." When the door was locked, he showed me where to hang my hat, and how he managed matters there. The rooms were whitewashed once a month; and this one, at least, was the whitest, most simply furnished, and probably neatest apartment in town. He naturally wanted to know where I came from, and what brought me there; and, when I had told him, I asked him in my turn how he came there, presuming him to be an honest man, of course; and, as the world goes, I believe he was. "Why," said he, "they accuse me of burning a barn; but I never did it." As near as I could discover, he had probably gone to bed in a barn when drunk, and smoked his pipe there; and so a barn was burnt. He had the reputation of being a clever man, had been there some three months waiting for his trial to come on, and would have to wait as much longer; but he was quite domesticated and contented, since he got his board for nothing, and thought that he was well treated.

He occupied one window, and I the other; and I saw that if one stayed there long, his principal business would be to look out the window. I had soon read all the tracts that were left there, and examined where former prisoners had broken out, and where a grate had been sawed off, and heard the history of the various occupants of that room; for I found that even there there was a history and a gossip which never circulated beyond the walls of the jail. Probably this is the only house in the town where verses are composed, which are afterward printed in a circular form, but not published. I was shown quite a long list of young men who had been detected in an attempt to escape, who avenged themselves by singing them.

I pumped my fellow-prisoner as dry as I could, for fear I should never see him again; but at length he showed me which was my bed, and left me to blow out the lamp.

It was like travelling into a far country, such as I had never expected to behold, to lie there for one night. It seemed to me that I never had heard the town clock strike before, not the evening sounds of the village; for we slept with the windows open, which were inside the grating. It was to see my native village in the light of the Middle

Ages, and our Concord was turned into a Rhine stream, and visions of knights and castles passed before me. They were the voices of old burghers that I heard in the streets. I was an involuntary spectator and auditor of whatever was done and said in the kitchen of the adjacent village inn—a wholly new and rare experience to me. It was a closer view of my native town. I was fairly inside of it. I never had seen its institutions before. This is one of its peculiar institutions; for it is a shire town. I began to comprehend what its inhabitants were about.

In the morning, our breakfasts were put through the hole in the door, in small oblong-square tin pans, made to fit, and holding a pint of chocolate, with brown bread, and an iron spoon. When they called for the vessels again, I was green enough to return what bread I had left, but my comrade seized it, and said that I should lay that up for lunch or dinner. Soon after he was let out to work at haying in a neighboring field, whither he went every day, and would not be back till noon; so he bade me good day, saying that he doubted if he should see me again.

When I came out of prison,—for some one interfered, and paid that tax,—I did not perceive that great changes had taken place on the common, such as he observed who went in a youth and emerged a gray-headed man; and yet a change had to my eyes come over the scene,—the town, and State, and country,—greater than any that mere time could effect. I saw yet more distinctly the State in which I lived. I saw to what extent the people among whom I lived could be trusted as good neighbors and friends; that their friendship was for summer weather only; that they did not greatly propose to do right; that they were a distinct race from me by their prejudices and superstitions, as the Chinamen and Malays are that in their sacrifices to humanity they ran no risks, not even to their property; that after all they were not so noble but they treated the thief as he had treated them, and hoped, by a certain outward observance and a few prayers, and by walking in a particular straight though useless path from time to time, to save their souls. This may be to judge my neighbors harshly; for I believe that many of them are not aware that they have such an institution as the jail in their village.

It was formerly the custom in our village, when a poor debtor came out of jail, for his acquaintances to salute him, looking through their fingers, which were crossed to represent the jail window, "How do ye do?" My neighbors did not thus salute me, but first looked at me, and then at one another, as if I had returned from a long journey. I was put into jail as I was going to the shoemaker's to get a shoe which was mended. When I was let out the next morning, I proceeded to finish my errand, and, having put on my mended shoe, joined a huckleberry party, who were impatient to put themselves under my conduct; and in half an hour,—for the horse was soon tackled,—was in the midst of a huckleberry field, on one of our highest hills, two miles off, and then the State was nowhere to be seen.

This is the whole history of "My Prisons."

I have never declined paying the highway tax, because I am as desirous of being a good neighbor as I am of being a bad subject; and as for supporting schools, I am doing my part to educate my fellow countrymen now. It is for no particular item in the tax bill that I refuse to pay it. I simply wish to refuse allegiance to the State, to withdraw and stand aloof from it effectually. I do not care to trace the course of my dollar, if I could, till it buys a man a musket to shoot one with—the dollar is innocent—but I am concerned to trace the effects of my allegiance. In fact, I quietly declare war with the State, after my fashion, though I will still make use and get what advantages of her I can, as is usual in such cases.

If others pay the tax which is demanded of me, from a sympathy with the State, they do but what they have already done in their own case, or rather they abet injustice to a greater extent than the State requires. If they pay the tax from a mistaken interest in the individual taxed, to save his property, or prevent his going to jail, it is because they have not considered wisely how far they let their private feelings interfere with the public good.

This, then is my position at present. But one cannot be too much on his guard in such a case, lest his actions be biased by obstinacy or an undue regard for the opinions of men. Let him see that he does only what belongs to himself and to the hour.

I think sometimes, Why, this people mean well, they are only ignorant; they would do better if they knew how: why give your neighbors this pain to treat you as they are not inclined to? But I think again, This is no reason why I should do as they do, or permit others to suffer much greater pain of a different kind. Again, I sometimes say to myself, When many millions of men, without heat, without ill will, without personal feelings of any kind, demand of you a few shillings only, without the possibility, such is their constitution, of retracting or altering their present demand, and without the possibility, on your side, of appeal to any other millions, why expose yourself to this overwhelming brute force? You do not resist cold and hunger, the winds and the waves, thus obstinately; you quietly submit to a thousand similar necessities. You do not put your head into the fire. But just in proportion as I regard this as not wholly a brute force, but partly a human force, and consider that I have relations to those millions as to so many millions of men, and not of mere brute or inanimate things, I see that appeal is possible, first and instantaneously, from them to the Maker of them, and, secondly, from them to themselves. But if I put my head deliberately into the fire, there is no appeal to fire or to the Maker of fire, and I have only myself to blame. If I could convince myself that I have any right to be satisfied with men as they are, and to treat them accordingly, and not according, in some respects, to my requisitions and expectations of what they and I ought to be, then, like a good Mussulman and fatalist, I should endeavor to be satisfied with things as they are, and say it is the will of God. And, above all, there is this difference between resisting this and a purely brute or natural force, that I can resist this with some effect; but I cannot expect, like Orpheus, to change the nature of the rocks and trees and beasts.

I do not wish to quarrel with any man or nation. I do not wish to split hairs, to make fine distinctions, or set myself up as better than my neighbors. I seek rather, I may say, even an excuse for conforming to the laws of the land. I am but too ready to conform to them. Indeed, I have reason to suspect myself on this head; and each year, as the tax-gatherer comes round, I find myself disposed to review the acts and position of the general and State governments, and the spirit of the people to discover a pretext for conformity.

> We must affect our country as our parents,
> And if at any time we alienate
> Our love or industry from doing it honor,
> We must respect effects and teach the soul
> Matter of conscience and religion,
> And not desire of rule or benefit.

I believe that the State will soon be able to take all my work of this sort out of my hands, and then I shall be no better patriot than my fellow-countrymen. Seen from a lower point of view, the Constitution, with all its faults, is very good; the law and the courts are very respectable; even this State and this American government are, in many respects, very admirable, and rare things, to be thankful for, such as a great many have described them; seen from a higher still, and the highest, who shall say what they are, or that they are worth looking at or thinking of at all?

However, the government does not concern me much, and I shall bestow the fewest possible thoughts on it. It is not many moments that I live under a government, even in this world. If a man is thought-free, fancy-free, imagination-free, that which *is not* never for a long time appearing *to be* to him, unwise rulers or reformers cannot fatally interrupt him.

I know that most men think differently from myself; but those whose lives are by profession devoted to the study of these or kindred subjects content me as little as any. Statesmen and legislators, standing so completely within the institution, never distinctly and nakedly behold it. They speak of moving society, but have no resting-place without it. They may be men of a certain experience and discrimination, and have no doubt invented ingenious and even useful systems, for which we sincerely thank them; but all their wit and usefulness lie within certain not very wide limits. They are wont to forget that the world is not governed by policy and expediency. Webster never goes behind government, and so cannot speak with authority about it. His words are wisdom to those legislators who contemplate no essential reform in the existing government; but for thinkers, and those who legislate for all time, he never once glances at the subject. I know of those whose serene and wise speculations on this theme would soon reveal the limits of his mind's range and hospitality. Yet, compared with the cheap professions of most reformers, and the still cheaper wisdom and eloquence of politicians in general, his are almost the only sensible and valuable words, and we thank Heaven for him. Comparatively, he is always strong, original, and, above all, practical. Still, his quality is not wisdom, but prudence. The lawyer's truth is not Truth, but consistency or a consistent expediency. Truth is always in harmony with herself, and is not concerned chiefly to reveal the justice that may consist with wrong-doing. He well deserves to be called, as he has been called, the Defender of the Constitution. There are really no blows to be given him but defensive ones. He is not a leader, but a follower. His leaders are the men of '87. "I have never made an effort," he says, "and never propose to make an effort; I have never countenanced an effort, and never mean to countenance an effort, to disturb the arrangement as originally made, by which various States came into the Union." Still thinking of the sanction which the Constitution gives to slavery, he says, "Because it was part of the original compact,—let it stand." Notwithstanding his special acuteness and ability, he is unable to take a fact out of its merely political relations, and behold it as it lies absolutely to be disposed of by the intellect,—what, for instance, it behooves a man to do here in America today with regard to slavery, but ventures, or is driven, to make some such desperate answer to the following, while professing to speak absolutely, and as a private man,—from which what new and singular code of social duties might be inferred? "The manner," says he, "in which the governments of the States where slavery exists are to regulate it is for their own consideration, under the responsibility to their constituents, to the general laws of propriety, humanity, and justice, and to God. Associations formed elsewhere, springing from a feeling of humanity, or any other cause, have nothing whatever to do with it. They have never received any encouragement from me and they never will."*

They who know of no purer sources of truth, who have traced up its stream no higher, stand, and wisely stand, by the Bible and the Constitution, and drink at it there with reverence and humanity; but they who behold where it comes trickling into this lake or that pool, gird up their loins once more, and continue their pilgrimage toward its fountainhead.

No man with a genius for legislation has appeared in America. They are rare in the history of the world. There are orators, politicians, and eloquent men, by the thousand; but the speaker has not yet opened his mouth to speak who is capable of settling the much-vexed questions of the day. We love eloquence for its own sake, and not for any truth which it may utter, or any heroism it may inspire. Our legislators have not yet learned the comparative value of free trade and of freedom, of union, and of rectitude, to a nation. They have no genius or talent for comparatively humble questions of taxation and finance, commerce and manufactures and agriculture. If we were left solely to the wordy wit of legislators in Congress for our guidance, uncorrected by the seasonable experience and the effectual complaints of the people, America would not long retain her rank among the nations. For eighteen hundred years, though perchance I have no right to say it, the New Testament has been written; yet where is the legislator who has wisdom and practical talent enough to avail himself of the light which it sheds on the science of legislation?

The authority of government, even such as I am willing to submit to,—for I will cheerfully obey those who know and can do better than

---

*These extracts have been inserted since the Lecture was read.

I, and in many things even those who neither know nor can do so well,—is still an impure one: To be strictly just, it must have the sanction and consent of the governed. It can have no pure right over my person and property but what I concede to it. The progress from an absolute to a limited monarchy, from a limited monarchy to a democracy, is a progress toward a true respect for the individual. Even the Chinese philosopher was wise enough to regard the individual as the basis of the empire. Is a democracy, such as we know it, the last improvement possible in government? Is it not possible to take a step further towards recognizing and organizing the rights of man? There will never be a really free and enlightened State until the State comes to recognize the individual as a higher and independent power, from which all its own power and authority are derived, and treats him accordingly. I please myself with imagining a State at last which can afford to be just to all men, and to treat the individual with respect as a neighbor; which even would not think it inconsistent with its own repose if a few were to live aloof from it, not meddling with it, nor embraced by it, who fulfilled all the duties of neighbors and fellow men. A State which bore this kind of fruit, and suffered it to drop off as fast as it ripened, would prepare the way for a still more perfect and glorious State, which I have also imagined, but not yet anywhere seen.

• •

The Witch

Shirley Jackson

• •

Shirley Jackson (1919–1965), a native of San Francisco, moved in her teens to Rochester, New York. She started college at the University of Rochester but had to drop out, for she was stricken by severe depression, a problem that was to recur at intervals throughout her life. Later she graduated from Syracuse University. She wrote a novel, The Road Through the Wall, *and three psychological thrillers:* Hangsaman, The Haunting of Hill House, *and* We Have Always Lived in the Castle. *"The Witch" is one of many short-stories produced by Shirley Jackson.*

• • • • • • • •

The coach was so nearly empty that the little boy had a seat all to himself, and his mother sat across the aisle on the seat next to the little boy's sister, a baby with a piece of toast in one hand and a rattle in the other. She was strapped securely to the seat so she could sit up and look around, and whenever she began to slip slowly sideways the strap caught her and held her halfway until her mother turned around and straightened her again. The little boy was looking out the window and eating a cookie, and the mother was reading quietly, answering the little boy's questions without looking up.

"We're on a river," the little boy said. "This is a river and we're on it."

"Fine," his mother said.

"We're on a bridge over a river," the little boy said to himself.

The few other people in the coach were sitting at the other end of the car; if any of them had occasion to come down the aisle the little boy would look around and say, "Hi," and the stranger would usually say, "Hi," back and sometimes ask the little boy if he were enjoying the train ride, or even tell him he was a fine big fellow. These comments annoyed the little boy and he would turn irritably back to the window.

"There's a cow," he would say, or, sighing, "How far do we have to go?"

"Not much longer now," his mother said, each time.

Once the baby, who was very quiet and busy with her rattle and her toast, which the mother would renew constantly, fell over too far sideways and banged her head. She began to cry and for a minute there was noise and movement around the mother's seat. The little boy slid down from his own seat and ran across the aisle to pet his sister's feet and beg her not to cry, and finally the baby laughed and went back to her toast, and the little boy received a lollipop from his mother and went back to the window.

"I saw a witch," he said to his mother after a minute. "There was a big old ugly old bad old witch outside."

"Fine," his mother said.

"A big old ugly witch and I told her to go away and she went away," the little boy went on, in a quiet narrative to himself, "she came and said, 'I'm going to eat you up,' and I said, 'no, you're not,' and I chased her away, the bad old mean witch."

He stopped talking and looked up as the outside door of the coach opened and a man came in. He was an elderly man, with a pleasant face under white hair; his blue suit was only faintly touched by the disarray that comes from a long train trip. He was carrying a cigar, and when the little boy said, "Hi," the man gestured at him with the cigar and said, "Hello yourself, son." He stopped just beside the little boy's seat, and leaned against the back, looking down at the little boy, who craned his neck to look upward. "What you looking for out that window?" the man asked.

"Witches," the little boy said promptly. "Bad old mean witches."

"I see," the man said. "Find many?"

"My father smokes cigars," the little boy said.

"All men smoke cigars," the man said. "Someday you'll smoke a cigar, too."

"I'm a man already," the little boy said.

"How old are you?" the man asked.

The little boy, at the eternal question, looked at the man suspiciously for a minute and then said, "Twenty-six. Eight hunnered and forty eighty."

His mother lifted her head from the book. "Four," she said, smiling fondly at the little boy.

"Is that so?" the man said politely to the little boy.

"Twenty-six." He nodded his head at the mother across the aisle. "Is that your mother?"

The little boy leaned forward to look and then said, "Yes, that's her."

"What's your name?" the man asked.

The little boy looked suspicious again. "Mr. Jesus," he said.

"Johnny," the little boy's mother said. She caught the little boy's eye and frowned deeply.

"That's my sister over there," the little boy said to the man. "She's twelve-and-a-half."

"Do you love your sister?" the man asked. The little boy stared, and the man came around the side of the seat and sat down next to the little boy. "Listen," the man said, "shall I tell you about my little sister?"

The mother, who had looked up anxiously when the man sat down next to her little boy, went peacefully back to her book.

"Tell me about your sister," the little boy said. "Was she a witch?"

"Maybe," the man said.

The little boy laughed excitedly, and the man leaned back and puffed at his cigar. "Once upon a time," he began, "I had a little sister, just like yours." The little boy looked up at the man, nodding at every word. "My little sister," the man went on, "was so pretty and so nice that I loved her more than anything else in the world. So shall I tell you what I did?"

The little boy nodded more vehemently, and the mother lifted her eyes from her book and smiled, listening.

"I bought her a rocking-horse and a doll and a million lollipops," the man said, "and then I took her and I put my hands around her neck and I pinched her and I pinched her until she was dead."

The little boy gasped and the mother turned around, her smile fading. She opened her mouth, and then closed it again as the man went on, "And then I took and I cut her head off and I took her head—"

"Did you cut her all in pieces?" the little boy asked breathlessly.

"I cut off her head and her hands and her feet and her hair and her nose," the man said, "and I hit her with a stick and I killed her."

"Wait a minute," the mother said, but the baby fell over sideways just at that minute and by the time the mother had set her up again the man was going on.

"And I took her head and I pulled out all her hair and—"

"Your little sister?" the little boy prompted eagerly.

"My little sister," the man said firmly. "And I put her head in a cage with a bear and the bear ate it all up."

"Ate her head all up?" the little boy asked.

The mother put her book down and came across the aisle. She stood next to the man and said, "Just what do you think you're doing?" The man looked up courteously and she said, "Get out of here."

"Did I frighten you?" the man said. He looked down at the little boy and nudged him with an elbow and he and the little boy laughed.

"This man cut up his little sister," the little boy said to his mother.

"I can very easily call the conductor," the mother said to the man.

"The conductor will eat my mommy," the little boy said. "We'll chop her head off."

"And little sister's head, too," the man said. He stood up, and the mother stood back to let him get out of the seat. "Don't ever come back in this car," she said.

"My mommy will eat you," the little boy said to the man.

The man laughed, and the little boy laughed, and then the man said, "Excuse me," to the mother and went past her out of the car. When the door had closed behind him the little boy said, "How much longer do we have to stay on this old train?"

"Not much longer," the mother said. She stood looking at the little boy, wanting to say something, and finally she said, "You sit still and be a good boy. You may have another lollipop."

The little boy climbed down eagerly and followed his mother back to her seat. She took a lollipop from a bag in her pocketbook and gave it to him. "What do you say?" she asked.

"Thank you," the little boy said. "Did that man really cut his little sister up in pieces?"

"He was just teasing," the mother said, and added urgently, "just teasing."

"Prob'ly," the little boy said. With his lollipop he went back to his own seat, and settled himself to look out the window again. "Prob'ly he was a witch."

• •

Should Princes Tell the Truth?

Niccolo Machiavelli

• •

Historian, playwright, poet, and political philosopher, Niccolo Machiavelli (1469–1527) lived in Florence during the turbulence of the Italian Renaissance. From 1498 to 1512, he served in the Chancellery of the Florentine Republic and held the position of secretary for the committee in charge of diplomatic relations and military operations. In fulfilling his responsibilities, Machiavelli traveled to France, Germany, and elsewhere in Italy—giving him the opportunity to observe numerous rulers and the strategies they used to maintain and extend their power. When the Florentine Republic collapsed in 1512 and the Medici returned to power, Machiavelli was dismissed from office, tortured, and temporarily exiled. He retired to an estate not far from Florence and devoted himself to writing the books for which he is now remembered: The Prince *(1513),* The Discourses *(1519),* The Art of War *(1519–1520), and the* Florentine History *(1525). Of these works the most famous is* The Prince.

In writing The Prince, *Machiavelli set out to define the rules of politics as he understood them. His work became a handbook on how to acquire and maintain power. Machiavelli's experience taught him that successful rulers are not troubled by questions of ethics. He observed that it is better to be feared than to be loved. As the following excerpt reveals, he believed that virtues such as honesty are irrelevant to the successful pursuit of power. The amorality of Machiavelli's book continues to disturb many readers, and its shrewd nature of politics has made the author's name synonymous with craftiness and intrigue.*

• • • • • • • •

Originally published in *The Prince*, 1513.

How laudable it is for a prince to keep good faith and live with integrity, and not with astuteness, every one knows. Still the experience of our times shows those princes to have done great things who have had little regard for good faith, and have been able by astuteness to confuse men's brains, and who have ultimately overcome those who have made loyalty their foundation.

You must know, then, that there are two methods of fighting, the one by law, the other by force: the first method is that of men, the second of beasts; but as the first method is often insufficient, one must have recourse to the second. It is therefore necessary for a prince to know well how to use both the beast and the man. This was covertly taught to rulers by ancient writers, who relate how Achilles and many others of those ancient princes were given to Chiron the centaur to be brought up and educated under his discipline. The parable of this semi-animal, semi-human teacher is meant to indicate that a prince must know how to use both natures, and that the one without the other is not durable.

A prince being thus obliged to know well how to act as a beast must imitate the fox and the lion, for the lion cannot protect himself from traps, and the fox cannot defend himself from wolves. One must therefore be a fox to recognize traps, and a lion to frighten wolves. Those that wish to be only lions do not understand this. Therefore, a prudent ruler ought not to keep faith when by so doing it would be against his interest, and when the reasons which made him bind himself no longer exist. If men were all good, this precept would not be a good one; but as they are bad, and would not observe their faith with you, so you are not bound to keep faith with them. Nor have legitimate grounds ever failed a prince who wished to show colourable excuse for the non-fulfillment of his promise. Of this one could furnish an infinite number of modern examples, and show how many times peace has been broken, and how many promises rendered worthless by the faithlessness of princes, and those that have been best able to imitate the fox have succeeded best. But it is necessary to be able to disguise this character well, and to be a great feigner and dissembler; and men are so simple and so ready to obey present necessities, that one who deceives will always find those who allow themselves to be deceived.

I will only mention one modern instance. Alexander VI did nothing else but deceive men, he thought of nothing else, and found the occasion for it; no man was ever more able to give assurances, or affirmed things with stronger oaths, and no man observed them less;

however, he always succeeded in his deceptions, as he well knew this aspect of things.

It is not, therefore necessary for a prince to have all the above-named qualities, but it is very necessary to seem to have them. I would even be bold to say that to possess them and always to observe them is dangerous, but to appear to possess them is useful. Thus it is well to seem merciful, faithful, humane, sincere, religious, and also to be so; but you must have the mind so disposed that when it is needful to be otherwise you may be able to change to the opposite qualities. And it must be understood that a prince, and especially a new prince, cannot observe all those things which are considered good in men, being often obliged, in order to maintain the state, to act against faith, against charity, against humanity, and against religion. And, therefore, he must have a mind disposed to adapt itself according to the wind, and as the variations of fortune dictate, and, as I said before, not deviate from what is good, if possible, but be able to do evil if constrained.

A prince must take great care that nothing goes out of his mouth which is not full of the above-named five qualities, and, to see and hear him, he should seem to be all mercy, faith, integrity, humanity, and religion. And nothing is more necessary than to seem to have this last quality, for men in general judge more by the eyes than by the hands, for every one can see, but very few have to feel. Everybody sees what you appear to be, few feel what you are, and those few will not dare to oppose themselves to the many, who have the majesty of the state to defend them; and in the actions of men, and especially of princes, from which there is no appeal, the end justifies the means. Let a prince therefore aim at conquering and maintaining the state, and the means will always be judged honourable and praised by every one, for the vulgar is always taken by appearances and the issue of the event; and the world consists only of the vulgar, and the few who are not vulgar are isolated when the many have a rallying point in the prince. A certain prince of the present time, whom it is well not to name, never does anything but preach peace and good faith, but he is really a great enemy to both, and either of them, had he observed them, would have lost him state or reputation on many occasions.

• •

The Declaration of Independence

Thomas Jefferson

• •

When in the course of human events, it becomes necessary for one people to dissolve the political bands which have connected them with another, and to assume among the powers of the earth, the separate and equal station to which the Laws of Nature and of Nature's God entitle them, a decent respect to the opinions of mankind requires that they should declare the causes which impel them to the separation.

We hold these truths to be self-evident, that all men are created equal, that they are endowed by their Creator with certain unalienable Rights, that among these are Life, Liberty and the pursuit of Happiness.

That to secure these rights, Governments are instituted among Men, deriving their just powers from the consent of the governed.

That whenever any Form of Government becomes destructive of these ends, it is the Right of the People to alter or to abolish it, and to institute new Government, laying its foundation on such principles and organizing its powers in such form, as to them shall seem most likely to effect their Safety and Happiness. Prudence, indeed, will dictate that Governments long established should not be changed for light and transient causes; and accordingly all experience hath shewn, that mankind are more disposed to suffer, while evils are sufferable, than to right themselves by abolishing the forms to which they are accustomed. But when a long train of abuses and usurpations, pursuing invariably the same Object evinces a design to reduce them under absolute Despotism, it is their right, it is their duty, to throw off such government, and to provide new Guards for their future security.

Such has been the patient sufferance of these Colonies; and such is now the necessity which constrains them to alter their former Systems of Government. The history of the present King of Great Britain is a history of repeated injuries and usurpations, all having in direct object the establishment of an absolute Tyranny over these States. To prove this, let Facts be submitted to a candid world.

He has refused his Assent to Laws, the most wholesome and necessary for the public good.

He has forbidden his Governors to pass Laws of immediate and pressing importance, unless suspended in their operation till his Assent should be obtained; and when so suspended, he has utterly neglected to attend to them.

He has refused to pass other Laws for the accommodation of large districts of people, unless those people would relinquish the right of Representation in the Legislature, a right inestimable to them and formidable to tyrants only.

He has called together legislative bodies at places unusual, uncomfortable, and distant from the depository of their Public Records, for the sole purpose of fatiguing them into compliance with his measures.

He has dissolved Representative Houses repeatedly, for opposing with manly firmness his invasions on the rights of the people.

He has refused for a long time, after such dissolutions, to cause others to be elected; whereby the Legislative powers, incapable of Annihilation, have returned to the People at large for their exercise; the State remaining in the mean time exposed to all the dangers of invasion from without, and convulsions within.

He has endeavoured to prevent the population of these States; for that purpose obstructing the Laws for Naturalization of Foreigners; refusing to pass others to encourage their migrations hither, and raising the conditions of new Appropriations of Lands.

He has obstructed the Administration of Justice, by refusing his Assent to Laws for establishing Judiciary powers.

He has made Judges dependent on his Will alone, for the tenure of their offices, and the amount and payment of their salaries.

He has erected a multitude of New Offices, and sent hither swarms of Officers to harass our people, and eat out their substance.

He has kept among us, in times of peace, Standing Armies without the Consent of our Legislature.

He has affected to render the Military independent of and superior to the Civil power.

He has combined with others to subject us to a jurisdiction foreign to our constitution, and unacknowledged by our laws; giving his Assent to their Acts of pretended Legislation:

For quartering large bodies of armed troops among us:

For protecting them, by a mock Trial, from punishment for any Murders which they should commit on the Inhabitants of these States:

For cutting off our Trade with all parts of the world:

For imposing Taxes on us without our Consent:

For depriving us in many cases, of the benefits of Trial by Jury:

For transporting us beyond Seas to be tried for pretended offenses:

For abolishing the free System of English Laws in a neighbouring Province, establishing therein an Arbitrary government, and enlarging its boundaries so as to render it at once an example and fit instrument for introducing the same absolute rule into these Colonies:

For taking away our Charters, abolishing our most valuable Laws, and altering fundamentally the Forms of our Governments:

For suspending our own Legislatures, and declaring themselves invested with Power to legislate for us in all cases whatsoever.

He has abdicated Government here, by declaring us out of his Protection and waging War against us.

He has plundered our seas, ravaged our Coasts, burnt our towns, and destroyed the Lives of our people.

He is at this time transporting large Armies of foreign Mercenaries to compleat the works of death, desolation and tyranny, already begun with circumstances of Cruelty & perfidy scarcely paralleled in the most barbarous ages, and totally unworthy the Head of a civilized nation.

He has constrained our fellow Citizens taken Captive on the high Seas to bear Arms against their Country, to become the executioners of their friends and Brethren, or to fall themselves by their Hands.

He has excited domestic insurrections amongst us, and has endeavoured to bring on the inhabitants of our frontiers, the merciless Indian Savages, whose known rule of warfare, is an undistinguished destruction of all ages, sexes and conditions.

In every stage of these Oppressions We have Petitioned for Redress in the most humble terms. Our repeated Petitions have been answered only by repeated injury. A Prince, whose character is thus marked by every act which may define a Tyrant, is unfit to be the ruler of a free people.

Nor have We been wanting in attentions to our Brittish brethren. We have warned them from time to time of attempts by their legislature to extend an unwarrantable jurisdiction over us. We have reminded them of the circumstances of our emigration and settlement here. We have appealed to their native justice and magnanimity, and we have conjured them by the ties of our common kindred to disavow these usurpations, which would inevitably interrupt our connections and correspondence. They too have been deaf to the voice of justice and of consanguinity. We must, therefore, acquiesce in the necessity, which denounces our Separation, and hold them, as we hold the rest of mankind, Enemies in War, in Peace Friends.

We, therefore, the Representatives of the United States of America, in General Congress, Assembled, appealing to the Supreme Judge of the world for the rectitude of our intentions, do, in the Name, and by Authority of the good People of these Colonies, solemnly publish and declare, That these United Colonies are, and of Right ought to be, Free and Independent States; that they are Absolved from all Allegiance to the British Crown, and that all political connection between them and the State of Great Britain, is and ought to be totally dissolved; and that as Free and Independent States, they have full Power to levy War, conclude Peace, contract Alliances, establish Commerce, and to do all other Acts and Things which Independent States may of right do. And for the support of this Declaration, with a firm reliance on the protection of divine Providence, we mutually pledge to each other our Lives, our Fortunes and our sacred Honor.

• •

Incivility in the Classroom
Breeds "Education Lite"

Paul A. Trout

• •

Paul A. Trout is an associate professor of English at Montana State University at Bozeman.

• • • • • • • •

Ill-mannered, uncivil students are certainly nothing new to higher education—remember the '60s? But over the last decade or so, the number of them on some campuses and in some classrooms has apparently reached a critical mass, provoking professors from across the country—and the political spectrum—to complain about them publicly (see "Insubordination and Intimidation Signal the End of Decorum in Many Classrooms," a news story in the March 27 issue of *The Chronicle*).

Although they don't agree on the causes of the problem, professors frequently identify the following: poor parenting and guidance; a youth culture that is profoundly contemptuous of authority and adult values (and that is embraced by a popular culture that glorifies in-your-face rudeness and coarseness); a marketplace ethos that fosters a demanding, consumerist attitude; and huge classes that are often dehumanizing and insulting to students.

One of the causes that tends to get overlooked is the "dumbing down" of elementary and secondary education. The educational pipeline is funneling to college more and more students who are not only academically underprepared but also hostile to the rigors and requirements of higher education. Although an overhaul of the entire education system would be the optimal solution, colleges can affect

From *The Chronicle of Higher Education* by Paul Trout. Reprinted by permission of the author.

student attitudes toward learning in much more humble ways—for example, in how we design the course evaluations that, in their current form, encourage students to trash their teachers. Evaluations can be worded instead to encourage students to reflect on the value of a rigorous education, and, at the same time, discourage instructors from lowering their standards in an attempt to win positive evaluations and mollify potentially disruptive students.

Of course, it won't be easy to change the attitudes of students who have spent 12 years in our typical elementary and secondary schools. In *Greater Expectations: Overcoming the Culture of Indulgence in America's Homes and Schools* (Free Press, 1995), William Damon, the director of the Center for the Study of Human Development, at Brown University, writes that elementary classrooms have been so stripped of challenging intellectual material and rigorous standards that many students "are sitting for hours in mental states that approach suspended animation." They are learning habits of "idleness, of getting by with the least possible effort, of cynicism about the very possibility of achievement," in effect, of "willed incompetence," says Damon.

High schools often exacerbate that condition. In *Why Our Kids Don't Study: An Economic Analysis of Causes and Proposed Remedies* (Johns Hopkins University Press, 1995), John D. Owen, a professor emeritus of economics at Wayne State University, says that in the typical high-school classroom an unwritten contract enables the teacher to trade fewer demands and lower standards for a minimum of conventional respect and cordial relations. By the time students get to college, Owen writes, they are experts at diverting instruction from "concentrated academic exercises towards genial banter and conversation," and at limiting how hard they will work.

The Higher Education Research Institute at the University of California at Los Angeles—which annually surveys 250,000 students—has found that "students are increasingly disengaged from the academic experience," with record numbers of them reporting little time spent studying, doing homework, or talking with teachers outside of class.

In other words, a sizable segment of students now entering college does not love to learn, is not used to working hard to learn, and does not have anything resembling an intellectual life. When those high-school graduates collide with college professors who have expectations and standards appropriate to training the nation's future scientists, professionals, and social leaders, they are understandably shocked. A science professor told me that he could provoke "real hostility" from students merely by presenting required course material. To a degree, classroom incivility is the way some students protest an alien academic culture that they deem onerous and unfair.

Let me support that view with a few comments from teaching-evaluation forms that my colleagues received last year, and that I read as a member of my department's performance-review committee. The students' remarks aren't rude in themselves, but they do reveal the degree to which some students feel aggrieved when requirements and standards are not as "comfortable" as they want them to be (assume "*sic*" throughout):

"It is unfair to drop someones grade because he/she missed to many days,"; "we were bombarded with information about authors that was boring with fact"; "who gives a damn if we call it elegy or loss? Are these terms used elsewhere in lit? I've never heard of them"; "he had a tendency to be critical on objective manners such as word choice"; "it is really hard to come to class when every day the material is being shoved down your throat"; "the instructor needs to lower her standards"; "ease down on exam grading"; "I also think 2 novels to read outside of class is a bit too much. It's hard enough to get through 1"; "she should have more concern for her students, their stress levels, and their GPA'S!"; "This course helped and I got a lot out of it but I feel that the proffessors expectations of us were *too high*. He didn't give much lieniancy toward what we wrote or toward our grades."

Remarkably, even students who acknowledge that high standards helped them learn nevertheless want professors to have lower expectations of them. Not quite *Mr. Holland's Opus,* is it?

Disgruntled students also fill out, in addition to forms that request narrative responses, numerical evaluation forms, which many colleges use to help determine retention, tenure, promotion, and merit pay. Given the significant number of students now demanding dumbed-down instruction, the numerical evaluation form may be the Trojan horse of higher education, *if* administrators still want to encourage professors to maintain high standards and challenging workloads. I write "if" because many students assume that administrators—the audience most students address in their evaluations—are their allies in the struggle over classroom standards, and that their friends in high places will *do* something to punish professors who expect too much.

Administrators can rebut that calumny by using evaluation forms that are more than student-satisfaction surveys. Instead of asking students to rate the Professor's "stimulation of interest," "concern for students," and "impartiality in grading"—categories that allow disgruntled students to make piñatas of their professors—evaluation forms should ask whether the course was demanding, whether performance standards were high, whether the workload was challenging, whether the grading was tough, whether the student learned a lot. Those kinds of questions make it a little harder for students who resent a heavy workload or low grades to give spiteful responses.

Some students may still act out in class their hostility to the rigors of college instruction, and some students may still give poor evaluations as payback, thereby encouraging professors to dumb down their courses and perpetuating the cycle that leads to resentful, uncivil students. Therefore, administrators and peer reviewers should supplement numerical and narrative forms with, for example, classroom visits, videotaped reviews, exit interviews with students, and alumni interviews. Faculty members evaluating teaching effectiveness should also examine a professor's self-assessment statement, syllabus, handouts, grading practices, and course design. More than ever before, professors must be protected from those students who use course evaluations and disruptive classroom behavior to get what they want: Education Lite.

Administrators and professors—and indeed students themselves—can do a number of other things to deter routine forms of classroom incivility. They can inform students of campus and classroom policies, confront the problem in freshman-orientation programs, manage the classroom in more-personal ways—such as using a seating chart to learn students' names even in large classes—and respond quickly and directly to rudeness in the classroom. Obviously, though, the problem is not likely to abate much until high schools produce college-bound graduates who actually enjoy learning and who take responsibility for their own intellectual development, and until colleges produce teachers and administrators who know how to accomplish that goal.

Until that Great Reformation, I intend to resist the persistent pressure to dumb down my requirements and standards any more than I already have. My hard-headedness may make some students angry, and they may act out their anger in class or express it on evaluation forms, but it could make *other* students happier. What I found while reading more than 1,000 teaching-evaluation forms this spring is that some students actually want challenging courses and high expectations. Let me quote from one such student: "She expected more from us than any teacher I have had up to this point. She did not waste a lot of time going over things we should already have learned. This was somewhat of a challenge to those of us who have been coddled by high-school English classes. I realize that I didn't really learn anything in high school. She warned us that she was a tough teacher. . . . You need to be pushed and challenged, especially early on."

I side with this student, and those like her, in the struggle for a *higher* education.

• •

Terrible Tragedy Confronts Nation

Jon Carroll

• •

The shootings in Colorado demonstrate the dark side of American culture—the rush to make pious pronouncements, the scramble to assign blame to the usual scapegoats, the assurance that we are all *surprised* and *saddened* and yet these sad events *do not change whatever beliefs we had before these sad events happened.*

It's a learning experience from which we don't learn. We merely say the things we said before—it's the guns, it's the media, it's the breakdown of family values, it's some weird cult subculture brought on by drugs, Marilyn Manson and fantasy role-playing games. Littleton, the Gathering.

Kids. They are so mysterious. What are they thinking, doing, believing? It was such a nice town. It was such a nice high school. No one suspected. Everyone was polite. We are baffled.

But wait: There Is violence stalking our children. It has a name: Dad. There is psychological terror stalking our children, and it has a name too: Mom. It is parents who injure their children—not cults, not the media, not the gun lobby; Mom and Dad. The home is not a safe place.

We are not interested in dealing with that reality. The newspaper does not publish a map of a split-level house with Billy's room carefully numbered (3. Victim crosses to bedroom and hides).

Daddy was drunk at the time. He was using legal drugs. Most of the violence against children is associated with legal drug use. Television is implicated, too; television is a fine thing to watch while you are getting loaded enough to go off on your kids.

"Daddy didn't mean it," says Mom. She has a prescription for Xanax that makes the noises go away. Is this an epidemic? Oh, we wouldn't want to go that far. It just happens every night. Mostly the people who do it were themselves beaten, by people who were themselves beaten, unto the generation when the only media available was the telegraph and "Goth" was just another tribe of dead barbarians.

What happened in that high school is nothing compared with what happens nightly in lovely homes across our nation, behind the nice doors, underneath the framed photos. Our miming of horror allows us to forget where the real violence is. Still is. Will be tonight.

Am I exaggerating? A little. Am I exaggerating more than the media reports about dangerous schools and dangerous clothing and dangerous movies? Oh, no. I am at least at the correct level of reality.

Not all moms and dads, I understand that. But it is useful to look at all the aspects of those much-praised "family values." As we search for answers. As we seek to learn what we already know.

In every class in every high school, there are kids who do not fit in. They are shunned by their classmates; high school is a cruel place. They are labeled by school administrators because they disrupt the system, and administrators by definition worship the system.

Right now, in the high school nearest you—a coterie of miserable kids. For many people, it is the worst time in their lives. Most of them get through on attitude and nerve and maybe a friend they found on the Internet.

Why do we pretend it is Happy Town? Why do we express surprise that any child should harbor profound resentment at his high school, at the charmless rigidity of the caste system, at the dumbed-down textbooks and the glorification of butt-kissing and the weirdly fascistic pep rallies?

Didn't we all go to high school? We managed to make it through without pipe bombs, but surely it is fruitless to pretend that the motivations of the two murderers in Colorado were mysterious or irrational.

"We look for the sermon in the suicide," Joan Didion wrote. We already know the lesson. Maybe we should turn off the television and pick up the telephone. Somewhere there are lost children who have not given up hope.

• •

Precise Language Exercises

. . . .

As critical thinkers, you must begin increasing your awareness in myriad arenas, beginning with language. You must begin taking a critical approach to language usage and language "abusage." Because, as Herman Hesse once wrote,
"words are the source of misunderstandings," it might become us to focus on making a conscious attempt to speak and write with precision; hence, what follows are
Precise Language Exercises (PLE). Internalizing the lessons inherent in PLE will
not only increase your awareness, but it will, ostensibly, make you a more mar-
ketable person, for we reward people who can speak and write with precision. Most
leaders, in politics, religion, and business, have followers for one reason: they can
speak or write with precision.

Consider Winston Churchill: "The truth is incontrovertible. Malice may attack
it, ignorance may deride it, but in the end, there it is."

Consider Elton John: "It seems to me she lived her life like a candle in the
wind."

Consider Mark Twain: "He knew not what to say so he swore."

Look at Elvis, Jim Morrison, Bob Marley! What about Shakespeare, Angelou?
We deify actors like Tom Cruise, Will Smith, and Julia Roberts, why? For one,
they're good looking, and in America we prize appearance above all (do you
agree?). But second, they can deliver their lines with precision.

Thus, embrace a critical spirit and a wanton desire to speak and write with precision by completing the following:

PLE I

When you engage in spoken or written discourse, the words you use must be selected with great attention to precision. You must make a concerted effort to use
words responsibly, noting both their denotations and their connotations.

Denotation: the explicit or direct meaning or set of meanings of a word or expression, as distinguished from the ideas or meanings associated with it or suggested by it; the association or set of associations that a word usually elicits for
most speakers of a language, as distinguished from those elicited for any individual speaker because of personal experience.

Connotation: the associated or secondary meaning of a word or expression in
addition to its explicit or primary meaning.

Take a look at the word *snake.*

Snake: Denotation: a limbless, scaly, elongate reptile, comprising venomous and nonvenomous species inhabiting tropical and temperate areas.

Snake: Connotation: serpent, Satan, devil, evil, poison.

For Discussion

1. List different words, noting their denotations and connotations.
2. Why is it important to be conscious of a word's denotations and connotations when composing an argument?
3. How can using certain words with consistently positive or negative connotations help determine how your listeners or readers interpret your argument?

_____

_____

_____

_____

PLE II

One of the principal reasons for learning to speak and write with precision is to transcend the mundane act of merely *attempting* to communicate an idea, a sensation, or a moment of wonder. When one has a moment of extreme clarity, a moment when her thoughts are being articulated so that others can see what she sees, this is a moment for pause and reflection. Because the fundamental frustration with language is this: how can I get my audience to see what I see? This, unfortunately, is subject to laws of flux and chaos. Too many variables exist to obfuscate meaning, to keep the audience from truly seeing what the speaker or writer sees. But by simply realizing this as a fundamental motivator for communicating with others, we can begin making a more conscious attempt to speak with precision.

For Discussion

1. Pick something in the room. Pretend you have been asked to describe it to a blind person. In at least two fully-developed paragraphs, describe (with precision) the object you picked.
2. Listen to a sound or a combination of sounds. Pretend you have been asked to describe it/them to a deaf person. In at least two fully-developed paragraphs, describe (with precision) the sound(s) you selected.

_____

_____

_____

_____

_____

PLE III

When a person doesn't engage in proper pronoun referencing, they often encounter certain challenges. Specifically, there exists a terrific distraction, for their prose is now replete with issues ranging from whether a person is singular or plural and whether that person somehow multiplied (or divided like amoebae).

The aforementioned, of course, was an example of how not to do it. Try changing *person* to *people*. You can also give *they* and *their* genders (he or she, his or her).

Repair These Sentences

1. When a person considers whether or not legalizing marijuana is a good idea, they begin questioning authority, which is a good idea.
2. People who oppose liberal immigration laws are hypocrites, for unless a person is one of the indigenous people, he is an immigrant himself.
3. Pam went to Jenny's house. She needed to talk.
4. Everyone should eat their vegetables.
5. Each Yankee took their at-bat.

Did you have a real good day? Or did you have a really good day? Did you play good? Or did you play well? Did you test real good? Or did you test really well?

Real vs. Really

If you can substitute *truly* in place of *real* or *really,* then you should be using *really.* Here is an example: "I had a *truly* great day." Here you can see that truly works quite well; hence, you can substitute *truly* with *really:* "I had a *really* great day."

If you can substitute *true* in place of *real* or *really,* then you should be using *real.* Here is an example: "He was a *true* man." Here you can see that *true* works extraordinarily well; thus, you can substitute *true* with *real:* "He was a *real* man."

Good vs. Well

Good is an adjective, so it must modify a noun. I had a *good* day. She is a *good* woman. If it's not modifying a noun, then don't use it. Do not test *good* or run *good.* Instead, test *well* or play *well.* How are you doing? I would submit that you're doing *well,* thank you.

And if someone calls you via telephone and asks, "May I please speak with John?" respond (assuming your name is John) by saying, "This is he." And if someone calls asking for Kate, respond (assuming your name is Kate) by saying, "This is she."

What if somebody says, "There's four ways to interpret this argument?" Though it is quite common to hear language abused in this manner, it's important to note that one should use *there's* responsibly. Since "There is four ways to interpret this argument" does not jibe grammatically, it is important to become conscious of such irresponsible word use. Use *there are* or *there're.*

Finally, is the class comprised of thirty students, or is it composed of thirty students? Does it comprise thirty students, or does it compose thirty students? Do rain forests comprise myriad trees, or are rain forests composed of myriad trees? Or are rain forests comprised of myriad trees?

The rule here is simple: for *comprise,* the whole makes up its parts; for *compose,* the parts make up the whole. For example, the United States comprises fifty states (here, the whole makes up its parts). In contrast, one might use *compose* in this manner: the United States is composed of fifty states (here, the parts make up the whole).

For Discussion

1. Create five sentences using *comprise,* and create five sentences using *compose.*

_____

_____

_____

_____

_____

PLE V

Have you ever been driving in a car and heard somebody say, "Hey, I need some money. Will you find an *ATM machine?*" Or have you ever purchased cologne, perfume, lingerie, a new jacket, a tool set, etc. and been offered a *free gift?* Have you ever viewed a television show that was *pre-recorded earlier?* Have you ever had a teacher who asked you to *collaborate together* with your peers? Have you ever been asked to write in your *daily journal?* Have you ever done something *irregardless* of the consequences? Have you ever attended an *annual* meeting *once* a year? Have you ever seen a *little kitten?* Or worse, have you ever seen a *very unique* kitten?

All of the aforementioned italicized words are redundancies.

For Discussion

1. Why should you make a conscious attempt to eschew redundancies?
2. List at least five redundancies that were not mentioned above.

_____

_____

_____

_____

PLE VI

Webster's Encyclopedic Unabridged Dictionary of the English Language defines vogue word as "a word or term that is fashionable for a time." Unfortunately, these fashionable words and terms become incessantly annoying, for they do not convey the appropriate meaning as per the speaker's or writer's intent. Here are two examples:

unique: existing as the only one or as the sole example; single; solitary in type or characteristics; having no like or equal; incomparable; unparalleled.

impact: the striking of one thing against another; forceful contact; collision.

Unfortunately, it is not rare to hear someone say something like this: "Oh, I had such a unique day. And I met a very unique person. And I saw such unique shoes at the shopping mall. My goodness, they had such an impact on me. In fact, I hope that when I'm donning these shoes, they'll impact the very unique person I met today." This is awful. It is especially awful when a person modifies *unique* by using *very* or *really*. Know this: in most cases, *unique* is inappropriate. And when you do find something that is the sole member of a class, the only artifact, something having no like or equal, try using one of the following words: inimitable, incomparable, matchless, peerless, unparalleled. As for *impact,* owning stock in XYZ Corporation will not impact your stock portfolio. It will affect your stock portfolio, or it will have an effect on your stock portfolio, but it will not impact it. Most often, the only things which are impacted include automobiles and teeth. Please make a conscious attempt to thwart any urges you may have to use *unique* or *impact.* These words embody the grossest form of "abusage," representing verbal bugaboos which strike fear in the hearts and minds of those who make a concerted effort to speak with precision.

PLE VII

Emphatic words, or words that emphasize, should be placed at the end of your sentences. Whether you are speaking or writing, know that your audience will focus more attention on that final word. Note the following claims:

Affirmative action is wrong because it is a form of reverse discrimination, and it does not target people at specific class levels.

Affirmative action is wrong.

The second claim is stronger because it ends with a well-placed emphatic word, unlike the claim which precedes it. You should also note this effect on questions:

Do those against euthanasia consider how much suffering cancer patients are forced to endure?

Do those against euthanasia consider how much cancer patients are forced to suffer?

Note how your mental picture was influenced by *suffer* in comparison to *endure.*

For Discussion

1. Create five statements or questions. Create at least one variant for each, noting how by simply manipulating the placement of the emphatic word, you have changed your audience's reception of the statement or question.

2. Note how some professional writers are better at implementing emphatic words than others. Offer examples from magazines, newspapers, short stories, and novels. To see how integral emphatic words are to audience reception of a concept or idea, read some contemporary poetry.

PLE VIII

Mark Twain wrote: "The time to begin writing an article is when you have finished it to your satisfaction." What does this mean?

For Discussion

1. Write a short response to this prompt: "What role does the media play in your life? How have the media helped shape you and your world?" Once you write your response, and once you've re-read it and proofread it extensively, push it aside and begin a new, more-informed written response to the same prompt.

PLE IX

Eschew verbosity (avoid wordy language) when speaking and writing.

Here is an example: "The stock market is doing well due to the fact that Intel posted strong earnings." Remedy this excess verbiage by writing this: "The stock market is doing well because Intel posted strong earnings."

Here is an example: "The stock market reached a point to where selling was not an option." Remedy this excess verbiage by writing this: "The stock market reached a point where selling was not an option."

Here is an example of spoken verbosity: "The stock market is, like, volatile. It, like, goes up and down and, like, makes me nervous." Remedy this excess verbiage by saying this: "The stock market is volatile. It goes up and down and makes me nervous."

If you wish to economize, to say more with less, or to sound like one who is on a first-name basis with the English language, you can begin by replacing *due to the fact that* with *because* and by replacing *to where* with *where*. Moreover, you would do well to use *like* when you are making comparisons or making an assertion; do not use it to fill the void between words, thoughts, or phrases. Unfortunately, people are often judged by how they speak.

As a side note, you may wish to observe how the sun doesn't really set or rise; the earth simply turns. And even though, colloquially, you may be "mad," its first definitions are usually "crazy, deranged, insane." You would do well to say "angry," especially if you're upset about something.

Critical Exercises

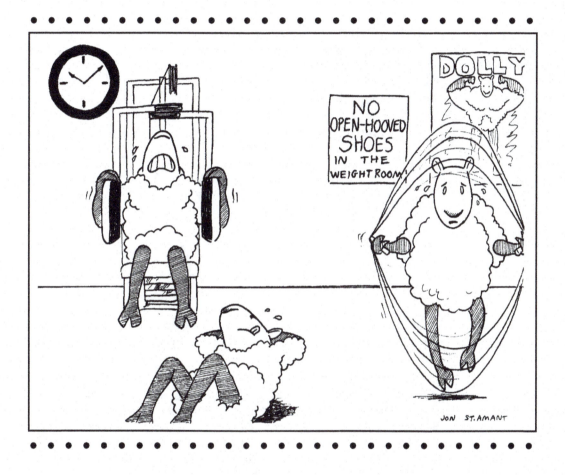

1. Who Should Survive?

   Task: Choose four of the following people to survive. List them in the order in which you would choose them, and indicate the reasons for your selection, i.e., why you chose these particular persons and why you placed them in this particular order.

   a. Dr. Dane—thirty-seven, white, no religious affiliation, Ph.D. in history, college professor, in good health (jogs daily), hobby is botany, enjoys politics, married with one child (Bobby).

   b. Mrs. Dane—thirty-eight, Jewish, rather obese, diabetic, M.A. in psychology, counselor in a mental health clinic, married to Dr. Dane, has one child.

   c. Bobby Dane—ten, white, Jewish, mentally retarded with IQ of 70, healthy and strong for his age.

   d. Mrs. Garcia—twenty-three, Spanish-American, Catholic, ninth-grade education, cocktail waitress, worked as a prostitute, married at age sixteen divorced at age eighteen.

   e. Jean Garcia—three months old, Spanish-American, healthy.

   f. Mary Evans—eighteen, black, Protestant, trade school education, wears glasses, artistic.

   g. Mr. Newton—twenty-five, black power advocate, starting last year of medical school, suspected homosexual activity, music as a hobby, physical fitness buff.

   h. Mrs. Clark—twenty-eight, black, Protestant, daughter of a minister, college graduate, electronics engineer, single now after a brief marriage, member of Zero Population Growth.

   i. Mr. Blake—fifty-one, white, Mormon, B.S. in mechanics, married with four children, enjoys outdoors, much experience in construction, quite handy, sympathizes with anti-black views.

   j. Father Frans—thirty-seven, white, Catholic, priest, active in civil rights, former college athlete, farming background, often criticized for liberal views.

   k. Dr. Gonzales—sixty-six, Spanish-American, Catholic, doctor in general practice, two heart attacks in the past five years, loves literature and quotes extensively.

2. Assume it costs $15,000/year for tuition at your university of choice. Additionally, assume it costs $10,000/year for room and board. Assume you will spend four years, or $100,000, pursuing your degree. If someone came up to you and said, "I will write you a check for $100,000 right now, but if you accept it you can never set foot on any college campus and you

can have no formal meetings with professors; moreover, you cannot engage in any 'formal' instruction like on-line courses and tele-courses," would you take the check?

(Do not rush to judgment. Instead, adhere to the activities of thinking: investigation, interpretation, and judgment.)

3. Complete these statements in a responsible manner (hence, avoid turning these statements into fallacious assertions):

   All English teachers . . .
   All students . . .
   All lawyers . . .
   All garbagemen . . .

   (In doing this exercise, it should become grossly apparent that certain words, unless used with severe precision, should be expunged from your spoken *and* written discourse: all, always, every, none, never.)

4. Take a critical look at several different newspapers reporting on the previous day's events. Look not only at local newspapers and their respective headlines but at newspapers with greater circulation, such as *The Wall Street Journal* and *USA Today.* Notice how editors of certain newspapers think one article is more important than the other (hence, some articles are buried, finding themselves on page nine, while others find themselves on pages one or two). Also, notice how articles which are, presumably, about the same event are written in different manners. Note language use and abuse. Note skewed language. Note ambiguous language. Most importantly, note authoritative language. For instance, one newspaper article might read: "Then, the woman proceeded to lie to both judge and jury." Conversely, *The Wall Street Journal,* a newspaper noted for responsible language, might have this to say: "Then, the woman proceeded to lie to both judge and jury, as told by two sources: Betsy Johnston of the *Miami Herald* and Bob Franco of *The Associated Press.*" Many would argue that *The Wall Street Journal* has reported this instance in a more responsible manner, for it does not offer a wantonly blanket statement implicating the woman. Instead, it simply reports what Betsy Johnston and Bob Franco believe they saw. Note how newspapers can construct or manipulate the opinions of their readers by using responsible *and* irresponsible language.

5. Note how the three mediums which compose the media (print, radio, and TV/film) have helped construct your reality. Pay special attention to gender roles and anything which may lead to desensitization (violence, vulgar language, fantastic imagery, attention shifts, reliance on image vs. intellect). Also, notice how people from certain ethnic groups are consistently portrayed. Again, note how the media have helped construct your reality, and note how they continue to play a major role in remodeling the way you see things.

6. After reading an assigned essay, identify the following on a 5 × 8 card:
   Claim
   Five points of significance
   Two facts
   Two opinions
   Logic (Was the essay logical or not? Why?)
   Example of precise language
   Evaluation

The purpose of this exercise is threefold: (1) It promotes thought. Students cannot simply read an essay right before class without giving it any thought. Instead, students must critically read the essay, for they are required to produce a responsibly written 5 × 8 card. (2) The 5 × 8 card helps reinforce what students should be learning to do throughout the semester: identify claims, distinguish facts from opinions, note logic and precision, and consistently evaluate essays and their assertions. (3) For professors of critical thinking, the 5 × 8 cards help separate those students who did the reading from those who did not. Collecting the 5 × 8 cards at the beginning of each class can provide a professor with a wealth of knowledge relating specifically to the quality of the forthcoming discussion and the quantity of "informed" participants.

Additional Exercises

Fallacies

· · · · · · · · · · ·

Apply the appropriate fallacy to each of the following assertions. After each, please explain why the assertion is fallacious.

1. The Toyota Tundra hugs corners like leather pants on a rock star.

   Type of fallacy: _____

   Why is it a fallacy?_____

   _____

2. If you were a Christian, you'd understand what I'm saying.

   Type of fallacy: _____

   Why is it a fallacy?_____

   _____

3. He's an atheist, so what he says will house tremendous bias.

   Type of fallacy: _____

   Why is it a fallacy?_____

   _____

4. George W. Bush's tax cut is a wolf in sheep's clothing. It is a Trojan Horse.

   Type of fallacy: _____

   Why is it a fallacy?_____

   _____

5. How can Bill Clinton advocate a draft when he was a draft dodger?

   Type of fallacy: _____

   Why is it a fallacy?_____

   _____

6. An apple a day keeps the doctor away.

   Type of fallacy: _____

   Why is it a fallacy?_____

   _____

7. Had Alexander Graham Bell not persisted, we wouldn't have the telephone.

   Type of fallacy: _____

   Why is it a fallacy?_____

   _____

8. Disrespect from students shows that we are witnessing the death of good parenting.

   Type of fallacy: _____

   Why is it a fallacy?_____

   _____

9. Since it can't be proven that TV causes violence, it can't be disproven either.

   Type of fallacy: _____

   Why is it a fallacy?_____

   _____

10. Terrorists attacked us, so we'll attack them.

    Type of fallacy: _____

    Why is it a fallacy?_____

    _____

11. You can eat just before you swim, but you'll either get a cramp or feel nauseous.

    Type of fallacy: _____

    Why is it a fallacy?_____

    _____

12. All religions are great.

    Type of fallacy: _____

    Why is it a fallacy?_____

    _____

13. Christianity is the true religion.

   Type of fallacy: _____

   Why is it a fallacy?_____

   _____

14. After the open-door immigration policy was reinstated, crime rose dramatically.

   Type of fallacy: _____

   Why is it a fallacy?_____

   _____

15. "Use Sprint long-distance for all your calling needs." (Michael Jordan)

   Type of fallacy: _____

   Why is it a fallacy?_____

   _____

16. Do you want to exercise or be overweight?

   Type of fallacy: _____

   Why is it a fallacy?_____

   _____

Refuting the Opposition

· · · · · · · · · · ·

Claim: Americans should welcome legal, first-year immigrants to America.

Claim: Americans should not welcome legal, first-year immigrants to America.

+	−
Immigrants aid in technological advancements (see "Geniuses from Abroad," Gilder)	America should focus on developing its own geniuses (see "How about Home-Grown Geniuses?", Krikorian)
Immigrants created America (see "The New Colossus," Lazarus)	Immigrants bring violence to America (see "Get out of Dodge!", Coleman)
Immigrants rely on welfare less than the native-born (see "We Should Always Lift Our Lamp to the World," Weld)	Immigrants contribute to a sense of disintegration and "fragmentedness" (see "Unchecked Immigration," Brimelow)
Immigrants generate $285 billion in income and pay more than $70 billion in taxes—far greater sums than the $5.7 billion they use in public assistance (see "We Should Always Lift Our Lamp to the World," Weld)	America is literally "out of room" (see "Gatecrashers," Kinsley)

The aforementioned represents four pros and four cons in response to the following question: Should Americans welcome legal, first-year immigrants to America? Based on the support provided, and after examining it within its context (because each supporting element comes from essays in Chapter 9), write a paragraph that refutes the opposition to your chosen claim (choose one of the two claims provided).

Remember, refuting the opposition comprises three parts:

Address the opposition:
- Some people argue . . .
- Many suggest . . .
- The opposition might contend that . . .
- Some maintain . . .
- Others assert . . .
- Arguably, one could oppose . . .
- Objections often surround this issue due to . . .

Identify with the opposition:
- This is reasonable. In fact, according to _____, [offer a quotation supporting the opposition]. This further substantiates the opposition's contention.
- This seems viable. In fact, according to _____, [offer a quotation supporting the opposition]. Because of this, it is easy to note whence the opposition's beliefs have come.
- This is specious. According to _____, [offer a quotation supporting the opposition]. Clearly, the opposition has grounds for its claim.
- This is, ostensibly, valid. In fact, according to _____, [offer a quotation supporting the opposition]. Here, it can be inferred that [link the quotation to the opposition's claim].

Refute the opposition:
- However, [refute the opposition's claim. Offer at least one example to advance your argument].
- Nevertheless, [refute the opposition's claim. Offer at least one example to advance your argument].
- Nonetheless, [refute the opposition's claim. Offer at least one example to advance your argument].

Now it is time to try your hand at refuting the opposition. First, articulate your claim. Then, address the opposition, identify with the opposition, and refute the opposition. Please do so in the space provided.

Claim: _____

_____

Address the opposition: _____

_____

_____

Identify with the opposition: _____

_____

_____

_____

_____

_____

Refute the opposition: _____

_____

_____

_____

_____

_____

Making Qualified Assertions

. . . .

Because few assertions are definitive, definitive language should not be employed very often. Definitive language includes the following:

All
Always
Every
Never
None

Unfortunately, even when the aforementioned words are not employed, assertions can still be made in a definitive manner. For instance, note the following:

People argue that affirmative action should not be supported.

The aforementioned assertion should be qualified by choosing one of the following words:

Some
Many
Few

Hence, the assertion more precisely (and less offensively) communicates the writer's sentiments in a more responsible manner:

Some people argue that affirmative action should not be supported.

While not obvious, if one writes "People argue that affirmative action should not be supported," the implicit word preceding "People" is "All." Hence, the assertion seems definitive and all-encompassing. For critical thinkers, such language irresponsibility is unacceptable.

Because so few facts exist, assertions must be qualified. This is especially germane to argumentation. Qualifying words include the following:

Reasonable
Perhaps
May

Could
Possibly
Might
Assuming
If
Considering
Presumably
Ostensibly
Arguably

When arguing, these words become quite effective:

Reasonably, however, some might object to this argument.
Some might argue that Mrs. Dane should not be chosen to survive. This is
reasonable.
This is, **perhaps,** why some might disagree.
Having unprotected sex **may** cause one to contract a Sexually Transmitted
Disease.
Smoking **could** lead to cancer.
One could **possibly** be involved in an accident when driving drunk.
Some **might** object.
Violent programming **might** cause children to become more violent.
Assuming Jean Garcia is Mrs. Garcia's child, Mrs. Garcia has proven that she
can procreate.

Use the following words (or derivatives thereof) to fill in the blanks in both body
paragraphs:

it is reasonable to infer   this suggests
further substantiated   ostensibly
perhaps   specious
some argue   seems
it could   seemingly
others might object   most
it is possible   many
it is reasonable to suggest   it is likely
may have
it is not unreasonable
one can surmise

The following is based on the "Who Should Survive?" prompt found in this book's Appendix. Adopting the following criterion, "ability to procreate healthy offspring," fill in the blanks with the appropriate words in order to more responsibly make qualified assertions.

1. Dr. Dane was not chosen to survive, for _____ _____ _____ that he _____ not have the ability to contribute to the procreation of healthy offspring. This is supported by examining Bobby Dane's IQ of 70. Since it can be _____ that Bobby Dane is Dr. Dane's biological son, _____ _____ _____ _____ _____

_____ that Dr. Dane _____ have contributed to Bobby's plight. It is, then, _____ _____ to surmise that Dr. Dane _____ not be able to aid in the procreation of healthy offspring. Some _____ argue that Dr. Dane has a Ph.D. in history and has botany as a hobby, _____ that he is, in fact, someone who should be chosen to survive. This is reasonable, for both are great qualities. However, they have nothing to do with the criterion for survival. Thus, Dr. Dane was not chosen to survive.

2. The first person chosen to survive is Mr. Newton. Mr. Newton is twenty-five years old, so _____ _____ _____ to infer that he can procreate. This is _____ _____ by his avocation as a physical-fitness buff. While this does not mean he's in good shape, _____ he is, and _____ it increases his chances of successfully procreating. _____ , nonetheless, argue that Mr. Newton's suspected homosexual activity could impede his ability to procreate. This is, unfortunately, fallacious.

Regardless of Mr. Newton's sexual preference, as long as he is physically capable, he can procreate. Hence, Mr. Newton satisfies the criterion for survival. Others, however, _____ object to Mr. Newton's black-power advocacy. This is _____ . However, it has nothing to do with his ability to procreate.

Stated vs. Implied Claim

· · · · · · · · · ·

Something many find useful when composing a satire is knowing how to distinguish between the stated and implied claim. While the stated claim is clearly articulated on the page (it is often typed in the introductory paragraph), the implied claim never appears in the text. Instead, the reader must infer, based on the contradiction between the support and the stated claim, in order to identify the implied claim. In a satire, the satirist is often attempting to sway the reader toward her implied claim. Hence, the stated claim is similar to a piñata. It appeals to the eye, especially when juxtaposing it with its support, but later its presence dissipates in light of a new claim, an implied claim.

Note the stated claim and the implied claim in the following examples:

1. There are many reasons why cyanide should continue being used to capture tropical fish. First, while ". . . 90 per cent of these fish are overcome by the clouds of cyanide and . . . die or are permanently injured," according to Ride Anouk from the *New Internationalist,* "[One] can get $300 for a single Napolean wrasse fish . . . [and] with fleets from mainland China, Hong Kong, Taiwan, and the Phillipines carrying drums of cyanide, this is big business." Making large amounts of money, however, is only one reason why cyanide should continue being used. Another reason is this: since tropical fish congregate, for the most part, around coral reefs, the cyanide not only harms the fish but the reefs as well. According to Ride Anouk, "Jamaica is just one of the countries mourning the death of its coral reefs—95 per cent of them are dead or dying." This is even more inspiring when noting a quotation excerpted from Don Hinrichsen's "BioScience: Coral reefs in crisis." According to Hinrichsen, "Coral reefs rank among the largest and oldest living communities of plants and animals on Earth. The soft-bodied invertebrates that make reefs evolved 200–450 million years ago. Most established coral reefs began growing 5,000–10,000 years ago." Regardless of cyanide's effects on coral reefs, however, cyanide should continue being used, for AZT, a treatment for people with HIV infections, is based on chemicals extracted from a Carribean reef sponge. Moreover, according to *The Hutchinson Dictionary of Science,* ". . . marine life in the reefs is a vital resource for battling cancer. More than half of all new cancer drug research focuses on marine organisms . . . The extinction

of reefs can mean the end of many life-saving drugs." Clearly, cyanide should continue being used to capture tropical fish.

Stated claim: _____

_____

Implied claim: _____

_____

2. There are many reasons why circuses should be supported. First, animals at circuses often bear the brunt of physical abuse. *www.circuses.com,* for example, shows video footage of Ringling Bros. Circus trainers whipping an elephant in the face and gouging it with metal hooks. Such abuse is justified, for the elephant probably refused to perform a trick. Second, circuses should be supported because, according to *www.circuses.com,* "Ringling Bros. Circus has opposed improvements to the lives of captive elephants, including proposed laws banning cruel training methods, such as electrocution and the withholding of food, and laws that would limit the amount of time elephants can be shackled by their legs." Again, such methods should be endorsed, especially since sometimes a circus can transcend physical abuse and enter the realm of mutilation. According to *www.circuses.com,* "Ringling has also invented a 'unicorn' by mutilating a baby goat—surgically moving his horns to the center of his forehead." Such information should be promoted, for droves would more readily frequent circuses if they were aware of all that is involved in preparing the animals for their "performance."

Stated claim: _____

_____

Implied claim: _____

_____

Identifying Types of Claims

· · · · · · · · · · ·

There are, primarily, three types of claims: claims of value, claims of fact, and claims of policy (note Chapter Three for details). Please identify the type of claim represented by each of the following examples. After identifying the type of claim, please explain why, specifically, it is a claim of value, fact, or policy.

1. Gays should be welcome in the military.

   Type of claim: _____

   Why? _____

2. It is irresponsible for the U.S. military to allow homosexuals to join.

   Type of claim: _____

   Why? _____

3. The "Don't ask; Don't tell" policy adopted by the U.S. military must be abolished.

   Type of claim: _____

   Why? _____

4. Homosexuals represent a reported 12% of the U.S. population; hence, it's a fact that homosexuals will be present in large organizations, especially the U.S. military.

   Type of claim: _____

   Why? _____

5. Animal experimentation should focus less on advancing the beauty industry and more on finding cures for HIV/Aids and cancer.

   Type of claim: _____

   Why? _____

6. **Animal** experimentation is wrong.

   Type of claim: _____

   Why? _____

7. Starbucks Corp. watched its revenue grow by over 80% per year during the 1990s due to its focus on customer service, employee benefits, and expansion.

   Type of claim: _____

   Why? _____

8. Doctors who perform pre-frontal lobotomies are causing irreversible brain damage.

   Type of claim: _____

   Why? _____

9. Employers ought to consider building "in-house" daycare facilities for their employees.

   Type of claim: _____

   Why? _____

10. It is unacceptable that few employers have built daycare facilities for their employees, especially since *Working Women* has observed that 52% of the 26 million working mothers in the United States send their children to daycare.

Type of claim: _____

Why? _____

True or False

· · · · · · · · · · ·

Please note whether each of the following is true or false. After doing so, justify your response by noting why each assertion is true or false.

_____ 1. Thus far, Microsoft has succeeded in creating the best operating system for personal computers.

Why? _____

_____

_____ 2. "Boy bands," like 'N Sync, can dance and sing, but they need to work on their ability to write music and lyrics.

Why? _____

_____

_____ 3. It is a better investment to buy a house than rent an apartment.

Why? _____

_____

_____ 4. Students want to learn.

Why? _____

_____

_____ 5. The New Balance 803 Trail running shoe should be used for cross-country running. It cannot be used for race walking or sky diving.

Why? _____

_____

_____ 6. Starbucks Corp. serves coffee the way Italians from Verona intended.

Why? _____

_____

_____ 7. Cyclists, because they do not succumb to injury as often as runners, are able to further develop their cardiovascular system and, hence, live longer.

Why? _____

_____

_____ 8. Abstract language, like "love" or "enthusiasm," convey meaning better than concrete language like "car" or "tree."

Why? _____

_____

_____ 9. All chairs have four legs.

Why? _____

_____

_____ 10. Lawyers go to court regularly.

Why? _____

_____

Read the following AFTER you have completed the exercise:

Unfortunately, True/False assessments are often guilty of the False Dilemma fallacy (found in Chapter 7). Because True/False assessments only offer two alternatives when many may be available, other options are not entertained. More importantly, after noting the etymology of "true," it becomes even more unreasonable to participate in True/False assessments. "True" comes from the Old English form of troewe, meaning "loyal" or "trustworthy." This comes from the Indo-Europoean base deru, which means "firm," "solid," "steadfast." This etymology maintains that "truth" must be unwavering, unbreakable, uncompromising. Based on this new information, you may wish to make a new decision regarding the aforementioned assessment. Did you label any of them "true?" If so, you may want to consider the assumptions you made, assumptions that, in reality, are not analogous to fact or truth.

Finding Objective Meaning

. . . .

Often, people have memorized one or two quotations, quotations constructed by somebody considered "wise." Such quotations, however, often employ abstract verbiage. As a result, the meaning of the quotation is often a reflection of the subjectivity in which the recipient is steeped. In other words, quotations often mean what we want them to mean. In the following quotations, articulate at least four different meanings, in your own words, for each one. Thinking critically, of course, should be done objectively, and this exercise should help promote objective thought by asking you to look at how a quotation may be interpreted, not just how you interpret it.

1. "Dog got to be man's best friend by wagging his tail not his tongue." (Zig Ziglar)

   Meaning: _____

   _____

   Meaning: _____

   _____

   Meaning: _____

   _____

   Meaning: _____

   _____

2. "The truth is incontrovertible. Malice may attack it, and ignorance may deride it, but in the end, there it is." (Winston Churchill)

Meaning: _____

_____

Meaning: _____

_____

Meaning: _____

_____

Meaning: _____

_____

3. "Once you have spent five minutes complaining, you have wasted five and soon begun what is called 'economic cancer of the bone.' They will soon haul you off to a financial desert and there let you choke on the dust of your own regret." (Jim Rohn)

Meaning: _____

_____

Meaning: _____

_____

Meaning: _____

_____

Meaning: _____

_____

4. "No problem can withstand the assault of sustained thinking." (Voltaire)

Meaning: _____

_____

Meaning: _____

_____

Meaning: _____

_____

Meaning: _____

_____

5. "If you do what you've always done, you get what you've always gotten."

Meaning: _____

_____

Meaning: _____

_____

Meaning: _____

_____

Meaning: _____

_____

6. "I'm a nobody who wanted to be a somebody. I should have been more specific." (Lily Tomlin)

Meaning: _____

_____

Meaning: _____

_____

Meaning: _____

_____

Meaning: _____

_____

7. "No one can make you feel inferior without your consent." (Eleanor Roosevelt)

Meaning: _____

_____

Meaning: _____

_____

Meaning: _____

_____

Meaning: _____

_____

8. "Confucius is reported to have said that if he were made ruler of the world, the first thing he would do would be to fix the meaning of words, because action follows definition." (George A. Steiner)

Meaning: _____

_____

Meaning: _____

_____

Meaning: _____

_____

Meaning: _____

_____

9. "Does the fairy godmother know she's make-believe?" (Laura Weinstock)

Meaning: _____

_____

Meaning: _____

_____

Meaning: _____

_____

Meaning: _____

_____

10. "Children must be taught how to think, not what to think." (Margaret Mead)

Meaning: _____

_____

Meaning: _____

_____

Meaning: _____

_____

Meaning: _____

_____

11. "It's a sad day when you find out that it's not accident or time or fortune but just yourself that kept things from you." (Lillian Hellman)

Meaning: _____

_____

Meaning: _____

_____

Meaning: _____

_____

Meaning: _____

_____

12. "Even if you're on the right track, you'll get run over if you just sit there."
(Will Rogers)

Meaning: _____

_____

Meaning: _____

_____

Meaning: _____

_____

Meaning: _____

_____

13. "The person who knows 'how' will always have a job. The person who
knows 'why' will always be his boss." (Diane Ravitch)

Meaning: _____

_____

Meaning: _____

_____

Meaning: _____

_____

Meaning: _____

_____

14. "No man really becomes a fool until he stops asking questions." (Charles Steinmetz)

Meaning: _____

_____

Meaning: _____

_____

Meaning: _____

_____

Meaning: _____

_____

15. "It is only with the heart that one can see rightly. What is essential is invisible to the eye."

Meaning: _____

_____

Meaning: _____

_____

Meaning: _____

_____

Meaning: _____

_____

*Now, articulate three of your favorite quotations. For probably the first time, you will be required to consider other meanings or interpretations to, ostensibly, timeless maxims. Don't fret, however. T.S. Elliott once observed, " . . . [they] had the experience but missed the meaning." Make sure that you attempt to experience things from other people's perspectives. How else can we attempt to transcend subjectivity?

1. " _____

   _____ "

   Meaning: _____

   _____

   Meaning: _____

   _____

   Meaning: _____

   _____

   Meaning: _____

   _____

2. " _____

   _____ "

   Meaning: _____

   _____

   Meaning: _____

   _____

Meaning: _____

_____

Meaning: _____

_____

3. " _____

_____ "

Meaning: _____

_____

Meaning: _____

_____

Meaning: _____

_____

Meaning: _____

_____

Detecting Bias

· · · · · · · · · · ·

In an attempt to become more conscious of bias, focus on noting that which is indicative of a predisposition, prejudice, or prejudgment. This is simple to detect in radio and television advertisements, political debates, and pep talks or pep rallies. What really smarts the critical thinker, however, is detecting bias in something disguised as "reporting."

In the following exercise, the first two quotations were excerpted from the "News Summary" component of the *Los Angeles Times*. The second two were excerpted from the "Commentary/Editorials" component of the *Los Angeles Times*. While the latter is expected to house bias, the former is not. In this exercise, try to, first, detect bias in supposedly objective writing (in "3 Weeks and a Lifetime Later, Bush Visits Another Classroom" and "Hooks of 'Hillbilly Heroin'"), and then distinguish between the goals of editorial writing and reporting.

1. On October 4, 2001, "3 Weeks and a Lifetime Later, Bush Visits Another Classroom," by James Gerstenzang, appeared in the *Los Angeles Times*. The following was excerpted from the article for your scrutiny:

"Using a first-grade classroom as a national living room, President Bush reached out Wednesday to comfort New York City children in a school near the destroyed World Trade Center—and, by extension, give the country a hug."

What language is not indicative of "reporting?" What gives us insight into the

writer's beliefs, intentions, motivations? _____

_____

_____

_____

Had the writer quoted certain parts of his sentence to indicate that they had been said by Bush or one of his advisors, what should be quoted and why?

_____

_____

2. On October 4, 2001, "Hooks of 'Hillbilly Heroin'," by Elizabeth Mehren, appeared on the front page of the *Los Angeles Times*. Its intention was, seemingly, to report on drug use in Machias, Maine (part of Washington County). The following was excerpted from the article for your scrutiny:

"Everywhere in Washington County, the need for treatment is a persistent theme. Many people do not know where to get help, or how. The state's two drug treatment facilities have waiting lists. Out-of-state rehabilitation is too expensive for most."

What is well-qualified and what is not? _____

_____

_____

How could Mehren have made her assertions more responsible? _____

_____

_____

3. On October 4, 2001, "Would We Really Want to Hold Bin Laden?" appeared in the "Commentary/Editorials" component of the *Los Angeles Times*. It *should* house bias; please note, however, that "reporting" should not. Hence, make the distinction between what George Franco writes below and what Gerstenzang and Mehren wrote in the aforementioned examples.

"Possibly the worst thing the Taliban could do to us would be to give Bin Laden into our custody. Luckily for us, the Taliban's leaders are stupid. Let's all pray together instead that God quickly grants Bin Laden the martyrdom he says he desires."

What bias did you discover? _____

_____

_____

What would it take to remove the bias or better qualify the assertions? _____

_____

_____

Compare Franco's bias to the bias that appears in the quotations by Gerstenzang

and Mehren. _____

_____

_____

4. On October 4, 2001, "Protesting the Protesters" appeared in the "Commentary/Editorials" component of the *Los Angeles Times*. Note the bias in what was excerpted from Ross Barrett's letter.

". . . all of us, young and old, must understand that our first and most urgent priority is to reduce and eventually stop opportunities for appalling acts like those committed September 11. It is pointless to argue about the rules of engagement. Those have already been decided by Osama bin Laden and his fanatic followers."

What bias can be detected in Barrett's diction? _____

_____

_____

What distinctions should be made between editorial writing and reporting?

_____

_____

Inference/Implication

Created by Julian Medina

• •

Reading and writing rely on the connotation and denotation of the words used to convey meaning. (Denotation is the exact meaning of the word; connotation is the suggested meaning of the word.) Re-reading and re-writing help clear up false impressions we may create or we may receive. False impressions occur in writing when ideas are erroneously extracted from statements that have been written down.

If false statements occur, it is the writer's responsibility to clarify. If false conclusions are reached, it is the reader's responsibility to revise those conclusions.

Between a reader and a writer, between a speaker and a listener, there is what is said or *written* and what is heard or *read*.

The writer (or speaker) states, implies, and suggests ideas to the reader. The reader (or listener) understands, infers, and assumes ideas from what has been read or heard.

Confusion and misunderstanding take place when a writer implies an idea with the use of certain words that is not meant to be inferred. Confusion and misunderstanding also happen when a reader infers an idea that the writer's words do not imply.

The writer:	The reader:
states	understands
suggests	assumes
implies	infers

The writer makes:	The reader draws:
statements	conclusions
suggestions	assumptions
implications	inferences

Reprinted by permission of the author.

Situation:

The newspaper reports that President Clinton is entering the hospital for treatment.

Legitimate assumptions:

The president is ill.

The president will receive treatment.

The vice-president will be nearby should there be a need to transfer power. (Executive power transfers when the president is under anesthesia.)

Unfounded assumptions:

The president is going to die.

The government will crumble.

The military will overthrow the legislature.

The stock market will collapse.

Correct inferences and implications are based on knowledge, past experience, and good sense. Looking at the situation above, we have to sort out the unfounded assumptions from those which are legitimate.

Our inferences might be different if we lived in a less stable country. They might be justified if problems had occurred in a similar experience.

Words create inferences and implications. Choose words carefully for their exact meaning. Read words that are written carefully for their exact meaning.

Writing Clues (1–13)

Created by Julian Medina

• •

1. Avoid the use of the pronoun "you" in all its forms: you, your, or you're.
2. Do not use introductory phrases that express attitude. Phrases such as "I think that," "I believe that," or "I feel that" are redundant and ineffective. They are indicative of a student's attempt to ignore detail and substitute opinion.
3. Avoid slang, cuteness, or inflammatory language. Use direct, concrete, neutral terms.
4. Avoid trendy references to current events. Politicizing assignments suggests a student's attempt to ignore detail and substitute opinion.
5. College language puts great emphasis on tendency and suggestion. For this reason *seems, appears, suggests,* and other less rigid verbs are used.
6. Avoid rhetorical questions as a means to solidifying or concluding an idea. A rhetorical question does not answer or direct the reader to conclusion; it may, in fact, cause the reader to reach a conclusion the author does not want. An example follows: "What do you expect people to do if they don't have jobs?"
7. Use a rhetorical question to begin a speculative paragraph.
8. Inference and implication are respectable modes of expression. Use them. Remember inference is the sense or meaning we infer or reach from what others say or do; implication is the sense or meaning we want others to infer from what we say indirectly or do.
9. Use the neutral terms *a person, a student,* or simply *one* rather than *you* in any of its forms. A person wishing to emphasize personal perspective may decide to use *I* or *we.*
10. Avoid imperative or prescriptive statements. They appear as commands and belong only in recipes or instructional material. (Each category on this list is an imperative/prescriptive statement; for example, the statement "Avoid imperative or prescriptive statements" is an imperative/prescriptive statement.

Reprinted by permission of the author.

11. Avoid outer-directed sarcasm. Light, self-directed sarcasm is occasionally effective in communicating a feeling. For example, the statement "I feel like a wet dog if I don't get enough sleep" is humorous because it is commentary on oneself. The statement "You look like a wet dog if you don't get enough sleep," however, is not because it assumes something about the reader of which the writer has no knowledge.
12. Never use a word you can't spell—consult a dictionary.
13. Never confuse the Constitutional First Amendment guarantee of freedom of speech with the dubious claim to the right to make money from saying atrocities.

Grammar

When writing an argument, it is important that you don't distract your reader by haphazardly applying commas, semicolons, and colons to your prose. Hence, what follows is a series of antidotes for ailing prose.

Commas

Here are some of the most commonly fractured comma rules:

1. Use a comma before a coordinating conjunction joining independent clauses. The seven coordinating conjunctions are *for, and, nor, but, or, yet, so*. These seven create an acronym: FANBOYS. An independent clause is a complete thought, one housing a subject and a verb. Here is an example: *We ate*. When joining two independent clauses via one of the FANBOYS, a comma must precede it. Here are two examples:

   We ate, and they danced.

   Dave studied German for seven years, but he still couldn't speak it fluently.

2. Use a comma after an introductory word group. Here are three examples:

   When Bob went jogging, he forgot to wear his shoes.

   Impressed with the film, Tom recommended it to others.

   After considering the ramifications of legalizing active euthanasia, the doctors at St. Luke's Hospital chose against its legalization.

3. Use a comma between items in a series, including the last two items in a series. Here are two examples:

   Many oppose affirmative action programs because they promote reverse discrimination, special treatment, and ill-will.

   Animal experimentation is essential because it saves human lives, provides the pharmaceutical industry with important data, and curbs the population of stray animals in society.

4. Use commas between coordinate adjectives. If you have two or more adjectives modifying a noun, a comma must separate each adjective. Here are two examples:

He was an old, ornery man.

When people with creative, right-hemispheric attributes enter English classes, they often excel.

Semicolons

Use semicolons between independent clauses. Here are four examples:

Many love to read traditional arguments; however, others prefer the satire.

Sheep are in need of someone to follow; thus, shepherds will always be in demand.

Cases of road rage are steadily increasing in California; conversely, cases of voluntary roadside assistance by motorists are on the decline.

The Prohibition benefited some and hurt others; it was, however, quite profitable for some bootleggers, like the Kennedys.

Here are examples of how *not* to use the semicolon:

When inmates complain of prison overcrowding; taxpayers have trouble listening.

One great example of passive euthanasia; an elderly person suffering.

The stock market is doing well; thus, helping small investors prepare for retirement.

Public schools are overcrowded in California; as a result, making it difficult for teachers to teach and students to learn.

Colons

Use a colon after an independent clause to emphasize the words that follow it. Here are five examples:

Joe should be allowed to pass for three reasons: he is a hard-worker, he has attended every class, and he has a good attitude.

Joe should not be allowed to pass for one reason: he is failing the class.

Day traders focus on one thing: market fluctuations.

These four people will survive: Dr. Dane, Mrs. Dane, Bobby Dane, and Mr. Newton.

After learning these grammar rules, one thing is certain: you will not trouble your professors with misplaced colons, semicolons, and commas.

Here are examples of how *not* to use the colon:

Some examples of euthanasia are: passive and active.

There are different types of affirmative action such as: class-based and race-based.

Sheila went to the store and bought: carrots, celery, potatoes, and a pumpkin.

Dashes

Use dashes to offer additional information in a sentence; usually, this additional information will be highlighted or emphasized as a result of the dash.

In "Just As Fierce," Katherine Dunn states: "In the rare case where a woman is seen as genuinely responsible, she is branded a monster—an 'unnatural' woman."

In "Femininity," Susan Brownmiller states: "Large numbers of women—those with small children, those left high and dry after a mid-life divorce—need financial support."

Ellipses

Use the ellipsis to indicate that you have omitted something from a quoted passage. Here is the original passage taken from D.H. Lawrence's *Sketches of Etruscan Places and Other Italian Essays*:

He did not reply, but obstinately looked as though he would be venomous if he could. He peered at the passport—though I doubt if he could make head or tail of it—asked where we were going, peered at B.'s passport, half excused himself in a whining, disgusting sort of fashion, and disappeared into the night. A real lout.

Here is the passage *with* the ellipses:

D.H. Lawrence writes: "He did not reply, but obstinately looked as though he would be venomous if he could. He peered at the passport . . . peered at B.'s passport, half excused himself in a whining, disgusting sort of fashion. . . ."

Here is the passage *with* the ellipses *and* parenthetical referencing:

D.H. Lawrence writes: "He did not reply, but obstinately looked as though he would be venomous if he could. He peered at the passport . . . peered at B.'s passport, half excused himself in a whining, disgusting sort of fashion . . ." (28)

Here is the passage with *an* ellipsis which does not connect one section of Lawrence's passage to another:

D.H. Lawrence writes: "He did not reply, but obstinately looked as though he would be venomous if he could. He peered at the passport—though I doubt if he could make head or tail of it—asked where we were going, peered at B.'s passport . . ." (28).

Brackets

Use brackets to insert explanatory material within quotations.
Here is an example from John G. Neihardt's *Black Elk Speaks*:

Then he painted High Horse solid white all over, and after that he painted black stripes all over the white and put black rings around High Horse's eyes. High Horse looked terrible.

Unfortunately, we do not know who "he" is. By using brackets, however, we can insert the necessary explanatory material:

Then [Red Deer] painted High Horse solid white all over, and after that [Red Deer] painted black stripes all over the white and put black rings around High Horse's eyes. High Horse looked terrible.

Another reason to use brackets is to insert the word *sic,* which means "so." It tells the readers that the mistake which appears in the quotation was the mistake of the person quoted, or it was the mistake of the person originally formulating the quotation; regardless, it shows the mistake was not yours. Here is an example:

F. Scott Fitzgerld was fond of dressing his characters in vivid colors.

"Fitzgerald" is improperly spelled; simply adding [*sic*] addresses and helps ameliorate the problem:

F. Scott Fitzgerld [sic] was fond of dressing his characters in vivid colors.

Glossary

audience: those who will hear, read, or view an argument.

abstract words: abstract words, like "sympathy" or "compassion," cannot be touched, drawn, or seen.

Ad Hominem: appealing to one's prejudice, emotions, or special interests rather than to one's intellect or reason—attacking an opponent's character rather than answering an argument.

Ad Ignorantiam: also known as "appeal to ignorance," that *ad ignorantiam* fallacy argues that a claim must be true simply because it has never been proven false.

Ad Misericordiam: an appeal to sympathy as opposed to one's intellect or reason.

addressing the opposition: when attempting to refute the opposition, the writer or speaker must first address the opposition by noting its fears, concerns, or objections surrounding the proposed claim.

Appeal to Ignorance: also known as *ad ignorantiam,* the appeal to ignorance fallacy argues that a claim must be true simply because it has never been proven false.

Aristotle's Deductive Syllogism: an argument of a form containing a major premise, minor premise, and conclusion.

assertion: a positive statement or declaration, often without support or reason.

bias: a particular tendency or inclination, especially one that prevents impartial consideration of a question; prejudice.

claim: in an argument, the claim is the assertion around which all of the supporting elements revolve. It is, ostensibly, the motivation for constructing an argument.

claim of fact: claims of fact attempt to prove that a condition has existed, currently exists, or will exist in the future. Claims of fact are supported by statistics and examples which can be verified.

claim of policy: claims of policy usually house the words *should, ought to,* or *must.* Claims of policy assert that certain conditions exist that call for a solution.

claim of value: claims of value make a judgment expressing approval or disapproval.

commentary: in developmental writing, "commentary" links the "example" to the "point." "Commentary" explains the relevance of the "example" (often a quotation) to the "point" (often an assertion relating to the topic sentence or claim). Without employing "commentary," writers naively assume a shared assumption with the reader.

concrete words: concrete words, like "tree" or "car," represent things that can be touched, drawn, or seen.

constitution: that which notes what a person stands for—beliefs, morals, principles, ethics—and why.

Contradictory Premises: a fallacy that occurs when the premises of an argument contradict each other.

deduction: reasoning by which we establish that a conclusion must be true because the statements on which it is based are true.

Dicto Simpliciter: this fallacy is committed when an argument is based on an unqualified generalization.

Doubtful Cause: also known as *post hoc,* the doubtful cause fallacy asserts that because one things has happened, the other thing happens. An example often cited to illustrate this fallacy reads: "After the rooster crows, the sun comes up. Therefore, the sun comes up because the rooster crows."

Either-or-Arguments: also known as false dilemma, this fallacy presents only two alternatives when many may be available.

example: in developmental writing, an "example" is often a quotation used to advance a "point." Since a "point" is an assertion, an "example" must be used to make the "point" believable or, at least, credible.

False Analogy: this fallacy makes a comparison between two things, but often the comparison is without the required connection or required evidence necessary to advance the argument.

False Dilemma: also know as an either-or-argument, this fallacy presents only two alternatives when many may be available.

Faulty Use of Authority: this fallacy is committed when an argument is delivered in an authoritative manner by a non-authority.

Hasty Generalization: this fallacy is committed when a generalized assertion is made in haste, often as a result of prejudice.

Hypothesis Contrary to Fact: this fallacy is committed when an argument attempts to draw supportable conclusions from a hypothesis, one that is, of course, not true.

identifying with the opposition: when attempting to refute the opposition, the writer or speaker must, after addressing the opposition, attempt to identify with the opposition by acknowledging the reasonability of the opposition's objections to the proposed claim.

induction: inference of a generalized conclusion from particular instances.

interpretation: deciding what the evidence (gathered from investigating) means.

investigation: searching for evidence and hunting for any data that will answer the key question about the issue. The evidence must be both relevant and sufficient.

judgment: reaching a conclusion about the issue. The conclusion must meet the test of logic.

point: in developmental writing, the "point" is the assertion made by the writer. In order to advance the "point," it must be coupled with an "example" and "commentary."

Poisoning the Well: this fallacy is committed when a writer or speaker attacks his opponent before giving him an opportunity to offer his argument.

Post Hoc: also known as doubtful cause, the *post hoc* fallacy asserts that because one thing has happened, the other thing happens. An example often cited to illustrate this fallacy reads: "After the rooster crows, the sun comes up. Therefore, the sun comes up because the rooster crows."

refuting the opposition: first, refuting the opposition refers to the activity comprising three parts: addressing the opposition, identifying with the opposition, and refuting the opposition. Second, refuting the opposition refers to what takes place immediately after the writer or speaker has addressed the opposition and identified with it. At this point, the writer or speaker attempts to disprove the opposition by revealing biases, prejudices, generalizations, fallacies, or unfounded assumptions.

ruminate: to chew the cud; to medicate or muse; ponder; to chew again or over and over.

reality: one's perception of that which exists in his or her world. This includes, but is not limited to, the definitions of words, cultural practices, societal preferences, and familial prejudices.

Slippery Slope: this fallacy is committed when an argument takes a "dangerous and irreversible course." If an argument claims that doing one thing will lead to another thing (usually something undesirable), and if the argument does not provide adequate evidence to support its claim, it is guilty of the slippery slope fallacy.

The Toulmin Model: an argument of a form containing a claim, support (evidence), and a warrant.

Two Wrongs Make a Right: this fallacy is committed when an argument attempts to sidestep the issue instead of addressing it.

warrant: a shared assumption. In arguments adhering to the Toulmin Model, the warrant cannot be corrupt (the general assumption must be shared); otherwise, the entire argument is faulty and, hence, unacceptable.

Index